THE CLIFF DWELLINGS SPEAK

Exploring the Ancient Ruins of the Greater American Southwest

BETH AND BILL SAGSTETTER

BenchMark Publishing of Colorado LLC

Denver

BenchMark Publishing of Colorado LLC
2217 Grove Street
Denver, Colorado 80211-4613

(303) 455-0789
FAX: (303) 455-1093

benchmarkcolo@worldnet.att.net

The modern photographs without attribution are by Bill Sagstetter.
The rare, antique books and pictures cited in the captions, are from the Sagstetter Collection.

First Edition

Printed in the United States

ISBN-13 Paperback: 978-0-9645824-2-2

ISBN-13 Hardbound: 978-0-9645824-3-9

WARNING:

This is a sight-seeing book to visiting cliff dwellings. Visiting cliff dwellings is usually an enjoyable and educational experience, but under some circumstances it can also be dangerous. You should not visit a cliff dwelling by yourself. Children must always be under constant uupervision by one or more adults. Your safety in a cliff dwelling depends on your personal judgment based upon your experience and a realistic assessment of the conditions.

There is no substitute for an experienced guide to help you safely enjoy your visit to a cliff dwelling. Therefore, the information provided in this book should only be used with caution. If you misinterpret the information contained in this book, you may be seriously injured or even killed as a result of the misunderstanding.

There are no express or implied warranties that this sight-seeing book contains accurate and reliable information. There are no warranties as to fitness for a particular purpose. Your use of this book expressly indicates your assumption of the risk of serious injury or death as a result of risks inherently dangerous in visiting a cliff dwelling and is an acknowledgment of your own responsibility for your safety.

The Navajo saw empty buildings perched in impossible places high on the cliffs and thought the ancient Pueblo people could fly.

— paraphrased from: Robert S. McPherson, *Sacred Land, Sacred View.*

All of the royalties from this book will be donated to these organizations devoted to preservation:

Canyonlands Natural History Association

Cliff Dwelling Research and Preservation Center/Group

Colorado Preservation Inc.

Crow Canyon Archaeological Center

San Juan Mountain Association

Telluride Historical Museum

Acoma Pueblo/Preservation Office

Laguna Pueblo/Preservation Office

Picuris Pueblo/Preservation Office

Pojoaque Pueblo/Preservation Office

San Felipe Pueblo/Presevation Office

White Mountain Apache Tribe/Preservation Office

Zuni Pueblo/Preservation Office

CONTENTS

FOREWORD

Cliff dwellings!

Perhaps no single kind of archaeological site north of the Mexican border conjures up such an immediate vision to so many people. To some, the mental image recalls the vacation they took to Mesa Verde National Park, with spectacularly preserved ruins of Cliff Palace, with its empty window-like doors staring back from across the canyon. To inveterate hikers traversing the backcountry of Arizona or southern Utah, a row of red stone rooms on a narrow ledge offers a more personal experience stemming from a sense of wonder and discovery. Turning a corner they may encounter an unexpected delight: intact houses left by Native Americans who moved on centuries ago but still remain connected to their ancestral homes through tales of ancient wanderings.

A few cliff dwellings have well over one hundred rooms, bordering on 200, but most have only one or two. Found along canyon walls, most are remotely located and some thwart the efforts of all but the most determined and robust would-be modern visitors. Regardless of size, grandeur, or remoteness, all seem mysterious in some way.

There are probably tens of thousands of cliff dwellings in the southwestern United States and northern Mexico, sprinkled across the canyon systems of Colorado, New Mexico, Arizona, and Utah, and extending into Chihuahua and Sonora. In some cases, those of Mexico are still in use by descendents of the original residents, but in the U.S. most were probably abandoned by about A.D. 1400, unless used by refugee populations. In the main, constructing pueblos in shallow caves or alcoves was not done much before A.D. 1150, although other kinds of houses were built earlier in such places. In terms of human history, cliff dwellings of this region were only used as a major form of architecture for about 250 years at the outside, and for any single cliff dwelling the primary construction footprint is generally limited to 30 — 40 years or less.

At one time these buildings were the homes of vibrant populations who confronted the same kinds of issues that one might experience in modern apartment buildings that were built by the residents as complete villages. Some of these villages also included public buildings or community gathering spaces serving social and religious purposes. Although at least some of these residents were undoubtedly kinfolk, probably not everyone liked their neighbors all the time. People prayed and played, changed their minds, made room for new arrivals, raised children from infancy to adulthood, and saw their relatives into the afterlife. In fact, a major factor in understanding these buildings may have to do with the length of a generation during those times. Whereas it is commonplace now for an adult person to know his/her grandparents, it was rare then, probably placing a premium on the early transmission of specialized knowledge. In many ways, the meaning of "family" is one way to reconnect with these homes.

More prosaically, these buildings were built from stones quarried out and shaped by harder stones, dirt that was dug from hillsides or trash deposits and mixed with what is now a rarity in these arid lands: water. Timbers were cut anew or recycled from older buildings. Clay soils became plasters and pigments became paint. But although the construction materials are straightforward, the combinations of them all are bewildering: rocks laid with or without mud, wattle-and-daub or jacal, upright slabs, cribbed log roofs, coursed mud, grass-impregnated mud bricks. The people who built the cliff dwellings were masters of building with such materials.

A modern visitor first entering a cliff dwelling of any size and complexity beyond just a couple of rooms is bombarded with the combinations and re-combinations of these various materials, the social and familial relationships of the people who lived in it, and the challenge of understanding the plasters, doorways, painted images, and artifacts found in many of them.

This book is about how to extract information and meaning from these remarkable and fascinating buildings. I encourage the reader to think in terms of the process as one of decoding the architecture that one sees during a field visit. Ultimately, doing so might involve visits to many cliff dwellings in order to develop a sort of "decoding manual." Fortunately for the reader, Bill and Beth Sagstetter have spent decades doing just that, at cliff dwellings throughout the southwestern United States and in the alcoves of northern Mexico.

Painstaking notes, thousands of photographs, and many hours of focused thinking have helped them define the major patterns of construction, use, and social history, as well as to delight in the idiosyncrasies of someone's personality, in many ways the opposite of "pattern." Their goal is to help the reader distill meaning from a number of seemingly disconnected observations, creating order from chaos and demystifying the mysterious, at least to a degree.

This is a truly different kind of guidebook, not to shorten your path or supersede your GPS coordinates, but to guide your observations and experiences once you've arrived.

— LARRY NORDBY

Research Archaeologist (ret.)
Mesa Verde National Park
Sr. Preservation Archaeologist
Western Mapping Co.(Currently)

MAY, 2009

This nineteenth-century canteen is decorated on
the side with designs of a deer and its breath line.
A corn cob would have been used to stopper it.
From the 2nd Annual *Bureau of American Ethnology,*

PREFACE

As we looked at the silent buildings clinging to the cliff face, the empty windows stared back at us, inscrutable. The walls were crumbling and the roofs were gone. Soon there would be nothing left. Yet living, breathing people had built these structures centuries ago. They had raised their families and lived out their lives here. But they were long gone now. Was this ruin also dead and gone now? We recalled a trip we had taken to a museum with a wonderful ancient Puebloan pottery display. One pot in particular fascinated us. On its side was the image of a probable deer, and into his body from his mouth was a painted line with a point at the end. We have heard this referred to as a *breath line*, but it has sometimes been called the spirit line or the heart line. This is a common element on pottery today, but it came late in the prehistoric era. To Pueblo people today, the breath is considered sacred; after all, it does disappear when we die. Was the breath line of this ruin gone? Was there no way for us to ever understand what went on here a millennium ago?

Early archaeologists developed techniques for understanding these ruins based on function. That is, which room was probably lived in, which rooms were for storage, which room(s) functioned as a ceremonial room. Gustaf Nordenskiold is considered the first to employ this technique in the 1890s in attempting to understand the Mesa Verde ruins. A. V. Kidder — sometimes called the father of Southwestern archaeology — as well as Jesse Fewkes and others, built upon these observational techniques near the beginning or the twentieth century before more scientific means began to be developed in the 1920s. These old observational techniques are not exacting like the scientific tests modern archaeologists employ today, and they did not work on open-air pueblo ruins. They gradually fell into disuse.

But when we stumbled upon these old techniques by reading the early archaeologists' works, we were ecstatic! Suddenly a whole new vista opened up to us. After many years of visiting ruins, we could finally understand more of what was going on at a ruin with careful observation. These older techniques breathed new life into the ancient ruins for us, allowing us to see them as not quite so inscrutable anymore.

This book is our attempt to share some of these late nineteenth-century ideas with you. Mind you, we are not archaeologists nor scholars nor experts. We are merely enthusiastic backcountry travelers who have been exploring, photographing and contemplating ruins since the 1960s. We have also read hundreds of books and papers on the subject and attended many lectures, as well as exploring most of the major libraries across the region.

This is a very exciting time in the study of Southwestern archaeology with new insights and new disciplines being brought into the study all the time. We have no doubt that scholars and scientists will be able to reveal new insights to all of us interested bystanders as time goes on. But in the meantime, we offer these observations with the hope that the information will increase your enjoyment of visiting cliff dwellings as much as it has ours.

Among some archaeologists today there is a surge in reemploying these early observational techniques. Jeffrey Dean reintroduced them and then developed them to new heights in his seminal 1969 paper, "Chronological Analysis of Tsegi Phase Sites in Northeastern Arizona." Arthur Rohn used them in his study of Mug House in Mesa Verde National Park, as did Robert W. Preucel's survey of old Kotyiti. And most recently, Larry Nordby in his book *Prelude to Tapestries in Stone: Understanding Cliff Palace Architecture* and Kathleen Fiero in her book *Balcony House: A History of a Cliff Dwelling* have made use of these techniques at Mesa Verde National Park. At sites where the artifacts have been removed, at sites where even archaeologists are not allowed to dig and in archaeological surveys these old techniques have proved to be invaluable again, offering insights as penetrating as procedures used by forensic scientists at crime scenes (some of which in fact originated with archaeology and physical anthropology).

So why just the cliff dwellings? Why not discuss the rich and complex and longlived Puebloan cultural heritage from the beginning to now instead of such a narrow time frame?

The subject is simply too complex and to do it justice in a book such as this. More is known about the ancient Puebloan cultures of the American Southwest than any other aspect of American archaeology. The sheer volume of facts and interpretations is daunting, and these facts sometimes conflict. This book is our interpretation of just a thin slice of this enormous body of information.

Also, it is possible for travelers to visit some cliff dwellings while the open-air pueblo ruins on the mesa tops are covered with dirt and unavailable for casual observation. The cliff dwellings have been protected by alcove or cave environments and are often in better condition than other types of ruins. Dating the ruins is a job for experts and laboratory tests. By choosing cliff dwellings — or the northern province's Pecos Classification of Pueblo III (PIII) — the timeline is narrowed down to a manageable few hundred years instead of nearly two thousand years of the past. Although there will be plenty of exceptions, the approximate date of cliff dwelling ruins can be generally assumed.

And then there's the lure of the cliff dwellings and the questions they inspire in us. People are visiting backcountry cliff dwellings already and have been visiting them for over a century — cliff dwellings by their very spectacular nature attract visitors. For many years the cliff dwellings have been so far away from anywhere that a person had to be very determined to reach them. That difficulty is what protected them but technology has made cliff dwellings more accessible than ever before. Information on specific sites is also more available than ever before. Whereas it took guides, equipment, stamina and gumption to reach "wild" cliff dwellings in the not so distant past, now most everyone can go to a cliff dwelling. That means it's time to organize the onslaught of visitors. It is time to enlist these restless, curious and determined backcountry travelers as partners in preservation.

We make several assumptions in this book. We begin by assuming that you are already at a cliff dwelling and that you are curious about what you are seeing and want to know more. Our emphasis is on the small, unrestored cliff dwellings that are common in the backcountry of the Greater American Southwest and not so much on the spectacular cliff dwellings at Mesa Verde National Park, the enormous Betatakin or Kiet Siel (pronounced Bet-TAT-akin and Keet Seel) at Navajo National Monument in Northeastern Arizona or any of the large, spectacular examples of cliff dwelling ruins. The larger more spectacular cliff dwellings are more complex and, hence, more difficult to understand. The small, backcountry ruins are the easiest to interpret because they are by necessity at their essence; in most cases the

What Is a Cliff Dwelling?

Cliff dwellings can be large, like Montezuma's Castle, above, or a small ganary like the one on the left. Not all are inaccessible — some can be entered easily, such as the one on the right.

For the purposes of this book, a cliff dwelling is any ruin that is in a cliff, either impossibly high on a wall in an alcove, or at ground level, but tucked up against the cliff wall. We will discuss the era from circa A.D. 1150 to circa 1450. In the study of the people of the northern realms, previously called the "Anasazi," this era is known to the archaeologists as Pueblo III (or PIII) and PIV era in the Pecos Classification System. In east/central Arizona in the Tonto Basin, this is referred to as the Roosevelt phase of the Classic era of the Hohokam people. In the far south, in Northern Mexico, this era has been referred to as the Medio period of the Casas Grandes culture.

Cliff dwellings include ruins large and small, and buildings built of stone, or jacal, and buildings pecked out of the volcanic rock such as at Bandelier National Monument. Those built of solid adobe in Northern Mexico that are also cliff dwellings.

A cliff dwelling does not necessarily have to have housed people. There are plenty of cliff dwellings that were used strictly for storage. With this book you'll learn how to tell the difference between them.

cave restricts the size of the dwellings, so there can be no extraneous rooms or spaces. Also, their message has not been obscured by early, well-meaning restorations.

Another assumption we make is that you are an experienced desert traveler and know that in the wilderness one is responsible for oneself. As such, you'll need to remember to bring plenty of water and a poncho or waterproof coat, and routinely carry some survival gear and a small emergency kit in a day pack or fanny pack. You'll need to wear heavy-duty hiking boots or shoes. Always take along a compass, maps and GPS, and most importantly, know how to use them. You *cannot* rely on a cell phone as emergency communication in this part of the country. It is essential that you travel with a companion because there are so many dangers in the desert. In other words, come prepared and never take any needless risks, knowing that if others have to rescue you, they put their own lives in danger.

It is even more important to **Tread Lightly!** in the desert than it is in other places. We hope you will make a dedicated effort to keep your impact to nature minimal while on your backcountry excursions, whether on foot, mountain bike, four-wheel drive or however you choose to travel.

Beyond that, we want to assume that our readers are *enlightened explorers.* An enlightened explorer is one who is sophisticated in her approach to what she finds. For example, this person can appreciate a field of wildflowers without picking them. She can spot relics and not be tempted to remove them, even to make "museum rocks." (A museum rock is a boulder or a window sill or some other flat surface at a ruin that visitors use for displaying artifacts that have been discovered at this site.) Her thoughts are concerned with the protection of the ruin and she is careful not to inadvertently damage it in any way. She is satisfied with being awed at the privilege of witnessing an ancient culture and lifeway. If she wants a memento, she photographs it. If she is looking for "art," she uses the experience to inspire her own artistic creation: An artist might paint a picture of the site, a musician write a song about it, a poet write a poem about it. But she does not remove *anything* from the site as a souvenir.

In 1879, a charismatic young man arrived at the Zuni Pueblo at the behest of the Smithsonian Institution. He was Frank H. Cushing, and his job was to record everything that was possible of this culture. It was recognized by scholars back East that much of the indigenous cultures in the eastern part of the country had already been lost, and they realized that with the remote Southwestern Pueblo cultures there was still a chance — still time to record what they could about these vanishing cultures.

A "museum rock," above, is where visitors have moved artifacts to a different place in order to "display" them. This practice is discouraged.

Cushing became one of the first *ethnographers*. An ethnographer studies one culture, its origins and its customs, and studies it intensively. Cushing chose to do this by actually talking his way into the Zuni Pueblo and making himself at home. He learned to speak their language, was inducted into a secret and prestigious war society, wore their clothes, ate their food and lived as a Zuni until 1884.

His insights into the Zuni people have been invaluable to scholars ever since. Because the descendants of the ancient people are still here is one of the reasons southwestern archaeology is so extensive. This is one of the few places in the world where archaeologists have someone to ask when they have questions about an artifact or a custom.

We relied heavily upon Cushing's and other early ethnographers' observations of how the Pueblo people lived before the onslaughts of the twentieth century. These early ethnographic works also contain beautiful artwork , some of which we have included.

We also relied on the earliest explorers and contacts pulling their observations from historical documents. The early explorers were able to witness the Puebloans at the first contact — before the coming of white men had impacted them greatly. Coronado and other Spanish conquistadors became our eyes and ears. But we used just their *observations* — what they actually saw — not their *interpretations* — that is, not what they thought about what they saw. For us, the prudent use of ethnography can provide insight into the culture.

Some archaeologists disagree with the idea that the modern Puebloans are a fertile source of information on their ancestors. Just look how much our *own* culture has changed in a thousand years, they point out. And the ancient Puebloan culture underwent major disruptions over the course of a millennium — too many to be able to draw a straight, unbroken line of cultural continuity back to the cliff dwellings. Certainly the move to the cliff dwellings was a sign of profound change and a culture under stress. Also, the first Europeans to arrive – the Spanish conquistadors – wrought many changes, including new plants, new livestock and new religion.

But for us a window of cultural continuity was established by a visit to Bandelier National Monument on the day after New Years, 1991. We took the walk to Alcove House along with a few other visitors. When we arrived at the kiva we were the only visitors who climbed down the ladder into the ceremonial room. There, on the floor at the edge of the round and otherwise empty room, was a small bundle. Of course we went straight to the bundle and looked at it but did not touch it. There was a cloud blower (a handmade tobacco pipe), a feather, a little man made of corn leaves, all this peeking out of a folded red, cotton flannel handkerchief so old it was frayed with age. We had visited this kiva many times, but this bundle had never been there. And it looked authentic, not something left behind by tourists. So we walked back to the visitor center and asked the ranger about it.

The ranger behind the counter looked at us stunned, and said, "What bundle?" She called to another ranger in the visitor center and they both darted out of the building, headed for the kiva. We heard her say as she filled in her colleague, "Nearby Native Americans must have used the kiva last night for a ceremony!" Bandelier National Monument is surrounded on three sides by Pueblo Indian reservations, and this was not the first time ancient facilities at the national monument had been secretly used by them for special ceremonies. This suggests to us that the Pueblo people themselves claim cultural continuity with their ancestors and the ruins.

Because of that experience and all the research we have done on the Pueblo people and the cliff ruins, we have come to the conclusion that — *for us* — the prudent use of ethnographic information from modern Pueblo people can provide a valid insight into life in the ancient ruins. In other words, we believe that some cultural continuity does exist although the ethnography must be used with *caution*.

That said, we have included chapters on ancient men and the women based on early ethnography. This will no doubt be controversial to some of our readers. But we have found it to be the breath line of the ruins for us, filling the empty buildings with some semblance of life. Besides referring to the early ethnographers for this information, we also relied on the memoirs and

The kiva at Alcove House in Bandelier National Monument.

biographies of Puebloans to try to "people" the ancient ruins that we all see in the backcountry. We found this information to be invaluable in addressing the question: Who were these people and how did they live?

In the chapter on preservation we do not emphasize the artifacts themselves, an approach that has been a longtime problem of many popular books on the subject. Instead we emphasize the *stories* the

artifacts and their context have to tell. We sincerely hope this approach will re-focus visitors to the ruins in a new and positive direction. We invite readers into this new way of thinking that the *real* treasure — the real discovery — is deciphering the story the artifacts have to tell you.

The chapter titled "The Architecture of Upheaval" will give the reader a quick, streamlined version of what seems to have been happening in the American Southwest about the time the cliff dwellings began to appear. And the landscape chapter will give a glance at the geography and usable plants important to the ancient peoples.

Pictographs and petroglyphs (sometimes referred to as *rock art*) always seemed inscrutable to us until we studied the ethnography of the Puebloans, especially their myths and legends. By understanding some of their symbolism, suddenly the symbols we saw on the rock walls began to make some sense. However, these are modern historic interpretations of the pictographs and petroglyphs. Again, what rock art means to Puebloans today may have meant something entirely different to their ancient ancestors. Differences in meaning might be particularly great for us, coming not only from a distance of a thousand years, but also from a different culture.

In all our years of exploring the backcountry, we have never seen a whole pot in place. But we used to see thousands of potsherds. Now even those are gone for the most part. So why have a chapter on pottery? Pottery was extremely important to the ancient people. Archaeologists have long used ceramic styles to determine cultural affiliation and boundaries. It takes a lifetime to master all the differences and nuances. However, knowing a few basics about it will help you to understand what you see in museums. We will paint the subject in broad strokes, with overall, general information. We will emphasize possible usage and function of things you might see in your travels.

The same is true of arrowheads. You might never encounter an arrowhead in the backcountry. But what you *are* likely to see is the *debitage* — the waste rock chips — from manufacturing one. These are very common throughout the Greater American Southwest.

We have also included a chapter on the fascinating origins of corn farming and some of the clever techniques the ancients used to be able to farm in this environment that was often hostile to farming corn.

A chapter on miscellaneous items we call by the Hopi word for variety, or a number of different things: *Hiihiimu*. This chapter includes a little on archaeoastronomy and the ancient highways that are still visible today. It also offers a little on towers and a few words on shrines.

But the heart of the book — the breath line — is the cliff dwelling structures themselves. In the twenty-first century, the artifactual legacy of the ancient ones of the Greater American Southwest is their architecture. The small, manufactured artifacts are mostly gone now, but the cliff dwellings themselves remain. We will give you observation techniques to help you spot clues as to the possible function of the rooms, buildings and structures.

The last chapter will present one way that people can meaningfully participate in the Southwestern archaeology today. It tells of how we came to be involved in this amazing world and explains why it still grips us to this day.

Following some of the chapters is a *field guide*. These field guides are intended to show you what you might likely see at a ruin. It is our hope that this book is a stepping stone to reading other books on the subject, because *The Cliff Dwellings Speak* is intended to merely scratch the surface of the subject. The field guides are one way to scratch that surface.

This book is intended as an intoduction to the archaeology of the Greater American Southwest. We sincerely hope it will inspire and enhance your backcountry travels as much as it has influenced ours.

We are told that our mindset from what is known as Western Civilization is an insurmountable obstacle to understanding the ancient Puebloan past. Although we may never fully grasp what it means to be a Puebloan — modern or ancient — we at least move one step closer to that understanding through research and study. However, we must acknowledge that the breath line back to the ancient past is a tenuous one: It is wispy and meandering and has gaps where the line of cultural continuity has been broken at certain critical times.

tread lightly! ®
ON LAND AND WATER

WHAT'S IN A NAME?

by Argie J. Miller

One compelling mystery behind these ancient sun-bleached structures sleeping in the desert is one that we will never solve: The mystery of what name the ancient people who lived there called *themselves*. Today we call the people who built the cliff dwellings the ancestral Puebloans. Even though we can't say what they would have wanted us to call them a thousand years ago, we can still glean important information from historic records written hundreds of years ago. These records were scratched by observers from Europe who first made contact with the descendants of the ancestral Puebloans.

The first written observations of this American culture were made by outside observers, specifically the Spanish explorers. Coronado was the first European to give us a written observation. In the seventeenth century the Spanish colonists noticed that the *Indios* (the word applied to the indigenous people in America) they found in the American Southwest were different from other indigenous people. These Indios were settled farmers with a rich culture, living in permanent villages, or *pueblos* in Spanish. As a result the European explorers referred to their new neighbors as the "Pueblo People." These village-dwelling people were distinctly different from other Native Americans who were foragers and hunters, who moved from place to place and lived in temporary housing.

The popular term we used until recently to refer to the ancestors of the northern Pueblo people is *Anasazi*. In the Navajo language the name *Anaasází* means "ancestors of the aliens" (that is, not Navajos) or even "enemy ancestors." The story behind the use of this word says that when the earliest explorers came to the Southwest, they would ask their guide — who was often Navajo — what those buildings were in the cliffs. The Navajo would answer, "Anasazi."

Our use of Anasazi is ascribed to rancher Richard Wetherill who is credited with discovering Cliff Palace in what is now Mesa Verde National Park. He attached the name Anasazi to the people who once lived in the abandoned stone buildings he found. Wetherill has been a controversial figure: Some consider him a terrible pot hunter, others see him as an early amateur archaeologist. This is paradoxical in that on one hand his actions mark the beginning of movements to recognize and preserve these valuable treasures, but on the other hand today these actions would be considered grave robbing. The Hopi people today, of course, resent their ancestors being named with a foreign name given by their enemies.

Edmund Nequatewa, a Hopi chief and writer, provides us with critical information about names given to ancestral Puebloans. In 1942 he published an article called, "Why the Spaniards called the Hopi, 'Moqui'" in the periodical *Plateau*. There Nequatewa noted that native tribes everywhere often came to be known to us not by names that members of their own tribe called themselves, but rather by names other neighboring tribes called them. The reason for this is because European people first coming to the area may learn of neighboring native people from members of another tribe. As the Spaniards approached the Hopi from the Rio Grande region, Nequatewa states in his example, they called the Hopi, *Moqüi* (pronounced MO-KWI). This is the name by which the Hopi were known at the pueblos to the east — the direction the Spanish were advancing from: Santo Domingo, Cochiti, Acoma, and Zuni, to name a few. After that, for some time the name *Moqüi* came into common use among the Spanish as well. Anglo-Americans, when they came to live in the region, pronounced the word *mo-ki*. Unfortunately, *Moki* in the Hopi language means *dead*. To be called "the dead ones" for obvious reasons Nequtewa confirms, was insulting.

Conversely, another example of this phenomenon involves the Navajo who call themselves *Dine*. Nequatewa recounted that the story behind the name *Navajo* originated in the seventeenth century when Rio Grande Pueblo tribes referred to them as *Apache de Navahu*, and the name was corrupted to *Navajo* in later times. A particularly chilling example of name transmutation is found in the literature when early linguists discovered an early Native American community that referred to their neighbors as "The Smallpox People."

Today we can ask the living descendants of these people — the Pueblo people of today who include the Hopi. The Hopi say they have lived in the American Southwest longer than anyone can remember, and that they have always been called *Hopi*. Their legends tell of constructing stone dwellings, raising their families and migrating to more suitable locations when it became necessary. The name the Hopi call their ancestors is *hisatsinom* (pronounced he-SAT-si-nom). This term means "Ancestral People."

Pueblo scholars, as do most archaeologists, use an anglicized derivation of Hisatsinom, the English term, ancestral Puebloan. This name refers to any culture in the American Southwest that centuries ago built and later abandoned the stone dwellings we find asleep in the desert today. This term, ancestral Puebloan, is meant to include all Ancestral Pueblo people in all the separate groups in Arizona and New Mexico.

Another complication is the Pueblo people do not have just one name for a person or landmark. Names are not standardized as they are in the Anglo culture. A person has many names — nicknames, we might say — and can be called one name at one time and another by a different person at another time. The same holds true for landmarks. A butte might be called "the tall butte" because of its size, or "the nearest butte" because of its location, or "the shrine to our Earth Mother" because it contains an alcove that is used as a shrine on occasion. Which name it is called depends upon the situation and sometimes the person who is referring to it.

And people are rarely called by their formal names, anyway. If you are with a friend, you would refer to him or her as "my friend." When with your father, you would refer to him as "my father." Or a grandparent would be referred to as "my grandmother," "or my grandfather." This is considered a sign of respect.

The disconcerting part of calling the ancestors of the Pueblo people by names like "Anasazi" is it separates the ancient ones from their descendants in the eyes of modern travelers. They look at a map, see there is no tribe called the Anasazi and are led to believe the old ones disappeared. That they "vanished." But they did not, in fact, vanish. In the following pages, you will discover what, indeed, might have happened to them.

ACKNOWLEDGMENTS

Writing a book is a lot like building a house. First of all, it's an enormous undertaking, one that will consume all of one's life until it is finished. It's an endeavor that must be undertaken with much thought and planning and consideration. It requires many different experts along the way — architects and master craftsmen and engineers who help erect a sound and functional structure. So it has been with *The Cliff Dwellings Speak.* We would like to introduce you to the many experts who took time from their busy schedules to help us design and build the book you now hold in your hands. We are grateful to each and every one of them — without any one of them this would have been a different, less fulfilling book.

We would like to thank the Tread Lightly! organization for allowing us to reproduce the *Tread Lightly!*™ logo. Because of their courtesy, this book is a more responsible book. (800) 966-9900.

As we have stated previously, we are not scholars — but we relied on scholars for guidance. We thank the archaeology scholars who took the time to read the manuscript and comment on it. We are grateful for their insights that have created a strong foundation for the book. First of all, we thank two archaeologists who are known for their work on cliff dwelling architecture: Larry Nordby, who wrote our wonderful Foreword, is retired Research Archaeologist for Mesa Verde National Park. And Jeff Dean, Professor Emeritus of Dendrochronology in the Laboratory of Tree-Ring Research at the University of Arizona, who read the manuscript and whose comments were greatly appreciated. Among archaeologists, they are recognized as two of the leading voices on the subject of cliff dwelling architecture.

Winston Hurst, scholar and archaeologist read the manuscript and gave us perceptive suggestions. He was also instrumental in the Telluride Blanket Project. Much of that story would have been lost without his contributions.

To Ruth Lambert, archaeologist and scholar at the San Juan Mountain Assoication, we owe our thanks for her guidance with the preservation issues. Because of Ruth and others like her, there will continue to be cliff ruins to visit in the future. We also thank her for reading the manuscript, her comments, and for her enthusiastic support of this book project.

We would also like to thank the archaeologists at the Crow Canyon Archaeological Center, Mark Varien and Jonathon Till and others who agreed to read the manuscript even with their heavy work schedules and time commitments.

John Kantner of the School of Advanced Research in Santa Fe is an archaeologist who also reviewed the manuscript. We are very appreciative for his comments.

Scholars Victoria Atkins, archaeologist at the Anasazi Heritage Center, and her husband Fred Blackburn, researcher, educator and author. Victoria alerted us to the quotation by David Hurst Thomas that is the epigraph for Chapter 1, which expresses so clearly what the book is about. Also thanks to Victoria for obtaining a fresh sample of Hopi parched corn so that we could describe it accurately for our readers. But most of all we thank Fred and Victoria for their work on the Telluride Blanket. Without their knowledge and perseverance, the Telluride Blanket story might never have been able to be told.

Cassandra Leoncini of Leoncini Consulting deserves special mention here. Not only is she an expert on the archaeology of the American Southwest, but she is also an expert in publishing of the American Southwest as well. We thank her for reading the manuscript and for her invaluable guidance.

History scholars also contributed much to this book. Andrew Gulliford, author, historian and professor of Southwestern Studies at Ft. Lewis College in Durango, Colorado, is a case in point. Andy urged us to include vernacular architecture in our discussion of cliff dwellings and we are thrilled at the result. He also came up with the name for a nameless type of ruin that we also included in the pages of this book. We are grateful to you, Andy, for your perceptiveness.

Rick Athearn is another historical scholar who contributed to the pages of this book. His expertise is on the point of contact between the Pueblo people and the Spanish conquistadors in the sixteenth century. Rick read the manuscript and his comments are much appreciated.

Linda Martin of Mesa Verde National Park is another historical scholar that we owe much to. Although on a tight schedule, she took the time to read the manuscript and share her comments with us. We are grateful to her for her insights.

We also thank the Denver Public Library and the Colorado Historical Society for their help and attention through this very long project.

Ken Detweiler, also a historical scholar, read the manuscript and contributed his "take" on the subject. We thank him for his astute input.

We are particularly humbled that seven of the twenty Pueblos agreed to read the manuscript. Because of this, *The Cliff Dwellings Speak* has veracity and authenticity. Thanks to the Acoma Pueblo, Laguna Pueblo, Picuris Pueblo, Pojoaque Pueblo, San Felipe Pueblo, San Juan Pueblo and the Zuni Pueblo. Mark Altaha of the White Mountain Apache tribe allowed us to visit a little-known and difficult ruin on their tribal land — and thus we able to piece together some of the jigsaw of the ancient people.

Several people volunteered to read the manuscript from the standpoint of the general public. We are grateful to them for taking the time to peruse a rough manuscript and offer advice. Thanks to: Rhonda Beck and Eric Rindahl, Steve and Charli Pierson, Bob and Eileen Gresham, Bud and Jackie Witman, Ewan Grantham and Ron Horn. Because of your efforts, *The Cliff Dwellings Speak* is more readable for all of us non-professionals.

Finally, we owe a debt of gratitude to the photographers who generously allowed us to include their fabulous photographs in the book: Andy Gulliford, Vaughn Hadenfeldt, Peg Hoffman and Ron Horn. Your generosity has helped us build a more beautiful and useful book.

We also thank Argie Jim Miller for his thoughtful discussion on the importance of names in the Pueblo cultures. Joe Pachak also deserves thanks for guiding us on two trips to the backcountry and sharing his expertise in rock art.

And finally to our long-time friend Mike Turner, who stood by us when we faced down banditos in Mexico, who was there shovel in hand when the Land Rover sank in quicksand, and all the adventures and mishaps — we thank him for his camaraderie under trying conditions. Without him many of these pictures would not exist.

We thank all the experts who helped us construct this book, but any mistakes are strictly our own.

Above, the photograph
William H. Jackson took on
September 9, 1874. Standing
is John Moss, Ernest Ingersoll is seated. Denver Public
Library Western History Collection (William H. Jackson,
#WHJ10667).

On the right, more than
a hundred years later, we
found the cliff dwelling and
matched Jackson's pho-
tograph. Our friend, Mike
Turner, stands, Bill Sagstetter is seated.

INTRODUCTION

They had seen a few mounds along the trail — ruined stone walls protruding from the dirt and covered with potsherds — but William Henry Jackson, photographer for the Hayden Survey, was impatient. Still the group pushed forward along the faint trail. Jackson had heard stories around the campfires of the San Juan Mountains in Southwestern Colorado, where he had been assigned for the summer of 1874. Prospectors loved to tell tall tales around the campfire, and Jackson knew that, but these tales were different. These tales were about a "lost civilization" and incredible cities built high in inaccessible cliffs. The place even had a name: Mesa Verde, the green tableland. Jackson wouldn't rest until he had seen cliff dwellings!

Jackson had immediately assembled a small interested group to make the trip. Besides the cook and some packers, Ernest Ingersoll, a naturalist, also accompanied the group.

Leading them was black-bearded John Moss. Moss was a well-respected man in the region: He was an experienced California prospector who had received funding from the Parrott Company to prospect in Colorado. He and his cohorts had founded Parrott City in the San Juan Mountains and Moss knew the region better than any white man in the area. Jackson had looked Moss up. Moss confirmed the unlikely-sounding story of a vanished civilization and even agreed to guide them there. Jackson couldn't have had a better guide to the region — the Utes were understandably upset about all the illegal mining activity taking place on their sacred lands and tensions were running high. But John Moss spoke the Ute language and had forged his own private treaty with them to be on their land. They let following a faint trail down the Mancos River.

By that evening — September 9, 1874 — Jackson was a little disappointed. He had seen nothing like what the campfire tales had described. They set up camp next to the Mancos River and ate a dinner of sowbelly [a kind of bacon] and bread. After dinner, they all backed up to the fire, warming their backsides and enjoying their second favorite pasttime around the campfire: making "ironical statements" and teasing Steve, their youngest packer. They told Steve he was going to have to carry all the heavy, new-fangled photographic equipment up to the top of the mesa so Jackson could photograph buildings the next day. The cliff to the north of them was a daunting 800 feet high. Looking concerned, Steve asked them to point out the exact spot. Trying not to laugh, Moss swept his arm at random toward the cliff face, "never dreaming ourselves that any were really there," wrote Jackson in his field journal.

"Yes," said Steve, "I see it."

They were thunderstruck! Jackson wrote: "I beheld upon my close observation there was something that appeared very like a house, the doors and windows" could just be made out in the failing light.

Suddenly everyone abandoned camp to investigate. Jackson wrote in his autobiography *Time Exposure*: "The first 600 feet or so we had a stiff climb but not a difficult one. Then we found ourselves facing a flat vertical wall rising some 200 feet above the ledge on which we were standing. Fifty feet above our heads, in a shallow cave, was a two-story house. But how to reach it?"

At this point all the others, except Ingersoll and Jackson, gave it up and returned to camp. But these two would not be stopped by the encroaching darkness and the sheer cliff — they continued on. They found an old juniper tree to clamor up and a series of crevices, and by helping each other, finally pulled themselves up onto the ledge they sought. Jackson wrote in his journal: "Then perched away in a crevice like a swallow's or bat's nest, it was, a marvel and a puzzle."

The next day Jackson took the sepia-toned photographs that would become famous and would introduce Mesa Verde and the cliff dwellings to an astounded public. The inset picture on our cover is an engraving of the photograph Jackson took that day. They named the cliff dwelling Two-Story House.

Ninety years later I read Jackson's account in the Hayden Geological Survey at the Denver Public Library as a college kid and I was awestruck! I could not rest until I had seen these amazing cliff dwellings.

And thus our life-long journey of exploring cliff dwellings began . . .

The broken arrowhead we found that day, side-by-side with an example of how it may have looked undamaged.

1

Partners in Preservation

It's not what you find, but what you find out.
— Archaeologist David Hurst Thomas

We worked our way up to the high windy ridge that would be our path to the cliff dwelling we sought. As we came to the final step onto the cap rock, rather than stepping up on it, we sat on it instead. To tired hikers like us, the cap rock looked like a perfect natural bench. Stretching beneath us was a 300-degree view of piñon pine and juniper forests punctuated by sandstone bluffs. The sharp aroma of sagebrush perfumed the air. The only sound was the whir of a hummingbird as it zipped by. We nibbled on trail mix and drank water as we admired the landscape. To our twenty-first-century eyes our perch seemed an ideal place to watch for game or to stand guard for the cliff dwelling.

As we sat there we happened to look down and noticed shiny chips of reddish rock fanning away from our feet. Each chip was no bigger than a fingernail. We don't know much about geology or stone, but even we could tell this type of rock did not occur here naturally — all around us was sandstone in various pale, gritty hues. No, this rock was out of context, and the only way it could have come here is if it had been brought here by a person. Archaeologists call these stone chips *lithic scatter* — the debris that results from making an arrowhead or a chipped stone tool. It appeared that someone who had sat on this very spot nearly a millennium ago had produced a chipped stone tool.

If we had been with an experienced *flintknapper* that day, he would have been able to tell us all kinds of information from the scatter of rock chips. He could probably tell us where the rock had originally been found. He could tell us what kind of rock it was — whether it was jasper or quartz, chalcedony or obsidian, or some other stone. He might have been able to explain to us

Lithic scatter is usually comprised of shiny chips of rock, which are the debris left from someone having manufactured a stone tool. It is a tell-tale sign of ancient human activity.

the theories of rock fracture. He certainly would be able to make a stone tool himself. But since we did not have the pleasure of traveling with such a person, what could ordinary travelers such as ourselves glean from such a finding?

As we looked casually at the stone debris, we saw the shape of an arrowhead outlined in the sandy dirt. To us it seemed impressive: It was about two inches long and was thin. Later we were told it was thought to be of the Archaic era, that is, much older than the ancient Pueblo ruins in the area. As we looked at it more closely, we saw that the tip of the arrowhead was chipped off and both of the tangs were also broken. This might well have happened naturally because of rock fall or a large animal like a deer or bighorn sheep stepping on it. But because it was still surrounded with the debris from its manufacture, we surmised that the arrowhead had probably broken while it was being made.

A possible story emerged from the rubble: Thousands of years ago someone who might have been watching for game began to make an arrowhead. However, when it was nearly complete it broke in his hands. Was he in a hurry, or was the stone of inferior quality? Or was he a young man just learning his craft? Whatever the reason, he discarded the broken arrowhead and it remained where it fell — unfinished and undisturbed and broken — for thousands of years.

We photographed the point and returned it to the divot that had been its home for so long. Although it was just a fistful of scattered rock chips and a broken arrowhead, this site still had a wonderful story to tell! Even we, as nonprofessionals, were able to discern some semblance of a story here.

What we took with us was a photograph and a story — a story about what might have happened in this very spot so long ago. Stories waiting to be told exist all over the Greater American Southwest: Stories about who passed this way before us. Stories about where they lived. Most all the canyons that we have visited in the Southwest contain some scrap of cultural remains — whether a stone tool, a rock art panel, building remains or pottery sherds. Our hope is to empower you to discern these stories as you travel in the backcountry in the American Southwest.

The key is being able to *see* the clues in order to piece together the stories like puzzles. This requires a highly developed sense of observation. We were not born with eagle eyes; it is something that we had to consciously develop. One of the best ways to develop one's sense of observation is to know what to look for in the backcountry. We hope this book will begin that process for you.

However, an artifact by itself tells only a partial story; what completes the story and gives it meaning is its *context* — what surrounds the artifact and relates to it. Therefore, protecting sites and their artifacts and context is of vital importance to preservationists. How to maintain the connection — those possible stories — is a problem that preservationists have been grappling with for decades.

But preservationists are only a single part of this endeavor. There are others who also hold keys to the stories locked in stone on the ledges that house the cliff dwellings. They too have stories to tell.

If we stood before a cliff dwelling on a narrow ledge today, what stories could be discerned from this site? A modern Puebloan, descendant to the ancient Puebloans, for example, might tell us what these buildings mean to him. If he were so inclined, he might explain to us how they were built and why.

If an *ethnographer* were also with us today, she could tell us about the descendants of these ancient people and their practices today, such as how they build their houses, make their pottery, live their lives. In particular, the early ethnographers —who lived with the Puebloans of the late nineteenth century in order to be able to study them up close and in depth — could tell us how the Puebloans did things before they had been impacted, even engulfed, by "Americans" and events of the twentieth century.

If an archaeologist were with us today on this ledge, he could give us an idea of how many folks probably lived in this dwelling. He could draw upon exacting scientific laboratory tests that could date this site and give us important information about the site — tests with imposing names like *thermoluminescence* or *dendrochronology,* or isotope tests that pinpoint where a corn kernel was grown or where a person came from originally.

An expert in *vernacular* (or folk) architecture who stood with us on the ledge today could tell us that Puebloan structures are the very essence of vernacular architecture. This scholar could explain to us the ramifications of vernacular architecture on nature and on the lifestyles of those who inhabited these structures.

And as we have seen, a preservationist would have yet another viewpoint about the treatment of cliff dwellings and other ancient structures in order for them to "speak" to future generations.

All these experts could provide us with important but differing viewpoints on ruins. They see the ruins from different perspectives. Through their eyes, we could see ruins in new ways — ways that would hopefully provide a deeper understanding and meaning to what we are witnessing.

But this is a *narrow* ledge and we could not possibly all stand here together today. Therefore, we have condensed many of their insights into the form of this compact book you hold in your hands. But if we are to be able to travel to the backcountry cliff dwellings without fences and guards, it is imperative we know the proper way to visit them before we start.

Preservationists' Point of View

In the words of archaeologist Peter Pilles, it is impossible for people to respect something they know nothing about. We heartily agree, believing that knowledge comes first and respect follows. Education, therefore, is the key to respect. Our purpose in writing this book is to provide readers with enough information to inspire love and respect for these fascinating places and the people who inhabited them. That is, in fact, how it happened for us.

But with this information comes responsibility. When we visit a backcountry site, for that moment in time we are its caretaker or guardian. We become temporary unofficial stewards of the site, protecting it for future generations of backcountry visitors. It is up to us to make sure it is not damaged in any way during our visit there. If we are to visit these sites as they are in the wild — without locked gates and guards — we must know the proper protocol for visiting a cliff dwelling.

However, each national park, state park, tribal park, national monument, and parcel of Bureau of Land Management or Forest Service land has its own rules for visitors. And these sometimes evolve and change. For example, in tribal parks you will need a guide to accompany you in the backcountry. At some sites, you are allowed to enter a ruin, look around it and take photographs. At others, such as Canyon de Chelly, the ruins are fenced and you are not allowed to enter them. Therefore, the only way to make sure you are aware of the rules of the places you visit is to stop by the nearest ranger station or visitor center and inquire. Obtain the needed permits and/or arrange for a guide, if necessary. Familiarize yourself with the rules for that particular place before embarking on your adventure. But there are some basic common-sense guidelines that are a starting point for visiting all cliff dwellings. They are the baseline for proper cliff dwelling visitation, with the understanding that these guidelines will be elaborated upon at each national park, tribal park and so on.

The Hopi people of northeastern Arizona are among the modern descendants of the ancient Pueblo people. They have a word, *qahopi*, (sometimes spelled *kahopi* and pronounced *kuh-HOPE- ee*). It basically means the wrong way to do something — not the Hopi way of doing things. Using their words, it is *qahopi* — wrong — to harm a ruin in any way, even inadvertently. This includes actions like leaning against or climbing on those old stone walls which might cause them to collapse. Or touching rock art panels, or tracing or outlining vague rock art in chalk for better photographs.

More obscure actions are also *qahopi*. Eating your lunch in a ruin can attract rodents burrowing for the crumbs, which can undermine walls and cause them to topple. For the same reasons, it is *qahopi* to camp or sleep in a ruin. Instead, camp nearby, safely away from the delicate structure. Keep children under close supervision for their own safety and also so they cause no accidental harm. Pets are not allowed in backcountry cliff dwellings.

Digging at a site is more than *qahopi*; it is illegal to dig on state or federal government land. In tribal park lands this law is also strictly enforced. Even archaeologists must submit reams of forms for permits to excavate. Digging without a permit is punishable by stiff fines and/or imprisonment, and vehicles and equipment will be confiscated.

It is also illegal to remove anything from a site including arrowheads, potsherds and even items that seem insignificant, like rock chips, for example. First of all, removing objects destroys the archaeological record and limits future research. Each artifact at a site is like a book — full of information and stories — that archaeologists attempt to decipher. Digging at a site destroys information. So to preservationists, removing or rearranging anything at a site is akin to burning a book or destroying a library.

This example of a "museum rock" is a niche in an ancient wall.

Then, from the modern Puebloan point of view, each object the ancients made was created with songs and prayers and thus is imbued with a spirit of its own. So when you find an artifact, leave it and its spirit where you found it. Don't remove it and its spirit from their places; they sing the same song and should remain together.

Some well-intentioned people move artifacts from their original place to a *museum rock*. A museum rock could be a boulder the size of a table or a window sill or the top of a wall on which people place artifacts they have found at the site

in order to display them. Apparently some folks think that this doesn't count as removing artifacts. But in fact it does destroy the story the artifact has to tell. Artifacts must be left *exactly* where they are encountered.

There are even special ways to walk in a cliff dwelling. It is *qahopi* to walk on the fragile midden (the soft discard area where inhabitants disposed of their refuse). The midden is often found in the front of a cliff dwelling, sometimes downhill or off the face of the cliff.

Also, attempting to retrace the steps of the ancient ones on the old hand-and-toe hold trails is foolhardy. People have been seriously injured or killed trying to climb the hand-and-toe holds etched by the ancients on the cliff walls. These holds have often eroded and are no longer negotiable, and using them hastens their erosion. Also, these hand-and-toe holds usually lead in only one direction; if you should become stranded halfway, there is no way down. Other hand-and-toe trails must be started with one particular foot — if you should begin up the trail with the "wrong" foot, you will not be able to complete the trail and could become stuck there.

If, in your backcountry travels, you should happen upon people vandalizing a ruin, do not confront them. Just observe them discreetly from a distance, make notes, and take photographs of their actions if you have a camera handy. If possible, write down vehicle license plate numbers at the trailhead parking lot if there is one, and report it to the nearest sheriff or ranger, or to site personnel at the nearest visitor center. Let us all become an army of unofficial stewards, protecting these very special cliff ruins for future generations of backcountry visitors. If you would like to become an *official* site steward, there are organizations you can join. (See Appendix B.)

Starting Your Adventure

Preservationists suggest that the best places to start are at the visitor centers and museums in national parks, monuments, tribal parks and other "official" sites. The techniques we offer in the following pages work best in the backcountry at small sites, but can also work in large, official sites. Because large spectacular ruins in parks and monuments are more complex, they are more difficult to understand. However, there are still plenty of reasons to visit large, official places. While there you'll be training your eyes to spot cliff dwellings. You'll be practicing the techniques we present in the book. Another reason to visit the visitor centers and museums at the parks is that you might never see an artifact like a pot or an arrowhead at the backcountry sites. The museums have artifacts on display that you can study and perhaps come to understand. And you'll be learning more about these fascinating

U.S. Geological Survey.

Plate XLVII.

AF. PHOTO-LITHO. CO. N.Y. (OSBORNE'S PROCESS.)

The old hand-and-toe holds are often no longer traversible because they have been damaged by weathering. Sometimes these "trails" only go one-way, if you climb up them, you might not be able to get back. Some of these trails must be started on a certain foot or they can not be negotiated all the way up. The 10th Annual Report of the Hayden Survey, 1878.

places, which with practice will make you a more astute, educated observer. Appendix A has a list of larger, official cliff dwelling sites.

Most serious cliff dwelling travelers also visit the modern pueblos, most of which are strung along the Rio Grande in New Mexico. A few more are scattered westward toward the border with Arizona, making a total of nineteen pueblos in New Mexico. Then the Hopi Mesas in northeastern Arizona make a total of twenty modern-day pueblos. The Pueblo people are the descendants of the ancient cliff dwellers and some of their present-day pueblos are open to visitors. Our understanding of the cliff dwellings has been enriched by visiting these very spiritual places. Meeting the cliff dwellers' descendants face to face has also increased our appreciation of the cliff dwellers immeasurably. We admire their accomplishments. We have respect for them, their culture, and their fascinating past.

Besides visiting ancient cliff dwellings and modern pueblos, you can read the many books that archaeologists and ethnographers have produced in more than a century of study. The more you know about the pueblo cultures, the more you will recognize in the ancient ruins. This is especially true of deciphering rock art — it is almost impossible to attempt to unravel its mysteries without the background knowledge of the culture's legends and past.

Like a magnifying glass, this book will enable you to fathom insights that might not be obvious to casual visitors. It is a new type of guidebook that will not give you specific directions to a cliff dwelling. There are already plenty of guidebooks on the market. This book will allow you the joy of discovering the cliff dwellings on your own. Once you are there, *The Cliff Dwellings Speak* will guide your eyes around the site you have found. You might even be able to identify which rooms were probably lived in, which were for storage, and which rooms were ceremonial rooms.

Since our discovery of the broken arrowhead, our greatest joy is to return again and again to see the artifact still in place, where it has rested for centuries. To see it in its home, where it belongs. As our knowledge has increased, we see the arrowhead with new eyes and the story is developed and elaborated upon. This joy is what we wish for you.

Why the ancient people moved to inaccessible perches in the cliffs is an enduring mystery of the Greater American Southwest.

Early explorers to the region were fascinated by these ruins and documented them. Above is an engraving made from a William Henry Jackson photograph taken in the 1870s. The 10th Annual Report of the Hayden Survey, 1878. On the right is a photograph matching the 1878 photograph.

46

2

THE ARCHITECTURE OF UPHEAVAL

After more than a millennium of living in moderately-sized communities spread evenly over the landscape [after A.D. 1250] in the space of about fifty years the entire population of the Colorado Plateau moved into about 100 very large pueblos that, geographically, were very unevenly spaced. The transformation was so rapid and so complete that it is unlike anything else that occurred in the history of Southwestern settlement patterns.

— *Steven A. LeBlanc*, Prehistoric Warfare in the American Southwest

We scrambled up rock fall and shimmied through a narrow crack. Then we inched across a stretch of slanting, deep red slickrock, and finally, there it was: a forgotten stone structure on a sandstone ledge so high and so remote only lizards live there today.

We considered the dwelling in front of us. There must have been a compelling reason for building here in this difficult place. Obtaining water would have been an arduous trip up and down hand-and-footholds, with a heavy pot on your head and perhaps a baby on your back. All household necessities like firewood had to be carried up and down ladders. Buildings were limited to the confines of a sometimes cramped sandstone alcove. Cornfields might have been far away. No doubt about it, this was an inconvenient place for a home. What could have driven these people to build in this forbidding place?

As we pondered this and studied the dwelling, a pair of ravens lazily flew by, wing tip to wing tip. At eye-level with us, they paused in their flight, cocking their heads to study the unusual sight of two humans in this uninhabited region. We turned our focus to the work of setting up the cameras.

Suddenly, a blood-curdling scream shattered the silence. The hair stood up on the back of our necks. We quickly glanced up just in time to see a falcon, perhaps a peregrine, silhouetted against the afternoon sun completing a dive. Black feathers drifted down from where one of the ravens had received a glancing blow. The other raven took off. Still aloft, the injured raven prepared himself for what he knew was coming — another attack. The falcon flew down the canyon in a wide loop, then up high above the mesa top, and dived after the raven again. But ravens are not called masters of the sky for nothing — this time the raven was ready for him. At the last possible moment, the raven flipped himself upside-down in mid-air and bunched his talons into fists, all the while maintaining his altitude. We watched in disbelief as the falcon and the raven engaged in a life or death battle, punching and slashing at each other with their talons.

After a few agonizing seconds, the falcon gave it up and swooped away down canyon, apparently seeking smaller and easier prey. The beleaguered raven flapped off in the direction his companion had taken. We were left in stunned silence with our mouths agape; we doubted what our eyes had just seen.

Later as we trudged across the mesa top back to our camp, we all but tripped over a pile of moss-covered stones at our feet. We paused to take a closer look: A gnarled piñon tree grew from the center of the stone pile. The stones were smaller than a loaf of bread and at a casual glance they looked natural. But as we looked more closely and walked the perimeter of the stone pile, we spotted colorful chips of rock and sherds of pottery, some decorated in black and white, and others a plain gray. It was then we realized this was not a natural pile of stones; this was an ancient, tumbled-down structure.

We automatically turned our eyes to the south of the stone pile. There we could just make out the dish-shaped depression in the dirt. From our research we knew that what we were seeing was the ancient pithouse/kiva. This ruin was what turn-of-the-last-century scholar T. Mitchell Prudden had named a *unit pueblo*. The ancient people lived in unit pueblos such as these before some of them moved to the cliffs. This site more than likely pre-dates the cliff dwelling we had just been in.

Unit pueblos date from the time the ancients were still living in small farmsteads scattered across the landscape, circa A.D.750–900. The unit pueblo was composed of a semi-subterranean pithouse like those they had lived in for centuries, only they had moved their storage up to the surface in stone structures; we could see the outlines of rooms among the moss-covered stones. This was the beginning of "Pueblo" times and is referred to as Pueblo I, or PI in the Pecos Classification. It was a time when the ancients were relying more and more on farming for their food and therefore needed more and more storage to contain it all. But they continued to live in their tried-and-true pithouses that had stood the test of time. They lived in these unit pueblos for centuries and the remains of unit pueblos pepper the landscape of the Colorado Plateau still today.

Then rather suddenly these ancient people began changing their living patterns about A.D. 1150. Experts in vernacular architecture tell us this is

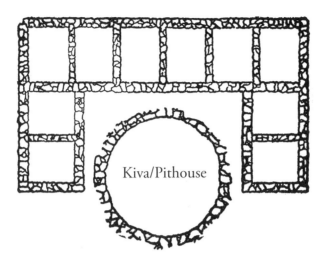

A diagram of a unit pueblo showing the semi-subterranean kiva/ pithouse and the arc of storage rooms behind it. From T. Mitchell Prudden's On the Great American Plateau.

The remains of a unit pueblo. The dish-shaped depression in the foreground was the kiva/pithouse; the piles of stones are what remains of a storage rooms.

rather unusual. Typically, house structures remain very stable throughout the generations. However, at this time the ancient people either flocked together into large open-air pueblo towns, or they began moving into cliff dwellings. Their ancient pithouse homes began evolving into ceremonial, subterranean kivas, and they lived now in surface rooms. Why this happened has been an enduring mystery in the American Southwest and is still to this day controversial.

Suddenly most of the ancient people moved into large pueblo towns. This is the Laguna Pueblo circa 1892, from William Thayer's Marvels of the New West.

The ancient people had often made casual use of alcoves in the cliffs since their early Basketmaker times. But the cliff dwellings beginning in the A.D. 1150s were much more elaborate and some had difficult access. These cliff dwellings were unprecedented. And this type of cliff dwelling would reappear again and again in succeeding generations.

However, most ancient Puebloan people lived in the large pueblo towns, and it's quite possible that the average ancient person never set foot in a cliff dwelling.

At first, early archaeologists thought ancient enemies moved nearby and drove the ancestral Puebloans to the cliffs or into large groups for protection. But archaeology has failed to pinpoint any other group moving into the area at that time. The *Athapaskans* — now known as the Apache and Navajo — would not arrive in the Southwest from Canada until the 1400s.

No one knows for sure why the ancestral Puebloans left their traditional farmstead homes out in the open on the mesa tops or on the canyon floors and moved into the cliffs, while others gathered together into large, defensible pueblo towns. But between A.D. 1250 and 1300, there is increased evidence of violence in the Mesa Verde and Kayenta regions that coincides with movement of large numbers of people in a short period of time, according to archaeologists Wilcox and Haas in Bernardini's paper "Conflict, Migration,

and the Social Environment." Other archaeologists surmise the *perception* of danger might have driven some ancient inhabitants to the cliffs and the rest into large pueblo towns.

A few others chose to live in cliff dwellings like this one in Canyon de Chelly, Arizona, instead.

There are several possible explanations for the changes developing at that time. Archaeologists have found indications that some areas may have suffered from deforestation about the time the northern ancient people moved into cliff dwellings. Wood was being used less and less in construction, and in some places uninhabited buildings were stripped of their wooden roofs in ancient times. The Hopi began using coal for their hearths and for firing pottery by circa A.D. 1000. There were also fewer large game animals such as deer in many places. Fewer bows and arrows were being made and used. More rabbits were being hunted and consumed. And of the rabbits, there were more jackrabbits, which are generally found in open areas — when for years cottontails had been the most common type of rabbit consumed. Cottontails prefer brushy, lightly wooded areas. This implies some areas had become more open and less wooded. Also, people began eating their turkeys, whereas in the past they relied on turkeys for their feathers.

By the late 1200s, an era of arroyo cutting occurred. An arroyo is a gully, a usually dry watercourse that drains certain areas only during thunderstorms and other periods of runoff. Formerly, streams meandered along soft alluvial

A dark arroyo, or gully, has formed in the soft alluival soil in the canyon bottom. This lowers the water table, making farming even more difficult.

canyon bottoms. Suddenly the soft dirt in the canyon bottoms was being washed away, probably from torrents, leaving the stream in the bottom of a gully. Arroyo cutting can be caused from deforestation. It can also be caused from extreme climatic conditions. Either way, its result is devastating to farmers: Arroyos lower the water table, making farming all the more difficult, if not impossible.

The ancestral Puebloans had become superb farmers. In other places such success has led to population increases. Steven LeBlanc in his book *Constant Battles: Why We Fight* discusses the theory that the ancient Puebloans may have been experiencing overpopulation. It is true, more structures have been noted after A.D. 1250, these new buildings filled every possible site and their inhabitants began farming the most marginal areas.

Certain pivotal dates have appeared in the prehistory of the southwest. One of these is for the Chaco Complex which withered and died between A.D. 1130 and 1150. The same fate occurred for the Mimbres culture in west/central New Mexico about the same time. But this "hinge point" date also appears "far beyond the boundaries of the Southwest," states archaeologist John Kantner in his fascinating book, *Ancient Puebloan Southwest*. "Groups as diverse as sea-faring societies in coastal California and the mound-building cultures of the Eastern Woodlands also exhibit substantial cultural change in the mid-1100s . . . The Toltec polity in Mesoamerica and the northern Mayan florescence in the Yukatan . . . both of these societies also effectively collapsed at about A.D. 1150."

Something profound was occurring, something so vast it could influence many different cultures in very different places. One possibility that could cause such disruption is climate change.

In other parts of the world there are ancient documents that chronicle what happens to people and cultures when the climate they have relied on for centuries changes. One of these climate incidents happened in Europe and has been called the Little Ice Age.

There is much controversy about when the Little Ice Age in Europe actually began. Archaeologist Brian Fagan in his book *The Little Ice Age* places the start date at A.D. 1310; some place it later. However, most scientists agree that it encompassed the1600s and 1700s and part of the 1800s — the coldest years.

Documents tell us what was going on during the Little Ice Age in Europe. As early as A. D. 1310, starvation became a serious problem there. A Norse colony in Greenland was abandoned, the people and livestock who remained starved when harbors iced over and no one could get in or out in the 1400s. Eventually wheat became so difficult to grow even in the robust farmlands of Europe that they began experimenting with growing other crops. It became so cold in Germany that only tuber crops could be grown. In England they began growing turnips; people could eat the turnips and the livestock could survive on the turnip greens. England in A.D. 1100 had more than fifty thriving vineyards. But by the late A.D. 1500s, there were none. By the 1600s, the height of the Little Ice Age, Russian peasants could not feed their children, so they sold them and survived on pine bark. In Poland food was so scarce at one point, robbers were hanged in front of starving crowds, and the hungry people cut the corpses down and ate them while the flesh was still warm. At this coldest time, some European farmlands would be inundated by glaciers. Indeed, some whole towns were engulfed by glaciers.

It's interesting to us that in Europe, the period from A.D. 1300 forward until the introduction of gun powder and cannons, represents the most active times for castle construction.

Although there is much disagreement about when the Little Ice Age began in Europe, everyone agrees it ended between A.D. 1850 and the late 1800s. But what was happening in Europe at that time can not be applied to the Greater American Southwest during the same era.

Scientists have not conclusively determined what happened in the Greater

American Southwest after A.D. 1150. However, it is known that after A.D. 1275, little rain fell for a generation. The Four Corners region, the northernmost region of cliff dwelling territory and high on the Colorado Plateau, was always a marginal area for farming corn. Ancient farmers had survived many droughts. However, this was not an ordinary drought or dry spell; for farmers this was a death knell. This era has sometimes been called the Great Drought.

The Mesa Verde landmass that is now a national park had a favored position in the Four Corners region. The high tableland sloped gently to the south, enjoying the favor of the warmth of the sun. And a steady breeze from the west kept blowing a constant new supply of fresh top soil onto the mesa, making for rich farmlands. No wonder the Mesa Verde was inhabited over such a long period of time! But some scientists believe it became cooler and drier there and in other areas of the Southwest. They surmise the ancient Puebloans might not have been able to continue growing enough corn even in this favorable place, and after A.D. 1250 the Mesa Verdeans were forced to move on.

The Mesa Verde enjoyed a favorable position in the region. But even Mesa Verde was deserted by A.D. 1300.

Whatever it was that happened in the Greater American Southwest beginning in A.D. 1150 had a profound impact upon the inhabitants. The ancient Puebloans had migrated often in their long past; it was a way of life for them. So they picked up and migrated again. However, there is a difference between their migrations before A.D. 1150 and after. This migration was unprecedented. As archaeologist Linda Cordell in her book *Archaeology of the Southwest* points out, before A.D. 1150, they typically migrated *locally*, usually no more than twenty miles or so. And this time, before they left an area they sometimes built cliff dwellings, something that had not happened before a migration in the past. And those who did not move into cliff dwellings left their scattered farmsteads of unit pueblos and gathered together in large pueblo towns up on high ground with grand vistas and a view of the surrounding valley. But after A.D. 1150 they all migrated out of the entire region, much further than they had wandered before.

But modern Pueblo people have their own ideas about why their ancestors left.

Their deities had always told them when it was time to move on — by failing to send rain at critical times in the planting cycle or their crops otherwise not thriving. And so they regularly migrated to new areas. The thousands of ruins scattered across the Southwestern landscape are mute testimony to ancient Puebloan migratory ways; it was an integral part of their way of life. Because of that, modern Puebloans do not like the word "abandoned" used in the context of cliff dwellings. These ancient sites are not abandoned, they say; the sites are still inhabited by the spirits of their ancestors. And they visit them often, leaving offerings and saying prayers.

The ancient people had lived in cliff dwellings only for a short while in their long, rich past — sometimes as little as twenty years, and in a few places as much as 150 years. And then, over the course of just a few generations, they left their lofty cliff homes.

The Great Migration from the northern reaches of the American Southwest must have been an incredible, unforgettable process. Family by family, group by group, the ancient people began slowly leaving the northernmost reaches of their former territories. The first to leave were the Virgin River Anasazi in Nevada and along the southern edge of Utah. Then those from the Southeast Utah country and Colorado left and slowly the area north of the San Juan River was emptied. By A.D. 1300 the area north of the San Juan River, including Mesa Verde, had been depopulated.

Some early sources imply the ancient people "vanished." They *did* retreat from the northernmost reaches of their original territory, but they did not vanish.

Where Did They Go?

In a lecture at the Denver Museum of Nature and Science, archaeologist Mark Varien stated the migrations cascaded north to south. The ancient people moved to places slightly warmer with permanent water sources. This implies weather that was slightly cooler and drier in general.

They moved south and east, some to the Rio Grande. In fact, many of their descendants still live in the area today. Strung along the Rio Grande in New Mexico, scattered westerly across New Mexico and in northeast Arizona are people who are the descendants of the cliff dwellers. In the United States they no longer live in cliff dwellings; they live in pueblos — flat-roofed houses of adobe and stone, stacked one upon another in a stair-step fashion. They were living in these pueblos when the Spanish conquistadors arrived, making some of these terraced pueblo towns perhaps the oldest inhabited towns in the United States.

THE MODERN PUEBLOS

THE MODERN PUEBLOS

Descendants of the Ancient Cliff Dwellers

Acoma

Cochiti

Hopi

Isleta

Jemez

Laguna

Nambe

Picuris

Pojoaque

Sandia

San Filipe

San Ildefonso

San Juan

Santa Ana

Santa Clara

Santo Domingo

Taos

Tesuque

Zia

Zuni

Pueblos are flat-roofed structures that appear terraced, much like the land. This engraving is from Frank H. Cushing, Century Magazine, *1883.*

Unfortunately, the northern migrants who moved south into Arizona encountered other ancient people who already lived there. In central Arizona, the Hohokam people had lived along the waterways for centuries in south/central Arizona. Their irrigation ditches total perhaps 600 miles in length and many are still in use today — all dug by hand with stone tools a millennium ago. In west/central New Mexico were the Mogollon people.

Sometimes the people migrating from the north already had a relationship with some of these southern people, say through trading or through marriage. These northern people of the Colorado Plateau were welcomed to join them.

But as the northern populations of the ancestral Puebloans continued to migrate into Arizona and as the numbers of migrating ancient people that had started with a trickle increased to a flood, the southern populations were overwhelmed. Swamped. Inundated. In Arizona the ancient cultures of the Southwest — the Anasazi, Mogollon, Hohokam — were thrown into a crucible — into a swirling mixture in which all were transformed — melded into a new culture called the Salado. The Salado are known by their distinctive pottery. No group came out of the crucible unchanged or unscathed, and probably no one person did either. But still each group retained some of its old traits, and some of its old ways of doing things remained — enough that archaeologists have been able to track the different groups. They have tracked the different groups by their pottery, by the shape of their skulls, by their house forms and by certain herbs used as seasoning. According to archaeologist Jeffery J. Clark in his book *Tracking Prehistoric Migrations: Pueblo Settlers among the Tonto Basin Hohokam,* the northern ancient Puebloans preferred to build their houses with shared walls and of several stories — like apartment buildings (think: urban), whereas the Hohokam and most Mogollon usually preferred their houses to be free-standing and unattached to others and of one story (think: suburban). Clark also points out the northern folks liked to flavor their foods with tansy mustard. The other groups apparently never touched the stuff. And there are other clues also — such as different species of seed corn that have been found, corn types that originated on the Colorado Plateau. So in ruins where archaeologists find pollen from the mustard tansy plant, and the ruins are in the form of room blocks, as well as other clues, they surmise they are seeing migrants from the Colorado Plateau.

By the 1300s the Hohokam irrigation ditches were becoming entrenched — arroyos forming in the irrigation channels — and there was no way to get the water up out of the gully to their fields. So this culture too began to dissolve and the people left their traditional homes. The area around Tonto National Monument that had once been part of the thriving Hohokam homeland, was vacated by circa A.D. 1450.

Perforated ceramic disks such as this are also a migration marker. They were apparently only produced by the Kayenta culture. Bureau of American Ethnology, #65, Kidder and Guernsey.

Everyone was migrating away, with many moving still farther south. Archaeologists have tracked them as far as northern Mexico. On the banks of what is called the Rio Casas Grandes today, a magnificent city suddenly emerged in the late 1300s where there had only been a small resident community in the past. Built of adobe, this city had sewers and a hidden interior well. A sophisticated ventilation system kept the place cool and pleasantly inhabitable. When Casas Grandes and its surrounding core areas were depopulated about A.D. 1450, some survivors moved to the west, both into the Sierra Madres, where cliff dwellings were constructed, and into the Sonoran Desert.

When the Spaniards arrived in the A.D.1500s, people who were currently living in the burned-out remains of this city told them it had once been called *Paquimé*, (POCK-ee-may).

Pedro de Casteneda, chronicler of the Coronado Expedition of 1540–1542, described the people they found: "In general, these villages all have the same habits and customs, although some have some things in particular which the others have not." In other words, the Spaniards saw them as more or less homogenous and sharing distinctive traits that separated them from the nomadic hunter-gatherer Native Americans of the Plains culture. So the Spaniards called them the *Pueblo* people — pueblo being the Spanish word for town — the people who live in towns. But that is not how the modern

Taos Pueblo circa 1892, the northernmost pueblo on the Rio Grande. From William Thayer's Marvels of the New West.

Pueblo people themselves see it. They see many differences among the different pueblos, and do not consider themselves a single, cohesive group.

What remains today of all the different groups are the different languages — four or five different language families with different roots that are spoken among the modern Puebloans. This is a marker that points to the possible different groups and origins that once inhabited the American Southwest.

The ancestral Puebloans who eventually settled along the Rio Grande also had their own problems to contend with. It is thought the reason this area along the second largest waterway in the American Southwest had remained so sparsely populated prior to the Great Migration was because cool air settled along its course, making the Rio Grande a little too cool for farming corn. They somehow managed to overcome this problem though no one knows exactly how. All they know is people began streaming into the area in the thirteenth century. And many Pueblo people are still living along the Rio Grande today.

For us, the cliff dwellings have become an architectural artifact of this Great Migration: the architecture of upheaval. The timeline for the cliff ruins roughly follows the timeline for the continuing migrations of the ancient peoples. Before they left a place or as they arrived in a new place, cliff dwellings were often constructed.

When Paquimé collapsed "in a frenzy of warfare and destruction" circa A.D. 1450, some of the survivors moved west into the Sierra Madres, Mexico, where they constructed cliff dwellings such as this.

We will probably never know the precise reason the ancient Pueblo people abandoned their northernmost region and settled in the well-watered valleys of New Mexico, Arizona and Mexico. But they did endure. And as we visit the cliff dwellings throughout the Greater American Southwest, what we are witnessing is the story of a turbulent episode in their past.

CLIFF DWELLING END DATES

These dates represent the last trees cut for timbers in the selected cliff dwellings above. Tree ring dating is called *dendrochronology*. Abandonment would have followed shortly after these end dates.

CLIFF DWELLING END DATE TIMELINE

Dates Cascade North to South

A.D.

Mid-1100s	Chaco culture collapses. Mimbres culture disappears, along with the Mound Builders and the eastern Woodland cultures. Toltec and Maya collapse. Virgin River Anasazi leave the Virgin River area and probably join with the Kayenta Anasazi.
1268	Cedar Mesa in SE Utah deserted — tree cutting all but ceased after late 1260s.
1275-1299	Cold drought begins.
1280	Mesa Verde: No more wood is cut, subsequently vacated.
1286	Betatakin and Kiet Siel are abandoned in an orderly fashion, residents seal doors and take portable tools with them.
1300	Area north of the San Juan River is depopulated, Salado culture rises to prominence. Area around the southern tip of the Colorado Plateau (Mogollon Rim) gains population.
1287	Gila cliff dwellings are vacated.
1348	Sierra Ancha cliff dwellings below the Mogollon Rim are depopulated: The last date is A.D. 1348.
1450	Tonto cliff dwellings are emptied.
1450	Paquimé: Looted, burned and then abandoned in a frenzy of warfare and destruction. Some survivors move west into the Sierra Madres where they build cliff dwellings.
1250—1540	Rio Grande population in New Mexico expands.
1540	Spanish conquistadors arrive marking the end of the prehistoric era and the beginning of the historic era.

The Colorado Plateau is a land of high mesas torn by deep, ragged canyons. Note the standing stone spires in the canyon. Off in the distance is a silvery sagebrush flat; sagebrush is an indicator plant for the Colorado Plateau. Mesa tops are cloaked in piñon pine (left) and Utah juniper trees (right).

3

LANDSCAPE: WHAT THE CANYON WREN SEES

The Greater American Southwest is an enormous area encompassing parts of five U.S. states and two states in Mexico — perhaps as much as 200,000 square miles. If the Greater American Southwest were a sovereign country, it would be considerably larger than Spain or France. This vast place is the homeland of the ancient Puebloans.

Standing on the edge of the Mesa Verde in southern Colorado and looking south, it seems we can see forever. The sun lights up distant canyons, layer upon layer, until the landscape is lost in the haze. Yet here in the northern realm of the Greater American Southwest we are seeing only a tiny fraction of the region. We love this land and all its different faces. We like to refer to the different areas as provinces. The provinces are different from one another: different plants and animals live there, and different farming and survival strategies are required. Just as the land and vegetation in each province have many differences, so it was for the people who lived there. Each province was home to different ancient Puebloans.

As we stared that day from the edge of the Mesa Verde, we heard the distinctive song of the canyon wren — its clear notes descending cascading down the scale is unforgettable and for us immediately evokes images of the Southwest. It reminds us that even with all the differences, there are also plants and animals that are indigenous to the entire Greater American Southwest. The canyon wren is one of these; its song can be heard throughout the entire region.

THE GREATER AMERICAN SOUTHWEST

The Different Landscapes

The Northern Province is the Colorado Plateau — one of the last places in the continental United States to be explored and mapped. This is the land drained by the roiling Colorado River, the largest river in the American Southwest. The Colorado Plateau hosts more national parks than anywhere else in the United States. A bird's eye view of the landscape would reveal a semi-arid land — high and dry — with flat-topped mesas cloaked in piñon pine and Utah Juniper trees. These forests have sometimes been called pygmy forests because in this climate the trees rarely grow to more than 12 to 14 feet high. Punctuating the forests are vast, silvery sagebrush flats. Sagebrush is so widespread on the Colorado Plateau, that it is an indicator plant for the region. Spectacular canyons slash this country, the Grand Canyon being the most famous example. This is the famed land of the red rocks and inhabited by *hoodoos* — standing sandstone pinnacles. It is home to smooth, narrow "slot" canyons as well as stone arches and windows eroded from the rocks.

It is also the home to *slickrock*, which cover acres and in certain places even stretch for miles. Dirt "islands" in the slickrock are filled with trees, grasses and sagebrush but the slickrock itself looks like frozen

Slickrock abounds on the southern Colorado Plateau, above. On the right, pothole pools are abundant, and below, tadpoles in a pothole pool live just a few weeks until the water evaporates.

The Sonoran Desert is the home of stately Saguro cacti.

sand dunes. And that is in fact what it is — sand dunes from another geological era that have turned to stone. But slickrock isn't actually slippery. So why is it called "slick"?

The earliest reference to slickrock we have encountered dates back to Dominguez and Escalante, the Spanish priests who explored the region in A.D. 1776. Their ponies slipped and struggled on the stuff, but we suspect it was the horses' iron shoes that made it treacherous. For unshod horses as well as for deer, elk and even cattle, it does not appear to be such a problem.

An eagle eye can spot potholes sculpted by the wind and rain in the slickrock; some are the size of a hot tub that could hold a half dozen or more lounging people. Others are not much larger than the head of a pin. During rainfall these potholes fill with water. Then, tadpoles come to life in some of the large pothole pools, their life cycles compressed into the few short weeks that it takes for the water to evaporate from those pools. They then lie dormant until the rains come again. On spring evenings the frogs serenade us, their songs made sweeter by the shortness of their lives.

Geologists love the Colorado Plateau. Here, the landscape is laid bare for them with little or no vegetation or dirt covering and concealing the ancient stone. So they can easily read the story the stone has to tell and answer the question of why the earth is such a brilliant, almost unnatural shade of red: Even just a trace of iron can create the brilliant red pigment we see today.

This is the homeland of the northernmost of the ancient pueblo peoples, those who have been known as the Anasazi.

The song of the canyon wren can also be heard in the Sonoran Desert. The Colorado Plateau drops off abruptly at the Mogollon Rim (pronounced muggy-own). Anyone who has ever stood in the Verde Valley of east-central Arizona has seen the great wall of the Mogollon Rim loom above him. It is an awesome sight. Here, below the rim, the habitat changes to Upper Sonoran Desert country. Here too are the statuesque Saguaro cacti and small trees that dominate the landscape, giving it a vertical sort of appearance. The spice-rack smell of the sagebrush on the Colorado Plateau changes to the pungent smell of the creosote bush. Cholla cactus and agave abound here.

Farming in the shadow of the Mogollon Rim is a very different proposition than up on the Colorado Plateau. This is the homeland of the Hohokam people. Their culture was centered near where Phoenix is today.
The song of the canyon wren can also be heard to the southeast and far south in the Chihuahuan Desert, the largest of the four North American

Rising above the Chihuahua Desert to the west are the Sierra Madre Mountains in northern Mexico, where the cliff dwellings are located. Tucked into this crumpled landscape are intriguing examples of structures unique to this area.

An eagle eye can spot the village strung along the ledge in the Sierra Madres, Mexico.

deserts. The Chihuahuan Desert is a low, shrubby place compared to the verticality of the Sonoran Desert. You won't find the majestic Saguaro cactus here. The evergreen lechuguilla plant, a type of agave, is one of the giveaways of the Chihuahua Desert. Punctuating this desert are mountain ranges, like archipelagos — chains of islands — in a desert sea. Since these archipelagos are higher, they are also cooler and moister than the surrounding desert, and here can be found forests and springs. The mountains are a wonderful resource to the people and animals who live in this desert or

Lechuguilla, a type of agave, is an indicator plant for the Chihuahuan Desert.

who pass through it in their migrations. Here were the ancient people who are referred to as the Casas Grandes culture. They built their magnificent city of Paquimé of adobe that was like cement in that river pebbles were incorporated in it.

Butting up against the southeastern side of the Colorado Plateau are mountains, another province of the Greater American Southwest sometimes referred to as the Mogollon Highlands. The song of the canyon wren is often heard here, too. These mountains stretch from mid-New Mexico across the border with Arizona to east-central Arizona. They nurtured a sub-group of ancient Puebloans referred to today as the Mogollon people.

*A cliff dwelling
in the Sierra
Anchas.*

*Photographer:
Peg Hoffman.*

The final leg of our journey takes us to the east of the Colorado Plateau where many of the descendants of the ancient Puebloans still live today. Here, bisecting the state of New Mexico is a great river — the Rio Grande. This river is the second largest river in the Southwest and has nurtured the ancient people who migrated here in the 1300s. Some archaeologists think that the people of the Mesa Verde were among those who migrated here when they left Mesa Verde in the late 1200s.

The Puebloans basically live between the two great rivers of the American Southwest, the Colorado River on the west and the Rio Grande on the east. And the song of the canyon wren can be heard throughout the entire landscape. It truly is the music of the Southwest.

This Land Then

But how did the ancient Puebloans see this land? We are told by ethnographers that today the Puebloans see themselves as part of this magnificent landscape, that the earth is the Puebloan's mother, for it is she who nurtures them. Perhaps it was true then as well.

Archaeologists tell us an ancient Puebloan would have seen a landscape — the plants, the wildlife — very much as it is today. The main difference would be fewer arroyos were present and they were much shallower than today.

The ancient cliff dwellers somehow found everything they needed to flourish in this harsh and rugged land.

What you would not see is the aromatic tamarisk that today grows thick in the bottoms of arroyos in canyons and along waterways. Sometimes called salt cedar, tamarisk is a European intrusion brought to the region in the last 150 years. Today we encounter an occasional barbed wire fence and cattle, horses and sheep. A thousand years ago an ancestor of a canyon wren flying overhead would see small farmsteads dotting the landscape below him. There would be well-worn paths leading down to water and to fields planted with beans, corn and squash. The only domesticated animals in times of old were dogs. Ancient people also had access to wild turkeys. But there were no cattle, sheep, donkeys, goats or horses. The sounds of a barking dog or the cry of an infant could be heard. In the distance there might have been a small pueblo village.

Instead of seeing a dry, empty land that some would call a desert, an ancient person would have seen a cornucopia, a place where everything you needed for survival was available if only you know how to tap into it.

Need a tool? There was plenty of fine-grained stone around that could be shaped, with a few deft hits, into a serviceable hammer, axe, scraper, knife or arrow point. Need a house? All around you was plenty of adobe mud, stone and/or timber to construct one. Need dishes? Clay suitable for making into pottery was abundant throughout the entire region. Need a basket? Yucca plants grew across the entire region, and their sharp, pointy leaves provided stringy fibers for making baskets that were water-tight when a coating of pine-pitch was applied to it. You could also make sandals from the leftover yucca, as well as rope. Even the roots were useful: When pounded, yucca roots produce a fine shampoo. And if you were hungry and it was the right time of year, you could eat the fruit or flowers of the yucca.

Although today we call what we see a "desert," we are told the ancient people saw their Earth Mother — a land that was rich in resources and could provide them with everything they needed. As we hike this land today, we try to envision it as these ancient ones might have. Although we are no doubt unsuccessful, still the act of trying keeps the landscape fresh and exciting for us.

The Dangers of the Landscape

Winter mornings in the desert Southwest are often crisp and clear, and such was the case on an early morning when we hiked up the Chinle Wash bottom with some of our Navajo friends. The winter sun had not yet reached the canyon bottom, and each of us blew a cloud of breath in front of us as we walked. Puddles in the sandy arroyo bottom were topped by a thin layer of ice. Our friends showed us some interesting ruins, and by the time we turned around it was late afternoon. Now the sun was warm and the air had changed from invigorating to almost balmy. The ice on the puddles was long gone. We stripped off our outer garments and stowed them in our packs.

When we were within sight of our vehicles, Bill, being the first in line, suddenly lurched forward and immediately sank up to his chest in quicksand. We had walked this very stretch of sand in the morning and the footing had been solid. But just a few hours later, this same bed of sand had somehow become viscous quicksand.

We were able to stop in time before we all were mired in the stuff, and lying on our bellies in the safe sand, we passed the end of a long stick to Bill. He was able to grab the stick and, hand-over-hand, slowly work his way out of the bog.

Quicksand can be found anywhere in the world where there is sand and water. And since the sandy-bottomed arroyos are often the thoroughfares of the region, there is bound to be quicksand present. In fact, some of the worst quicksand occurs in the American Southwest. During the wet season, backcountry travelers had better be prepared to encounter quicksand at some point in their trip.

Quicksand can run the spectrum from sluggish to super-quick. It can even appear like dry sand on the surface and be virtually impossible to recognize until you step in it. This happens when water evaporates from the exposed outer layer of sand and forms a crust. A bed of sand can be quicksand at

Escaping Quicksand's Grip

*I*f you should become mired in quicksand, the first thing to remember is not to panic. This is often the most difficult of all the steps. There are actually far more dangerous things in the region than quicksand. But when one plunges in up to his chest, as Bill did, the pressure exerted by the water and sand gives a suffocating, constricting feeling, and it's hard not to panic. It's comforting to remind oneself at this time that most quicksand bogs are rarely more than four feet deep and therefore you won't be sucked under by it. Quicksand is also much more buoyant than water, and if you fling yourself on your back, you'll float. Quicksand doesn't like to be disturbed, so make your movements slow motion and smooth. If no one is there to pass you the end of a long stick like we did with Bill that day, use very slow-motion swimming motions to free yourself. This must be done **very** slowly — excruciatingly, frustratingly slowly. And eventually you'll work your way out.

Our early days in the Four Corners region in the 1960s. When we first became stuck in quicksand, the area around the Land Rover was dry sand. By 2 a.m. the Rover was on its side.

If it's your vehicle that's mired, stop at the first sign that your wheels are slipping. Your instincts will tell you to gun the motor and put all the power you can to the wheels, but don't do it. If you spin the wheels to try to get free, you'll only succeed in digging yourself and your vehicle to bedrock.

Clear all people and pets from the vehicle and cut the engine. Even the vibration of the engine running is enough to disturb the quicksand and keep it working on your vehicle. A crowd of people bustling around the floundering vehicle trying to be helpful will also just cause it to sink more. Therefore, one person and one person only should place a large flat slab of stone under the bumper of the vehicle where it's mired. This will act as a base for the jack. Flat stone slabs are common to arroyos in the Four corners region, but other devices work well also — one tour guide successfully used the grill from a barbeque as a base. Travelers who spend a lot of time in the region often carry a piece of plywood with them to use as a base.

Then using a HighLift or Handyman Jack, place it under the bumper and on the base. Pump the jack up **one notch,** then back off and let it rest a minute or two. If you stand there and just pump the jack on up, you'll only succeed in jacking the jack and the stone down into the quicksand. Repeat this process until the wheel begins to rise out of the goo. Then, using more flat stone slabs of stone, build a "road" where the tire will travel, far enough to clear the bog. It's a slow process, but the first time we were mired in quicksand it took us twelve hours to get out and the last time it only took us twenty minutes to free the vehicle.

one time and merely wet at another — and even dry sand at yet another time. What determines which characteristics the bed of sand will have is an underground water source. The pressure exerted by the underground water — will determine how volatile the quicksand will be. With surface water, the sand is just wet sand.

Since it is made up of water, quicksand can freeze in cold weather, which is what happened to us that day in Chinle Wash. First thing in the morning, the ground and the quicksand were frozen solid, plenty solid enough to walk across or even drive a vehicle over, for that matter. But when the sun hit the sand and warmed it, the quicksand became viable. The most typical type of quicksand we have encountered in the northern region of the Southwest has the consistency of Jell-O. If you stomp your foot on it, hard ripples will undulate out in slow motion from the point of impact. Then, when you go to remove your booted foot, the sand is reluctant to release it. It feels like your boots are being sucked in deeper, but quicksand doesn't actually suck. What's really happening is that a vacuum is being formed when you attempt to remove your foot. When you finally are able to yank your foot free from the quicksand, the hole left by your boot fills with water. This is our test to determine if it is quicksand.

Besides quicksand, there are other dangers in the desert that await the unwary, inexperienced and unprepared.

One beautiful summer day, the sun was hot and the sky overhead was clear, although we could see a summer storm way off in the distance. But where we were was dry and sunny as we hiked up a shallow, unintimidating arroyo. Suddenly we noticed a dirty, foamy trickle of water slithering toward us in the sandy bottom of the arroyo. It was so innocent looking that it was hard to believe its implied threat.

But we were immediately alarmed. Experience has taught us this was a very dangerous sign. We scrambled up the bank of the arroyo, turned around and looked down. Already the trickle of water had transformed into a shallow sheet of water covering the bottom of the creek. Then it started rising — slowly, almost imperceptibly, it rose. Bits of debris were swept along by it. We were watching a flash flood in action.

The American Southwest is crisscrossed with arroyos and canyons that were created by runoff. A simple unimpressive arroyo can drain an area miles away. The water is very destructive to anything in its path. Walking in a canyon or an arroyo can be an extraordinarily dangerous pastime. One must always be aware what's happening miles away in the area that is drained by the canyon or arroyo; it does not have to be raining where you are for a flash flood to occur. And once you spot the innocent-seeming warning signs, you have very little time to seek high ground. Terrible tragedies have occurred when hikers were caught in smooth, narrow slot canyons and could not reach high ground in the few short minutes, (or maybe even seconds) of warning they had.

Deserts are lands of extremes. Although it can get so hot as to create sunstroke during the daytime, it can get cold enough to cause death by exposure at night. It can be hot and very dry, but when it does finally rain or snow, roads can become impassable. So the weather is not something to be taken lightly.

We have never felt so alive as when hiking in the American Southwest. All our senses are — and must be — engaged. Although we have had some encounters with rattlesnakes and scorpions, our awareness of them has kept us from ever being bitten or stung by them. However, it should be considered a medical emergency if a person should be bitten or stung, and he should be taken to the nearest medical facility. Less dangerous to humans are the tarantulas: In the fall, herds of tarantula spiders can be seen crossing highways and trails. Unsettling perhaps, but not dangerous.

Every part of us is challenged by these natural surroundings. Our endurance and sense of balance are constantly called upon by the long hikes and scrambling up and down the cliffs.

We find a keen sense of observation is absolutely necessary — first in keeping track of our location, watching for landmarks and anticipating danger. And also in spotting cliff dwellings and rock art panels.

Our intelligence is challenged in reading the topographical maps, the compass and the Global Positioning System (GPS) — and also in attempting to understand what we are looking at once we've found it. Finally our sense of discipline is challenged by the long distances to be traveled and by being careful of the dangers. And once we have reached our goal, we have to remain ever cognizant so as not to damage what we've found.

Pueblo people tell us the Earth Mother provides all of this. We see it simply as the place that draws us back again and again. All we have to do is hear the familiar descending cascade of notes of the canyon wren, and we know we are home.

The ancient people used hundreds of the plants in their environment; this field guide represents just a few. Most, though not all those shown here, occur throughout the entire region of the Greater American Southwest. These are some of the most useful plants and how they might have been used, based on ethnographic studies.

Rice Grass

Rice grass was an extremely important food source for the ancient people. It was a major staple before they began farming; it continued to be important after agriculture was established. Rice grass seeds were critical in the late spring and early summer before their crops came in. It was also rice grass that nourished them during droughts.

Prickly Pear Cactus

Prickly pear cactus is common in the Greater American Southwest, there are a dozen or so different speicies. Flowers can range from yellow, to red, to purple. Both the fruit and the pads are edible, if one can get past all the spines. It was one of the few sources of natural sugar for the ancient people.

Yucca

There is probably no other plant that was more useful to the ancient people than yucca. It is found throughout the entire Greater American Southwest region. There are at least two varieties, the narrow leaf yucca (above) and the broadleaf yucca on the facing page. Much of what a household needed to function could be made from the stringy, spiked leaves: sandals, baskets, rope, mats for sleeping. Cloth could also be made from it by weaving the fibers together, sometimes they wove other materials with the yucca, like feathers or strips of rabbit fur, making sturdy, warm robes for winter. The fruit pods are edible on yucca (above, center), and so are the flowers. But the roots are toxic to ingest. However, the roots make a fine shampoo. The sharp point of a leaf, with the stringy fibers left attached to the tip, made a functional needle and thread. It is from the yucca leaves that they made paint brushes. No ancient Puebloan's house could be without a constant supply of yucca plants.

Yucca

Yucca basket, tightly woven.

A sandal made from the tough, stringy fibers of a yucca plant. There were many different types of weaves on sandals, this represents only one.

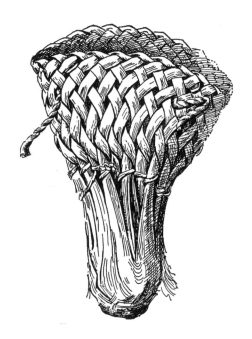

Yucca basket, loosely woven.

A yucca rope.

The ancients made many different types of baskets, more so before the development of pottery. All these artifacts are from the *Bureau of American Ethnology*, Bulletin 65. Kidder and Guernsey, 1919.

Sunflowers

An ancient Puebloan carefully carved these sunflowers from wood, and then painted them yellow and orange. To the Aztecs and Incas, the sunflower was a symbol of their sun god. Sunflowers would have been very useful to the ancient people: the seeds are nutritious and the ancients undoubtedly made use of them for nourishment. The oil was used to grease their cooking slabs. Sunflowers are also an indicator of good farmland, very important for people who migrate a lot. Sunflowers are a New World plant, so when the Spanish conquistadors arrived, sunflowers would have been one of the many plants that were unfamiliar to them. From the *Bureau of American Ethnology,* Bulletin #65, Kidder and Guernsey, 1919.

Mormon Tea

Mormon tea is scattered throughout the entire Greater American Southwest region. It has been valued through the ages for its theraputic qualities, particularly as a decongestant and for easing respiratory problems. Traditionally it is brewed into a tea, hence the name.

John Kantner in his book, *Ancient Puebloan Southwest*, tells an ancient tragic story uncovered by archaeologists. A three or four year old child had died in the late 1200s, and the burial was studied by archaeologists. The child had not suffered a long, lingering death — that would have etched a record on the bones. No, this child had been healthy until he died of some deadly, fast-moving disease. When they studied the stomach contents of the child they found his last meal was of rice grass, and the child drank some Mormon tea shortly before his death. The burial contained items for his trip to the next world as was typical of that time: "A ceramic canteen, a leather bag containing rice grass seeds, three baskets made of yucca, cottonwood spoons, a ... pendant and several other wild plant foods ... [also] a few seeds of domesticated squash." Kantner asks the question: Could it have been a respiratory ailment that took this young life?

Each morning Puebloan people say prayers and await the sun as it emerges from its eastern, morning kiva and begins its journey across the sky to its western, evening kiva. This romanticized depiction appeared in Harper's Weekly Magazine, *May 22, 1875. Sagstetter collection.*

4

PUEBLOAN DESCENDANTS: THE MEN

My grandfather advised me to keep bad thoughts out of my mind, to face the east, look to the bright side of life, and learn to show a shining face, even when unhappy ... And to always walk the Hopi Sun Trail.

— Don Talayesva, in Sun Chief, The Autobiography of a Hopi Indian.

It is still dark out and no one is rustling about yet. The sky is dark, but it is beginning to lighten at the eastern horizon. Then you hear your cue — the gobble of the turkeys heralding dawn. You step out onto your rooftop and watch the sky turn colors: first a deep purple, when you can just make out the silhouette of man. Then to yellow, in which you can see a man's breath. And finally bright red, where you can see the man in full.

When the sun kisses the horizon, you go to where there is a pottery bowl of water and splash some on yourself. It is icy cold, but it wakes you up instantly. If it is winter, you might substitute a quick roll in the snow while completely naked. Your people believe that this morning ritual will make you strong and healthy and brave.

You say your prayers to the sun as it climbs up from its eastern, morning kiva and begins its journey across the sky to its western, evening kiva. As you pray, you sprinkle sacred cornmeal as an offering to your father, the sun.*

Your day as a Puebloan man has begun. Perhaps it was similar a thousand years ago for the ancient Puebloan people.

The archaeological record reveals that an ancient Puebloan man would stand about 5 feet 5 inches tall. In your role as that man, you would cut the sides and bangs of your thick, black hair in a sort of Prince Valiant page-boy look, with your long hair in the back caught up in a *chongo*, a knot. All your hair would then be held in place with a colorful headband. You would wear sandals or go barefoot in the summer and wear a breech-cloth. In the winter you would add an outer covering of a "wearing" blanket made of feathers or

Early ethnographer Frank H. Cushing identified this man as the governor of the Zuni Pueblo. Note the knot of hair at the base of his neck. Today this is sometimes called a chongo. Although the name is probably modern, the practice of knotting the hair may be ancient because we have seen similar knots depicted on males on ancient Mimbres pottery. From Frank H. Cushing, Century Magazine, 1883.

* From the *Book of the Hopi* by Frank Waters

rabbit fur woven around a yucca base. About the time of the cliff dwellings, cotton blankets also became popular. You would be kept lean from all the hard work and activity.

After your prayers are said, you would hear the familiar voice of the Town Crier call out:

> *Ye dweller of the north arise,*
> *Ye dewller of the west arise,*
> *Ye dweller of the south arise,*
> *Ye dweller of the east arise.* *

Sometimes called the Crier Chief, the Town Crier might go on to assign jobs that the community needs done, such as cleaning the irrigation ditches or the village spring. If it is summer, he might announce that the Sun Chief has said this is a good time to plant your squash. It is the Town Crier's job to announce when there is a visitor to the pueblo and such things as if someone has something they would like to trade. In other words, he was the pueblo's newspaper, an important position in the pueblo. On this day, the Town Crier might announce that in three days the Hunt (or Bow) Chief wants your help.

Now it is time to begin your day's work. If you were a single man, you might look for something useful to do for the community. Among the Zuni, young unmarried men collected firewood and piled it in the plaza for everyone to use.

But say you were a married man with a family. You would head out to your cornfields, which might be several miles from the Pueblo. Although your fields were already planted, you would still have much work to do weeding and chasing away pests. Nothing would go to waste. Any edible plants found growing independently in your cornfields (read: weeds) would be taken home to your family, and these "weeds" would be cooked and eaten.

The same with pests: A rabbit that has discovered your cornfields would be quickly dispatched by your *throwing stick*. This is a straight, flat stick that you throw much like an Australian boomerang, but this one does not return to you after being thrown. Or you'd use a hooked cane-like stick that you could insert in the rabbit's hole and pull him out. Or simply throw a stone. Then you'd take the rabbit home for dinner.

You are a practical man: You would have just rid your cornfield of a serious threat and at the same time provided your family with meat and rabbit fur. Archaeologists call this *garden hunting* and it provided an important source of day-to-day protein for families. Archaeologists have found mostly rabbit bones in the household debris of the ancient ruins.

Although ancestral Puebloan men were perfectly able to take the rabbit out with an arrow from their bows, they wouldn't waste a valuable arrow for something like a rabbit when it could be easily killed by a simple stick or a stone that did not require such intense labor to produce, as an arrow does. Curved-neck canes are often pictured in ancient rock art, and throwing sticks are a common find for archaeologists.

After a man killed a rabbit, he might have brought it very close to his face to experience its last breath — its breath-line. Breath is important to modern-day Puebloans; they know that breath is a sign of life and, as such, is sacred. Therefore, singing is also sacred. In the winter or anytime one can see his breath, that is sacred. Smoke is also important in that it represents clouds — rain clouds — that bring life-giving moisture to Puebloan corn crops. Smoking tobacco in a pipe — or *cloud-blower* as it's often called — is still important to the Pueblo peoples today. We know it was also important to their ancestors because archaeologists have often found cloud-blowers in the ancient ruins. As was mentioned earlier, the breath-line is often pictured in rock art and on pottery.

When a man had down times in his corn fields or on guard duty, or any time when his body might be at rest, his hands were busy, producing. The early Spanish conquistadors commented on how industrious the Pueblo people were. They might be in the kiva, joking with their friends or telling

Above, a Puebloan man prays over rabbits. From the 23rd Bureau of American Ethnology, 1904, Stevenson.

Below, digging sticks on the right, left are crook-necked canes, from Bureau of American Ethnology, #65, Kidder and Guernsey, 1919.

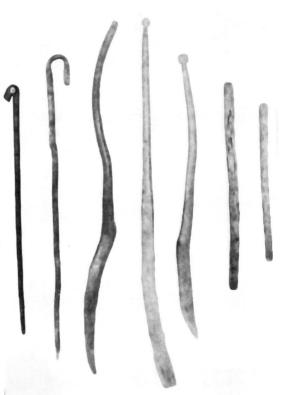

Spanish conquistadors wrote that the Puebloans were very industrious. Whenever Puebloan men were otherwise at rest on the terraced rooftops or in the courtyards, their hands were always busy, as on the left. Frank H. Cushing, Century Magazine, *1883.*

Even in the cliff dwellings today we can see evidence of their industriousness: At right, a sandstone boulder in a cliff dwelling is covered with abrasion marks. This is where ancient Puebloans worked stone into tools, for example, sharpening an axe head. Abrasion marks abound at cliff dwelling sites.

ancient legends to the young men, but their hands would be busy weaving. It is possible to see the results of this industriousness still today.

Around cliff dwellings, there are gouges in the sandstone cliff faces, abrading marks in the sandstone bedrock. This is where an ancestral Pueblo man rested and rubbed stones against the natural sandstone outcroppings to sharpen them into an axe, or rubbed sticks to straighten them for arrow shafts. These grinding marks are ubiquitous, reminding us the men's hands were usually busy, at work manufacturing every item they needed to survive. Just as they wouldn't waste a perfectly edible weed or rabbit, they wouldn't waste their rest time, either.

Every time an ancient Puebloan man made something, he probably also said a prayer while he was doing it. Pueblo people of today believe everything has its own spirit, even things they manufacture with their own hands, like an arrow point. As such, it needs a prayer to go along with its making, so that it will fly true when its time has come. Everything a Puebloan man or woman makes has its own song, has its own prayer that is part of its creation. This song helps the person connect with the object they are making, helps them focus and keep out any unwanted, unharmonious thoughts. And as their hands are always busy, so is there always a song and a prayer on their lips.

This song is not belted out like a Broadway musical — no, these are gentle songs, "under the breath" we might say. More like the breeze that whispers through the pine needles, so that we almost have to strain to hear it. At the end of the act of creation, at the end of the song, the song tapers off, the notes descending, reminiscent of a canyon wren's call.

The corn fields a man cultivated belonged to his wife and her family. As did the crops that resulted from his hard work. If he should decide to divorce, all of this would stay with his wife and her clan, as would the children. So what belonged to the man? What belonged to him was his clan kiva and all that it implied. To him fell a vital part of the pueblo life and culture. Today the men of the pueblos are in charge of guiding their people through this world, of keeping the universe in harmony. They are in charge of the ceremonies. Without their ceremonies this world would cease to function, and there would be no rain without their rain dances. The sun would cease to shine and there would be illness and starvation for all.

This is an awesome responsibility that the men take very seriously. All winter when the crops are in the storage rooms, when the weather is cold and life would be unbearably boring inside the pueblo, that is the time when ceremonies are at their peak. It is in winter that the pageantry of the ceremonies fills the pueblos with color and dancing and joy. In the modern pueblos today, this is the time when the kachinas arrive, hopefully bringing

Puebloan men are responsible for the ceremonies that keep their world in harmony. From the 23rd Bureau of American Ethnology, Stevenson.

A Puebloan man lays a feather paho at a shrine. Below is an example of a feather paho. Some are elaborate, this is a rather simple version. Both are from the the 23rd *Bureau of American Ethnology*, Stevenson

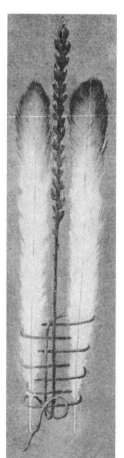

with them the promise of rain in the next season, with the fertility of many new babies and often with gifts. The kachina culture arrived late in the cliff dwelling era, so these dances might not have been performed in the cliff dwellings.

Today at home, modern Pueblo men are thought of as being very loving fathers. Mothers and fathers rarely spank their children. They fear that if they hit their children, it might break that loving bond between them and the child might lose its will to live. When a child needs to be disciplined, the parent sends for the mother's brothers — the child's uncle. Uncles are responsible for a child's conduct, they are the "enforcers." In the past, when a Puebloan boy ran afoul of the white man's law, early American social workers visited the boy's parents for disciplinary action. They would become confused when his parents referred them to his uncles.

So an ancestral Puebloan father, relieved from the responsibility of disciplining his children, was free to love his children unreservedly. Early ethnographers reported that fathers were often seen dandling babies in their cradle boards on their knees. They sang to their children on their laps at the close of the day and passed a baby in its cradle board from lap to lap of the extended family group.

There are no livestock animals available to any ancient native North Americans — sheep, cattle, horses and goats came with the Spanish. Nor were there any small domestic house cats. But the ancients did raise dogs and turkeys. Archaeologists have found wear marks on some dog skeletons that indicate they sometimes, but certainly not always, carried packs. Dogs were also raised, as evidence of puppy litters have been found at sites indicating they were being raised for a particular purpose. For what, we can only speculate. Amazingly, dogs could climb the ladders into the pueblos according to Gustaf Nordenskiold, a young Swede of a prominent family visiting Mesa Verde in 1891. But we don't know if or how dogs got into the cliff dwellings.

Koyongo, Hopi for Turkey

When Coronado arrived at the Zuni Pueblos in A.D. 1540, his chronicler described each Pueblo man as having his own herd of turkeys. The second Spanish contact with them in A.D. 1581 recorded: "There is not an Indian who does not have a corral for his turkeys, each of which holds a flock of 100 birds."

A Picuris Pueblo man told us that his ancestors passed down stories of herding their turkeys down the Rio Grande every fall to trade with the other pueblos. Any birds that did not sell were released into the wild over the winter. Then they were rounded up again in the spring.

A turkey tail feather has a distinctive flat top as in the one above. Sometimes we can recognize this distinctive shape in rock art and pottery designs. Below, wild turkeys are common in the back country even still today.

Blaine Turner of Arvada, Colorado, was an adolescent during the Depression. He felt very fortunate to get a job on a farm on the eastern plains of Colorado herding turkeys. He says they were very intelligent. Whenever they would encounter a rattlesnake, the turkeys would gather around it in a circle and gobble loudly until he came over and killed it with a shovel. Then the turkeys would calm down and go on their way again.

Turkeys have beautiful iridescent feathers in a golden, copper color, which is probably the main reason the Pueblo people treasured them. Ancestral Puebloan people needed a nearly endless supply of feathers for prayer sticks and for making the beautiful feather blankets they wore in the winter.

Turkeys are long-legged birds, and although they are strong fliers for short distances, they prefer to run from danger — which makes them suitable for herding. Turkeys like to roost high in cottonwood trees at night, trees that might have been cut around the cliff dwellings since wood was so precious to the cliff dwellers. So roosting in a cliff dwelling might have been a good alternative to a cottonwood tree for a turkey.

Pueblo people today have certain ceremonies dedicated to the turkey, and turkey feathers still figure prominently in prayer sticks and certain rituals. And the ancient city of Paquimé, later known as Casas Grandes in what is now the state of Chihuahua in northern Mexico, had an entire plaza devoted to turkeys. Surrounding the perimeter of this plaza were many unroofed pens made from adobe. Archaeologists discovered hundreds of turkeys buried under the floor of this plaza. Archaeologist Charles di Peso thought that the residents of Paquimé might have been raising turkeys to trade.

Besides garden hunting and raising turkeys, the ancestral Puebloans may have also taken part in communal hunts directed by a Hunt or Bow Chief, as their descendants have in modern times. Everyone in the village showed up for these hunts and they become as much a social occasion as for the opportunity to get meat for their families. At a pre-selected place everybody formed a huge circle, almost a mile in diameter. Then, on cue everyone started walking toward the center, closing the circle. Any rabbits in the area ran toward the center. When the circle was small enough, the men went in for the kill. Even the dogs participated.

This man is identified as the Bow Chief. In some pueblos the Bow Chief was in charge of game or wild food supply. He also organized rabbit hunts. From Frank H. Cushing, Century Magazine, *1883.*

CHIEF PRIEST OF
THE BOW.

This technique worked in open areas. In canyon country, the topography was used to the hunter's advantage. The group in this case would walk up a box canyon, trapping the game at the "box." At other times a long net might be strung across the mouth of a canyon and the game herded into the net. Archaeologists have found some of these extraordinarily long nets in their scientific excavations.

Ancestral Puebloan hunters had many choices for hunting weapons besides the bow and arrow. Deadfalls were used to catch animals on occasion. In this technique they would prop up a slab of sandstone with a stick. The size of the sandstone slab depended on the size of the animal sought — a small one to catch a desert rat and a large one to catch a coyote. They would place bait under the rock, then attach a string to the stick and tug on the string to pull the stick away when the animal was under the rock. The sandstone slab would fall on the prey.

Ancient hunters could fashion a snare from a single human hair for catching bluebirds.

When hunting deer, they might choose to simply run it down. The Puebloan people were and still are accomplished runners. Deer are fast, but only for relatively short distances. To run a deer down, they would stay on him, not allowing him to stop and rest. Finally when the deer was exhausted, they would go in for the kill. After the Hopi kill any large animal like a deer, they smoke tobacco in front of its nostrils and ask forgiveness. But by far the most common meat staple for modern Puebloans and their ancestors was the rabbit, both the cottontail and the jackrabbit.

Were these ancient farmers competent with bows and arrows? Don Talayesva in *Sun Chief* tells of the time when he was a boy that his father gave him a small bow and several arrows. He practiced with these over and over again until he became quite proficient at it. Then the inevitable day came when he lost one of his arrows. When he told his father, his father was furious with him, the most angry little Don had ever seen him. We take from this story that arrows were "expensive," that they required a lot of effort and materials to make. That they were used sparingly and as a last resort.

The chronicles of Coronado tell an interesting story: "One of the soldiers inadvertently, but none the less, in disregard of strict orders, became separated from the main party, and the Indians who were nowhere to be seen, at once attacked him. In reply to his cries the Indians who had tried to seize him suddenly disappeared. When everything seemed to be safe, Samaniego [the commander] raised his visor, and as he did so an arrow from among the bushes pierced his eye, passing through the skull." We take from this story that the ancient Puebloan men were extremely fast and accurate with their bows and arrows.

Trading

Archaeologists find at sites many objects that do not "belong" there, things like marine sea shells a thousand miles inland from the nearest beach. They find particular sherds of pots that were made in a different place and by a different hand than the people of the place they are studying. When scientific tests are run on the potsherds, archaeologists' suspicions are confirmed: the clay composition of the pot can be identified as coming from many miles away. Sometimes too, high quality stone for stone tools is found very far from its source. Macaw feathers are found in the American Southwest, thousands of miles north of the tropics where these colorful and noisy parrots live and thrive.

This has been attributed to trading. By the time the Spaniards arrived, the Puebloan people were experienced and enthusiastic traders. Although they might be staunch enemies with a particular nomadic tribe, at certain times in the summer and fall all the peoples would submit to a truce so that they might all trade. The nomads pitched their tents next to the pueblos and exchanged slaves, buffalo hides, buckskins and jerked meats for corn, beans, squash, tobacco and the beautiful woven items of the pueblos. The Smithsonian's *Handbook of North American Indians* explains: "Initially the Spaniards opposed such contacts with the enemy — the nomadic people of the Plains — but a desire to share in the profits caused them to put aside their objections and enter wholeheartedly into the commerce. . . . It became so important that in the late eighteenth century [the annual trade fair's] date was fixed in the fall to immediately precede the departure of the annual trading caravan to Chihuahua."

Don Talayesva in *Sun Chief* tells that he began as a child learning the nuances of trading. When he was in the kiva, listening to the stories of the older men while they wove, they would send him to other kivas to conduct trades. If this were for a head of livestock, the seller would make a stick figure of the animal from twigs. Young Don would have to bargain with the men of the other kivas and understand what constituted a fair trade. If the deal was struck,

Trading constituted a big event in the pueblos, one which people remembered fondly. Evidence of trading abounds in the Greater American Southwest. From the 23rd Bureau of American Ethnology, Stevenson.

then the buyer kept the stick figure as proof of purchase.

Women engaged in trading, too. In *Me and Mine*, Helen Sekaquaptewa described if a woman had something she wanted to trade — say, *piki* (wafer-thin flat bread) — she'd take it to the plaza and the Town Crier would announce what she wanted in return — say, flour tortillas. She'd leave the piki on a tray or *plaque* (flat, basket-woven tray) covered with a cloth in the plaza, then she'd leave. When she returned in an hour or so, her piki would be gone and in its place would be the flour tortillas.

But the serious trading would occur when a stranger came to the pueblo to trade. A trader could be of a tribe that might have been an enemy, but he would be welcomed into a Puebloan's home as a friend and treated like visiting royalty over night. The Hopi people remember fondly when a Zuni traveler/trader would arrive at their pueblo with a pouch of their excellent Zuni turquoise to trade. The actual trading would begin in earnest the next day.

If the trader brought items like buckskin or buffalo robes, the men handled this trading in a businesslike fashion. But if the trading was for food items, the women lined up to make their offers. Helen Sekaquaptewa described it: The trader might say, "This rabbit meat cries out for good Hopi beans." Or, "These piñons want piki." The women would bargain hot and heavy, "I don't have piki on hand, will you take ground corn meal in its place?" Everyone would gather in the plaza to watch and "enjoy all the drama."

Archaeologist Charles di Peso surmised places like Paquimé in northern Mexico were lively trading centers, with traders there acting as brokers particularly between the pueblos in what is now the American Southwest and the culture centers to the south.

No one can know for sure that ancient Puebloans conducted trade centuries ago similar to trade in the recent historic past, but there is sound evidence that they were indeed trading. And we can still see the evidence of that with our own eyes today.

Every time you encounter a sherd of pottery "out of place" — like seeing a sherd of Mesa Verde black-on-white pottery at a site that produced polychrome pottery — you are seeing the evidence of this ancient trading. Turquoise in areas where there is no turquoise, is also evidence of trade. Or a chip of obsidian rock, where there is no obsidian source nearby. Or shells from the Pacific Ocean strung into a necklace. Or feathers of the Macaw from the tropical south. These are all examples of trade.

"Your children will eat. Your granddaughters, your grandsons want for nothing. Therefore, even though I am tired, I have planted. Therefore, I am not lazy, I have toiled hard in all things." Parsons, *Pueblo Religion*, volume 2. The picture is from the 23rd *Bureau of American Ethnology*, 1904, Stevenson.

Amystery emerges concerning what happened when an ancient Puebloan man died. Men in their prime of life are under-represented in burials. There are burials of young, adolescent males and boys, and old men, but few men in their prime. What happened to these men?

Archaeologists toss around several possibilities that might account for this. One possibility is there may have been a special burial for warriors. This was the case for some plains Native Americans. A warrior was buried on a raised platform and left open to the sky, where he could be welcomed to the heavens. Archaeologist Steven LeBlanc, in his books *Constant Battles: Why We Fight* and *Deadly Landscapes: Case Studies in Prehistoric Southwestern Warfare* (coedited by Glen Rice), argues that Puebloan men could have died in battles and their scattered remains may yet be discovered by archaeologists.

When people die, it is believed by modern Pueblo people they go to the skeleton house — that place in the west where the dead travel. Cemeteries are also known as "skeleton houses." For all important journeys, prayer sticks or prayer feathers are placed in the ground, and so they would be for this, the most important journey a person would undertake.

At the ancient cliff ruins we visit, there are clues all around us — clues as to who these men were. For example, when we see the grinding marks on sandstone outcroppings around Puebloan dwellings, what we are *really* seeing is evidence of their industriousness that so impressed the Spanish conquistadors. When we observe tiny corncobs scattered in the ruins, what we are actually witnessing is their ability to wrest a living from a harsh and unforgiving land. When we encounter the remains of their kivas, we are seeing the locus of their greatest responsibility: maintaining the coherence and harmony of their intriguing world.

When you put all these clues together, they form a window to the past. The people we see there are shadowy and indistinct. Although we might never know them precisely, still we can have an inkling of who they were and what they did.

Who was the ancient woman who created beauty in this remote, inhospitable place? The ancient woman was an ancestor of the modern Pueblo people. Two maidens from the Acoma Pueblo bring water from the well circa 1920. From *American Indians: First Families of the Southwest.* The inset photograph shows the plastered wall decorated with a *dado* that we saw that day.

5

PUEBLOAN DESCENDANTS: THE WOMEN

They were "Wives, mothers, firekeepers."
— Polingaysi Qoyawayma, No Turning Back

We scrambled up the cliff face and there it was: the outer wall of a cliff dwelling peppered with openings. Gingerly we looked in one of the larger doorways and let our eyes adjust to the dim light. The room was beautifully stuccoed with adobe mud. The upper part of the wall was off-white; the lower part was tinted brown. These two-toned wall designs are called *dados*, and although they are rare in the backcountry today, at one time they were common.

A shaft of light shone through the doorway and side-lit one wall, emphasizing its irregularities. The stucco had been hand-smoothed, and as we peered more closely at the wall we saw slight indentations in the surface. It took us a moment to realize these were handprints. Looking closer still, and recalling the words of archaeologist Florence Lister in *Pot Luck*, we could make out the ridges and grooves of the actual fingerprints: fingerprints of the person who had participated in building this home. Pueblo women typically plaster the walls of homes today. And judging from the dainty size of the fingertips, these were probably the fingerprints of a woman.

It is the Pueblo women of today who own the houses and probably did in the past, too. We realized this woman had not only left behind her home for us to find, but she had also left her personal identification — her fingerprints. As we gently hovered our fingers over the marks in the plaster but without touching the ancient adobe plaster, we felt a connection across the centuries, a link with this woman who had stood in this exact spot and had helped to build this structure a thousand years ago. Who was this woman? What can we know about her?

At top, a young unmarried Puebloan girl has her hair styled in the butterfly by her mother. From *American Indians: First Families of the Southwest*. Beneath it is a reproduction of an ancient rock art design, from *Bureau of American Ethnology*, #65, Kidder and Guernsey.

Archaeology can tell us certain physical things about her; anthropology can suggest other possibilities. If we were to step back in time and peer out one of the doorways, we might see such a young woman ascending the trail toward us. We would know at a glance that she was unmarried because her glossy, black hair would be swept up in whorls covering her ears, similar to Princess Leia's in the first *Star Wars*. The Pueblo people today have a hairdo called the "butterfly" and it is beautiful. A similar hairdo is sometimes depicted in ancient rock art and pottery designs, so we know it is an ancient tradition, popular during the time of the cliff dwellings and also centuries before.

We would know she was returning from fetching water because balanced on her head would be a large pottery jug today called an *olla* (OY-ah, a Spanish word) that holds water. These jugs are heavy, even without the water. Archaeologists have found marks on the bones of the neck and spine of the skeletons of these ancient women that indicate they carried heavy loads on their heads. And until recently, fetching water for the household was a duty of young Puebloan women.

Although the trail is rough and difficult for us, her footsteps would be confident. After all, she would have lived here her entire life, as had her ancestors. We can assume she could easily scamper across a boulder-strewn canyon or up a seemingly inaccessible cliff with ease while carrying a heavy load.

She would stand barely five feet tall. She would be thin as hard work and subsistence food would keep everyone lithe. Archaeologists have found marks on nearly every skeleton they have encountered that suggest most people had experienced hunger at some point in their lives.

Her clothes would have been well-made, particularly considering the era. They had no wool yet; sheep would come with the Spanish. But they did weave cotton, which was grown in the warmer areas in the southern parts of the region. Her clothes would be of this. Coronado's chronicler admired Pueblo women because he considered them and their attire "modest."

She would wear an outer robe-like garment that in modern times has been called a *manta*, a Spanish word meaning "cloth." This manta is actually a long length of cloth, as much as seven feet long and two to three feet wide with tassels on the corners. It is folded over her body length-wise, slung over the right shoulder to leave her left arm free. This garment hangs to below her knees and is cinched closed at her waist with a colorful sash. Pueblo women have been wearing this garment since the first contact with Europeans. However, archaeologists have found an intact manta stashed in an ancient pot at Wallace Tank, Arizona, and when they carbon dated it, it dated to circa A.D. 1250—1325. This manta is on display at the Center of Southwest Studies in Durango, Colorado. So there is evidence that Pueblo women have been wearing the mantas for many centuries.

In the coldest weather she would cover it all with a cloak — sometimes of turkey feathers or sometimes of rabbit fur cut into delicate strips and painstakingly interwoven with yucca. This material is surprisingly warm, lightweight and comfortable. Archaeologists have found scraps and even whole blankets of it, and it is a wonder to behold. The skill required to cut the rabbit fur into such thin strips with stone tools and then to plait it into a whole cape is impressive to consider.

On her feet she would wear sandals made from yucca fiber or perhaps be barefoot.

She might wear jewelry of sea shells from Mexico or California and charcoal-colored *heishi* (pronounced HEE-shee) beads. These

A Puebloan woman dressed mostly in the traditional fashion goes for water about the turn of the last century. The silver jewelry is a modern additon, as are the white leggings. From the 23rd Bureau of American Ehtnology, *Stevenson.*

were tiny pieces of shell or sometimes stone that were ground into beads and then strung into necklaces. Others might wear turquoise jewelry. A few copper bells, imported from the south, have occasionally been found by archaeologists. Someone might have worn these or used them as dance regalia.

Although she would be thin, her face would be round and open. It is thought this was caused when mothers placed their babies on a hard cradle board, which made a flat spot on the back of the baby's head and changed the shape of the skull. Rancher Richard Wetherill noticed this about the skeletons he found in the Four Corners region in the 1890s. Earlier skeletons had skulls that were longer and narrower, later skulls were more rounded. He thought he had found a different race of people, but it was probably an example of a change in style. Perhaps a round, full face might have appeared robust and healthy even in the direst of times. The Pueblo people of today no longer place babies on cradle boards and in historic times they carried a child on their back until it was one year of age.

Marriage

When this woman married, her work would be that of a wife, a mother and a fire keeper, according to *No Turning Back.* The fire was the heart of the home, anchoring the family and all their activities that would have been centered there. So the fire keeper was vitally important; someone had to bend over the hearth day in and day out. When we see the blackened, sooted walls of the living rooms of the cliff dwellings, we are seeing the remnants of her work done eight hundred years ago.

As was mentioned before, modern-day Pueblo women are in charge of the everyday affairs of the household, and men are in charge of the ceremonial aspects of their lives. Soon this young woman would have her own family. As a married woman her hair would be short. Apparently a woman's hair was a valuable resource, as archaeologists have found it braided into twine and combined with other materials.

Who would our young Pueblo woman marry? She would not marry a member of her own clan — that was considered incest even if the couple were technically not related. Whoever the young man was, her parents would have to be beseeched at some point. Marriages were not *arranged,* per se, but her parents had some say-so about the marriage in that the young man would become a part of the young woman's family group and marriage creates a series of reciprocal responsibilities to each family group. For example, if someone of your clan or father's clan shows up at your doorstep, you are obligated to feed them and house them. You might also call upon your in-

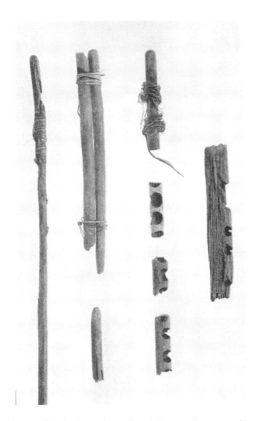

On the left are examples of a firekeeper's tool kit. Early archaeologist A. V. Kidder reported that fire starters were discovered in most cliff dwellings he visited. On the photograph's right are the base sticks, or as he called them, the hearth sticks. To their left are drill sticks. The hearth stick rested flat on the ground, then the drill stick was twirled in the socket of the hearth stick until friction created a spark which would fall onto the tinder. In a different ruin he discovered a drill stick and a hearth stick tied together as if for a traveling kit, second from the left. Bureau of American Ethnology #65, *Kidder and Guernsey.*

laws for help when building a house, for example. And there are ceremonial duties, too.

Some of the Pueblo people of today have a wedding ceremony or ritual that is performed. Among the Hopi, for example, the young woman must go to the prospective in-laws' home and grind corn for three days so they can see how industrious she is. While she is doing this a beautiful trousseau is being woven for her in the kiva by her future male in-laws. But with other Pueblo people marriages are more casual, where the young groom simply takes up residence with his prospective bride's family.

Our young ancestral Puebloan matron would be a woman of substance. As a female member of a matrilineal society, the woman owned any house they might build, or any farmland they should cultivate. She would also own the crops that were harvested from her ancestral lands. Her children would be members of her clan, and her children would inherit through her. The young husband would live and work side by side with his new in-laws. Farmland he cultivated would also belong to the wife's clan. But if this land was not farmed, ownership would revert back to the wife's clan.

Once the corn was harvested and in the storerooms, it was the wife's responsibility. Anyone needing anything from any of the storerooms would ask her first. She had to budget its contents carefully so it would last until the next harvest.

If the marriage did not work out, divorce was an option. When the marriage was finished either the wife would place her husband's possessions outside the door or the husband would pack up his belongings — his sandals, cloud blower, bow and arrows and his feather box — and move back to his clan, which meant his mother's house or, if she was no longer living, an older sister's house. Or he could live in his clan's kiva. The Pueblo people believe in living in harmony, and if that is not possible, then it is better to dissolve the marriage. Both are free to remarry and there is no stigma to divorce. There are no illegitimate children among the Pueblo people; all children stay with their mothers, and all are recognized as members of her clan.

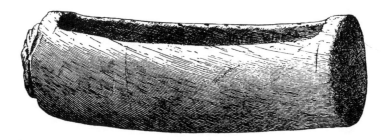

Two examples of feather boxes, which were used to store feathers. The feathers were used in pahos, prayers and ceremonies. Both from *8th Annual Bureau of American Ethnology*, V. Mindeleff.

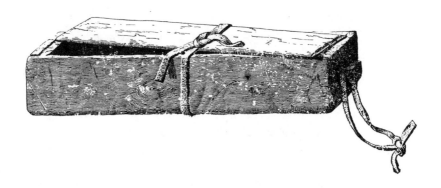

This mother and child were of the Santa Clara Pueblo, circa 1920. From American Indians: America's First Families.

Children

Childbirth claimed many a young woman's life. Most female skeletons the archaeologists uncover prove to have died in their twenties. Childbirth would have been one of the reasons.

When our young ancestral Puebloan woman was ready to deliver, she would be tended by her mother, aunts and sisters. A bed of clean, warm sand was prepared for her on the floor of the house. Among the Hopi and Zuni women of today, massage is one the techniques they use to help the mother during labor. If a problem should arise, they send for the shaman or medicine man. Although nineteenth-century Zuni medicine men used fetishes and

These Puebloan youths prepare for a foot race. From the 23rd Bureau of American Ethnology, Stevenson.

herbs in medical treatment, their treatment had some real medical value at that time according to nineteenth-century anthropologist Matilda Coxe Stevenson. After the baby's arrival, they tied the umbilical cord with a strand of the mother's hair.

When an infant was born he was kept in a darkened room for twenty days among the Hopi and four among the Zuni. Then his mother and the female members of his father's family presented the baby to the Sun Father at dawn on the twentieth day and claimed him as a member of both his mother's and father's clans. Facing the east, the mother-in-law says to the Sun God: "May you live always without sickness, travel along the Sun Trail to old age, and pass away in your sleep without pain. And your name shall be _____." The shaman names the child among the Zuni, while among the other Pueblo people it is his mother. He is rarely called this name, because Pueblo people feel it is wrong to call a person by his name too often. Instead, they refer to people by their relationship. Our young mother would call her new baby "my son" or "my daughter." The child would refer to her as "my mother." He will call his friends "my friend." This name would be his name only until he was older. Later, he would earn new names that might be different on different occasions. And he would also have nicknames that he would be called.

Infants were carried on their mother's back in a cradleboard — among more recent Pueblo people, a child was carried on the back for as much as a year. The baby was wrapped and then the cradleboard was padded with soft juniper bark, which is so absorbent it also served as a diaper. Modern Pueblo women say the cradle board kept the baby safe and made it easier to handle him or her.

Children learned by imitating their parents. Little girls tagged along after their mothers when they were collecting clay for pots. And when the mother pinched a bit of dirt and brought it to her mouth and tasted it, the little girls would also grasp a little fistful of dirt and taste it, too — thereby learning how to test for the correct soil composition for pottery making. Big sisters could be seen carrying their baby brothers on their back, just like their

The caption of this picture reads "Learning to weave belts." From the 23rd Bureau of American Ethnology, Stevenson.

mothers did. Bands of nearly naked young boys could be seen stalking any hapless rabbit, raven or such that ventured too close to the pueblo. For practice, boys would weave a hoop from twigs and dried grass, hang it up, swing it back and forth and take turns shooting arrows through it with their pint-sized bows. By doing so, they would become as proficient with these items as their dads and uncles were. Boys also collected firewood, and all children guarded the fields from pests like crows and rabbits.

In modern times, Pueblo people initiate youngsters into the tribe. When girls are initiated they are given a colorful kachina doll, usually carved by their father, grandfather or uncle. The dolls have incredibly detailed costumes that are culturally correct and in brilliant colors. Today these are very popular with collectors. The doll is presented to the girl during a kachina dance, when one of the spectacularly dressed dancers in a long line steps out of the line as he reaches the girl and hands it to her. As a gift directly from the kachinas, the doll is cherished.

This child has a broken leg which is in splints. From the 23rd Bureau of American Ethnology, *Stevenson.*

We can guess the ancestral Puebloans loved their children as all parents do. But this point is driven home when you see the child-sized crutches on display at the Mesa Verde National Park Museum. Someone carefully carved these from forked tree branches nearly a thousand years ago and then padded the fork. There are not many wear marks on these crutches, and we are left to

7

Most of a woman's life would be spent grinding corn. From Century Magazine, Frank Cushing, 1883.

wonder if the child did not survive long enough to put the crutches to much use.

But sometimes a mother's medicine did not work. Every Puebloan knew that serious illness was caused by *witches*! Then the medicine man was sent for to counteract the witch's evil work. Tragically, sometimes even the magic of the medicine man didn't work.

Archaeologists tell us that perhaps as many as 50 percent of all children died in childhood. When families buried their young, they would place a small possession with the child. Even if the family was very poor, their infant might be buried with a pretty potsherd. Children were often buried in an unused room or perhaps under the floor of the family's habitation room so that the child's spirit could remain with its family in the rafters of the house. The Hopi of today believe that the spirit of a dead child can be born again and again to them.

A Woman's Work

Most of a woman's life would have been spent on her hands and knees, grinding corn. Study of the ancient bones shows the type of wear that would have occurred in this activity. In their living room or on a plaza there would be a series of three grinding bins (sometimes four), each one with a *metate* (the stone base) and a *mano* hand stone in it. These metates were of different levels of coarseness. One would be very coarse for the first grinding.

107

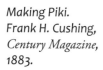

Next to this coarse metate would be a hand-held pecking or hammer stone, for keeping the surface rough. The middle one would be of medium coarseness, and the last would be of fine coarseness for finishing the meal to a fine powder — so fine it could immediately dissolve in water and make a refreshing drink called *piñole*. Or it could be used to make the delicious wafer-thin bread that the Hopi call *piki* (PEE-kee) and all Pueblo people are famous for.

A woman's hours of grinding were shared by the other female members of the family and sometimes friends. Often they would work in threes, using the long tedious hours of grinding as a time to chat. Young men knew that young women could be found here and came to the window to chat, joke and tease their favorites.

Among the Zuni, a flute player sat in the doorway to the grinding room playing music for the women to work by. And there were special grinding songs created for the purpose of accompanying grinding, the gentle beat of the song matching the rhythm of the stones in motion. Still today, a Pueblo person's life is lived accompanied by the gentle, rhythmic hum of the grinding stones and the rich smell of parched corn.

It was common to eat two meals a day, breakfast about eleven in the morning after everyone had put in a good day's work, and dinner after sunset when the work for the day was done. If you were lucky enough to be invited to our young Pueblo woman's house for dinner, you might experience what Frank

Making Piki.
Frank H. Cushing,
Century Magazine,
1883.

A young wife dresses her husband's hair with a dried grass hairbrush, Cushing. Inset, an ancient grass hairbrush discovered at the turn-of-the-century by Kidder and Guernsey. *Bureau of American Ethnology, #65.*

Hamilton Cushing described with a Zuni family in the 1880s. First of all, you would not be offered any water — you were expected to have quenched your thirst at the spring or well before coming. Everyone knew how much work a dipper of water represented for the young women of the household and would be too polite to ask for it. Everyone lounged on mats on the floor in a circle and our Pueblo hostess brought in a pot of carefully flavored corn mush and set it in the middle of the circle. With it might be some wafer bread (the piki of the Hopi was known as *he'we* among the Zuni) rolled and piled high on a basket tray. When Major John Wesley Powell visited the Hopi in 1869, he claimed he loved the colorful (since it was made from different colored corn) piki bread best. This paper-thin wafer bread is said to taste similar to corn flakes. When it is still warm and fresh it has a distinctive, unforgettable flavor, but as it cools and dries it is still quite tasty and can be stored a long time.

Each member of the group would dip his index and middle finger in the mush up to his first knuckle and scoop the mush to his lips. It was considered rude to plunge your fingers in deeper than the second knuckle. This takes practice as it's *hot*! And each person would take a piece of bread and sop up the stew with it. Along with the meal there was a lively repartee and much laughter. Cushing said he had rarely experienced such a jolly time as at these family meals. The Pueblo people of today still love to tease each other.

Besides grinding corn, our young Pueblo woman would also need to "gather" just as her hunter/gatherer ancestors did. Even after the ancestral Puebloans began farming corn there were times of famine and times of want before the corn ripened, times when the corn in the store rooms and granaries was beginning to run short. In these lean times the family would be dependent upon the Pueblo woman's skills in the ancient art of gathering. She would know which wild plants were edible and which were not, what was toxic and what was merely unpalatable, but not poisonous.

She would also know where the important wild foodstuff grew. She would know where to go to find rice grass. She would know where the most succulent prickly pear cactus could be found and how to remove the spines and prepare it as a nourishing meal for her family. Anthropologist Ruth Underhill wrote that Pueblo women could make use of more than two hundred different wild plants.

She would also know where to go to find these plants at different times — a place on the cooler north side of a hill where a certain plant might ripen a little later than usual or on the sunny south-facing side of a slope where it might be gathered a little earlier than usual — thus extending the wild harvest a little. There still is today among Southwestern people certain areas where a family has traditionally gone to collect piñon nuts in the fall.

She would know how to prepare wild foodstuff in such a way as to be palatable, soaking bitter tasting plants to remove the bitterness and then drying and grinding them to make edible meals from an otherwise unusable plant food. She would know that the prickly pear cactus has fruits as tasty as figs and how to burn off the long needles. Sometimes the cactus pads were boiled and sometimes eaten raw.

She would know which *parts* of the plant were edible and which parts were toxic — such as the yucca plant. No plant was more usable than the yucca. The flowers were edible, as were the fruit, but the roots were toxic if eaten. The roots, however, made a splendid shampoo. One modern-day Pueblo woman had her hair badly burned by chemicals at a beauty shop. She went home and shampooed her damaged hair in the traditional way — with the roots of the yucca plant — and her hair was restored to its natural beauty. Ancient Pueblo women knew all this and more.

These women also knew all the rules of etiquette for collecting wild plants. Among the Tewa a *wild* plant could not be owned (read: weed), and was OK for anyone to claim, even if it grew in the middle of your cornfield. But plants that were cultivated by the sweat of one's brow — such as corn, beans and squash — belonged to the person or clan who cultivated it.

This elderly woman was one of the few to live to such an advanced age — to be able to follow the Sun Trail to old age. From the 23rd *Bureau of American Ethnology,* Stevenson.

But food collection and preparation were just a part of what our ancestral Pueblo woman did. Nearly every household item would have to come from her hands. Don Talayesvma wrote in his autobiography: "My own mother was my best friend and my earliest memories are of her. She was always busy as a bee or an ant, cooking, grinding corn, bringing water, making baskets out of rabbit weed or pots out of clay." It was more than likely women who made the twined bags, sandals, belts and other non-loomed textiles, and baskets. From their hands probably came every inch of string and rope that was used, and the mats they ate and slept on. The nets that the men used for hunting might also have come from her hands. Her fingers would be constantly moving, day in and day out, rarely at rest, busy manufacturing much of what her family needed to get along.

Physical problems she might encounter as she aged would be arthritis from the hard physical labor and lifting of heavy loads. She might also have problems with her teeth. As they ground the corn with sandstone manos and metates, bits of sand found their way into the corn meal. After years of chewing the sand along with the corn meal, ancestral Puebloan teeth wore down alarmingly, so much so that abscesses are sometimes discovered in their ancient jawbones. Anemia was also a problem since their diets were short on iron and short on protein as well.

Burying a loved one in 1883. Frank H. Cushing, Century Magazine.

Very few ancient Puebloan women would have the privilege of living to be age forty. Most women died young — in their twenties was common. Archaeologists have calculated that ancestral Puebloan women lived seven years less than men, the opposite of today in our culture. When our young Pueblo woman died, she would be buried in a flexed position in the clothes her in-laws created for her on her wedding day. Among the Mimbres people a pot would be "killed" (a hole punched in the bottom) and it would be placed over her face. The Hopi place a small cotton mat over the face. The fluffy cotton symbolizes the clouds and is supposed to help her on her journey to join the Cloud People. She would be wrapped in her robe and then the robe held closed with twine wrapped around it. She would be buried with some of her tools and possessions.

What can we know about these women? What can speak to us from the depths of time? We sense they were lovers of beauty — they beautified their world wherever they went. They plastered the insides of their homes, and then decorated the plaster with designs. They plastered the interiors of the kivas with breathtaking murals. It was also they who plastered the outside of their homes. They decorated their pottery with designs that are still considered fine art even after a thousand years. And they decorated themselves with jewelry and with colorful sashes.

And we can still see traces of the beauty they created yet today — in a tantalizing sherd of decorated pottery or in a plastered wall bedecked with geometric designs or in a scrap of a kiva mural. And we know this is the ancient ones' legacy. Looking across the abyss of time, we can say they walked in beauty, leaving cultural footprints in nearly every canyon, across most mesa tops in the American Southwest — and it touches our twenty-first century *bahana* hearts.*

* *Bahana* is the Hopi word for white man. It sometimes is also spelled *pahana.*

Above, this magnificent cliff dwelling intrigued us from across the canyon. It stretched for perhaps a quarter of a mile along the ledge; pictured here is just a part of it.

6

BARRIERS TO ENTRY

The ancient stone buildings were perched in a long ragged line on the cliff ledge. They stretched from way out on the point to the crotch where the two cliff walls met. In front of them gaped a drop-off of hundreds of feet.

We considered these buildings across the canyon from us. Cliff dwellings are often near springs. This one had a large pothole pool that looked deep — a lot of water for this area. Even from our vantage point, we could see a hanging garden around the pool. Plants draped from the walls, grass grew — it was a tiny, hidden oasis tucked into the cliff face. No doubt about it, this was a very special place. We longed to see it, to feel the coolness of it on our faces, to explore its mysteries.

But how to get in? It looked impregnable — the access to these ancient ruins was designed by the builders to be dangerous. This one was no different. The perpendicular cliff face looked sheer — no chance of entry that way. The sandstone rim rock above it was overhung — we saw no promising route off the rim to the ledge. We left discouraged, but returned again and again on later trips.

It took us several trips, but we finally found the way into the cliff dwelling. As is true with most cliff dwellings, there was only one way in. This time we spotted a breach in the massive sandstone rimrock on the wall opposite the cliff dwelling. From this distance it looked like a hairline crack in the slickrock traversed laterally down across the slickrock *caprock* to the crotch. In a couple of places, bushes peeked up over the edge of the crack, letting us know it might just be wide enough to be traversable. And at the end of the

The "hanging garden" overlooks the pothole pool.

crack, where there was a dangerous drop-off to the cliff dwelling's ledge, there was a stunted tree. On foot, we found the crack and decided it was indeed trekable, but the exposure was daunting. We inched our way across the steep slope of the slickrock on the ten-inch wide path formed by the crack, all the while aware of the empty windows watching our every attempt — every move we made. When we finally made our way to the stunted tree at the end, we used it as a ladder to scramble down onto the ledge by the side of the pool. We had made it!

This large pothole pool is under a pour-over and contains more water than is typical for this region. It is perhaps eight feet across.

A freestanding wall blocked the ledge and the entrance to the cliff dwelling. In it was a doorway and two loopholes.

Now this is where *we* would have built our home — near the water, protected from the wind, and with a beautiful view down the canyon. The "hanging gardens" made it a cozy and delightful place for a home in the desert. And indeed, we did find some foundations of one-time structures. But the stones from the walls were no longer there, suggesting they had been dismantled in prehistoric times and moved. The people had started out in this sheltered spot but had found another place and moved the buildings and themselves.

We left the hanging garden and continued along the ledge to the cliff dwellings, where we encountered a freestanding wall with a small doorway in it, blocking the ledge. We find these man-made walls often in our backcountry treks. Sometimes these walls will have a T-shaped doorway; this one had a rectangular doorway in it. In many ruins we see, the lintel is low so a visitor has to stoop to enter. This one was missing its lintel so it is hard to tell if it was the case here. This doorway was the sole entry to the ruin, almost like a gateway. Puncturing this wall were two holes, a broomstick could have passed through them easily. Looking through the holes, we could see that one pointed to the pathway. The other pointed down sharply toward a blind spot behind the stone wall.

We continued on along the ledge, and there, among the clusters of buildings, were the remains of a tower — a square tower. It seemed odd that there should be a tower here; the ledge was already high so a tower would have

Out near the point, the ledge narrowed until it was impossible to continue on.

served no function as a lookout. It seemed somehow redundant.

Out near the point the ledge eventually became so narrow we could not continue and another building blocked our path. The hot wind battered us, pitching sand in our eyes and buffeting us. We leaned against each other so as to not be blown off the ledge. The weather out here was intensified by the wind. But back in the alcove with the hanging gardens and pool, it was quite pleasant. Yet, *this* is where they had moved to! Why on earth would someone choose to build here, out on the point with the wind and intensified weather, away from the water, instead of staying by the lovely and protected pool?

It was then as we turned our attention back to the cliff dwelling that we realized that from way out here near the point, you could see the crack we used to gain entry to this place. If you lived by the pool, you couldn't see anyone approaching down the crack to the ledge. But out here on the point, you had a clear view of anyone approaching the dwelling and attempting to gain entry.

Suddenly the unanswered questions about this place were beginning to make sense. It dawned on us that this place may have been defensive. Here security trumped all other considerations. Safety was more important than the distance from water, more important than being out of the wind and in a cozy, protected nook, more important than the complications of bringing firewood and other household necessities up a cliff face. Safety mattered more than the location of the cornfields or the ability to add rooms to one's home at will. If it is true, as psychologists tell us, that safety is one of the most basic of all human needs, then nowhere is this more evident than in many cliff dwellings.

This cliff dwelling had, in fact, layers of defenses. The first line of defense was to funnel any intruders to single file in the narrow crack that was the access to this place while in clear view of the occupants. Then there was the freestanding stone wall with its low doorway. This is a common defense around the world called a *choke point*. A choke point, or bottleneck, channels intruders one-at-a-time and is easy to defend by a small number of people. The small short doorway forces each person to enter stooped over and headfirst, making each of them vulnerable to being clobbered on the head by the defenders. Perhaps even women and children could have mounted a creditable defense of this place if the men were away.

And the tower. It was probably not here to be a lookout, which is why it seemed redundant. It is a truism in battles that he who has the high ground has the advantage. Was the tower here to provide "high ground" on the ledge itself? If the wall entry were breached, the tower could provide a last-ditch place to defend their home.

There are other examples of similar structures with layers of defenses such as these. If one defense were breached, the whole structure would not necessarily be lost. But these secure places are halfway around the world. They also rely on great walls and incorporated heights into their defense. They contain towers and have restricted entry gates. And they reached their heyday about the same time as cliffs dwellings. They are called *castles*.

Archaeologist Kathryn Kamp points out in her book, *Life in the Pueblo*, that we know conflicts were a way of life in Europe in A.D. 1200 because there are records still in existence that tell us as much. However, even if these documents did not exist, she continues, we would still be able to surmise as much from what the *architecture* of that time tells us. It was at this time that the thirteenth century medieval castles reached full flower in Europe. The hallmark of castles in A.D. 1200 is a successive series of architectural defenses.

The first consideration for a castle was the site; the best was considered to be a hilltop, making it easier for the inhabitants to see approaching intruders and assuring the advantage of high ground. Oftentimes surrounding this hill is a moat or ditch. Sometimes it held water; sometimes just the steep sides of the ditch were a difficult enough obstacle to discourage an attacker weighed down with heavy arms. This had to be dug by the castle builders.

Then came stone walls. Some castles have a thick, outer stone wall surrounding the entire structure called a *curtain wall*. This wall is bracketed

U. S. Geological Survey.   Plate **LXXIX**.

Cliff Fortress.

The 10th Annual Hayden Survey, 1878.

by towers, which were used for observation and also for storage. The walls are pierced with loopholes through which arrows could be launched, but the loopholes also functioned as ventilation, illumination and observation. Sometimes there are two outer walls, one inside the other, so that if one were breached, the whole castle would not necessarily be lost.

Between these two walls is a large courtyard area called a *bailey*. Here, in the protected place behind the curtain wall, the day-to-day activities of the castle took place — the workshops, stables, household activities and marketplace. This is where the peasants would live. The peasants worked in their fields all day outside the castle walls and retreated behind the castle walls whenever danger appeared, and at night.

The castle *keep* is a tower, either square or round, that was the most secure place in a medieval castle. It is usually in the heart of the castle, and this is where the lord and his family lived. The entrance to the keep is often on the second floor; sometimes it could only be entered by a ladder which could be pulled up after them. If all the castle walls were breached, the keep would be the last place of retreat.

A castle keep was not a comfortable place to live. It was intended for defense, not comfort, and the rooms were dark and cold and drafty. But if the lord's family was uncomfortable, it was even worse for the peasants.

As a peasant your house inside the castle walls would be small and cramped. Your entire family lived in one room. It would have no chimney or fireplace and mantle. The fire was on the floor in the center of the room with a hole in the thatched roof for the smoke to escape. You cooked on the dirt floor,

Like castles, some cliff dwellings often have an outer wall protecting the courtyard. This one has a curtain wall, complete with a choke point entrance.

121

Many cliff dwellings could only be reached by a ladder or a series of ladders, like this one. On the ledge beneath the dwellings are ladder socket holes that stabilized the base of the ladder, inset photograph. The ladder led to the choke point entrance above.

Photographer: Andrew Gulliford ©.

ate on the floor and slept on the floor. *Everyone* slept on the floor huddled together — including visitors, chickens, goats and other livestock. Such was medieval European life about A.D. 1300.

Life in the American Southwest circa A.D. 1200 to 1300 was not a lot different from the life of a peasant about the same time in Europe.

If the architectural features of castles tell a tale of medieval conflict, what does the architecture of the cliff dwellings tell us about A.D. 1200 in the American Southwest? Some of what architecture accomplished for defense in European castles, nature provided in the American Southwest. The landscape in the American Southwest is obligingly jagged — steep, unscalable cliff walls, and also towers and turrets are provided by nature in the form of hoodoos and pinnacle rocks. The canyon bottoms provide an obstacle similar to a moat. From a home high in the cliffs one would have a good view of all approaches to the site, and there would only be one or two possible approaches to the dwelling.

Ladders were sometimes used to get up to the cliff house, and they could be pulled up at night or at any sign of trouble. Cliff dwellers also used ladders within the cliff houses to get from floor to floor. The ancient people also pecked hand-and-toe hold trails up steep slickrock expanses. These hand-and-toe holds were difficult enough to ascend eight hundred years ago, but are impossible to negotiate today because they have weathered in the intervening years.

The entrance to the cliff dwelling area might be a choke point like the one in the freestanding wall we saw in the cliff dwelling described earlier.

Some cliff dwellings have an outer curtain wall, but not all do. Under the protective overhang of the sandstone alcove, and behind the curtain wall (if it has one) is a courtyard. Here all the day-to-day activities took place: grinding corn, arrowhead and stone tool manufacture, cooking, pottery making, basketry making, caring for children. And with a dog as an early warning alarm system for those long, dark nights, as much safety could be achieved as was possible in that day and age.

This curtain wall is made of stone and is pierced with small holes and vent holes for the fires. Early explorers and archaeologists called these small holes

This structure with loopholes overlooks one of the largest bodies of water in the area.

loopholes. The loopholes overlook approaches to a site. In addition to observation, the loopholes could also serve as ventilation and illumination. It was possible to even launch arrows from these apertures, if necessary.

But did the ancient people use the loopholes in that fashion? No one can ever know. However, there is an ethnographic account where the loopholes were employed. David Roberts in his book *The Pueblo Revolt* quotes from Governor Diego Jose De Vargas who traveled to Jemez Pueblo in northern New Mexico in A.D. 1694, to quell the Pueblo Revolt. Vargas wrote in his report: "From their loopholes they had wounded and injured many."

Towers, particularly in the Mesa Verde region, were often constructed over or connected to the subterranean kiva, or ceremonial room, because the men were vulnerable while in the kiva. Again there are ethnographic examples of this. Awat'ovi (uh-WAT-uh-vee, a Hopi Pueblo in northeastern Arizona) was attacked and destroyed about A.D. 1700. The attackers waited until they knew the men would be in the kiva for a certain ceremony. Then, just before dawn when they would be asleep, the attackers pulled up the ladder out of the kiva so no one could escape and threw burning greasewood down into the kiva. The men all perished hideously in the inferno. Having a connecting tower to the kiva would enable folks in the kiva to turn the tables and go from vulnerable to having the upper hand while under attack.

Although the ancient people were safer than they had been before in scattered farmsteads, life in a cliff dwelling could not have been comfortable. The living rooms were drafty and smoky and oppressively dark. Unless there was a spring or seep on the sandstone ledge, it was an arduous and dangerous trip to get water. Without the curtain wall, it would have been a full-time job keeping toddlers away from the cliff edge. Also, there had been lively trading between areas before some of them moved into the cliff dwellings. Once these few moved into the cliffs, most of the trading came to an abrupt end.

A difference between European castles and American Southwestern cliff dwellings is that in Europe there were standing armies, battlegrounds and written records of conflicts. Archaeologists have not discovered battlefields in the American Southwest, nor is there any evidence that there was anything like standing armies. In the Southwest conflict would have been confined to raids. But perhaps the *perception* of danger made dwelling in the cliffs more attractive.

We know because of written records that castles were built for defense. No one knows why the cliff dwellings were built, but after forty years of visiting these fascinating ruins, we see strong parallels between the two.

Definition of Barriers to Entry

We like to refer to all the layers of defense as *barriers to entry*. Our definition of a barrier to entry is: Any obstacle, natural or man-made, that must be overcome in order to gain access to the dwelling. Some sites have more barriers to entry than others.

The barriers to entry are the first things you notice when you approach a cliff dwelling. First, is the height of the cliff dwelling in the cliff wall. Actually, some cliff dwellings are not that high up on the cliff. Their access is straightforward enough for cattle or horses today to wander into the buildings. Others are impossibly high, and one can only speculate how on earth the ancient people came and went.

Sometimes the approach to a dwelling requires walking on a ledge so narrow that only one person at a time can approach the dwelling. In others this obstacle is compounded so that the ledge is narrow, but there is also an overhang so low that one must negotiate on hands and knees. Balcony House at Mesa Verde National Park is an example of having to leave on one's hands and knees. Sometimes on these ledges one must navigate slickrock that slopes steeply to the edge of the cliff while being buffeted by strong winds that take your breath away and make you dizzy. During access there is no question that one would be vulnerable to a simple push by defenders.

Above, some ledges are not only narrow, but are also under an overhang and must be negotiated on your hands and knees.

As was mentioned before, many cliff dwellings have a freestanding wall with a small doorway in it to restrict entry to one at a time, and anyone must enter bent over. Sometimes there is more than one such wall and doorway. Another wall, well inside the ruin, apparently exists so that if the first one fails, there is a back up.

Not all cliff dwellings were actually lived in. Sometimes the buildings that were built in caves with dangerous approaches were intended as granaries — more on this later. Some were apparently used as a place to retreat to when danger appeared, as castles were often used. But they were not intended to be lived in for any length of time.

This natural crack funneled intruders to single file — but apparently it was not enough. The inhabitants filled in the crack with masonry so that everyone had to enter not only single file, but also on their hands and knees. This ruin is Balcony House at Mesa Verde National Park.

So was it dangerous living in a cliff dwelling? We sense it was. Ethnographically, we know that Zuni women have a prayer that is recited while climbing up and down ladders. And in the past a feather paho was sometimes attached to ladders to prevent accidents. But for us it was brought home personally by an incident that happened to Bill in the early 1970s while he was making a film of the Tarahumara people of Northern Mexico. The Tarahumara have many technical similarities to the Pueblo people to the north — they are farmers of corn, beans and squash, and some of them live in cave and cliff dwellings. They reside in an extremely remote part of Mexico, and their culture has remained more untouched than most other Native American cultures because of it.

Deep in an unmapped region, Bill stopped to ask directions of a Tarahumara man. Although they each spoke only a little broken Spanish, they managed a conversation. The Tarahumara man eventually asked if Bill could take him to the nearest missionary clinic because his wife had fallen out of the cliff dwelling and was hurt. He took Bill to see his wife who was deep in the cave in a safe place. She was curled into a fetal position and unable to move. Bill, who had some medical background, took one look at her and knew it was an old injury, possibly a broken back.

Although Bill was headed in the opposite direction, of course he changed his plans and agreed to take them to the clinic. The men took all the sleeping bags and anything else that was soft, and made a bed for her in the back of Bill's Land Rover. Their two adorable children squeezed into the back seat. It was a long, grueling drive on primitive, two-rut roads. And every time that old Land Rover lurched, the Tarahumara woman in the back moaned.

Eventually, after driving all night, they made it to the clinic. Bill dropped off the Tarahumara family, indicating he'd be back later and continued on his way. On his way back through he stopped at the clinic again and asked for the Tarahumara couple. His intuition was confirmed: she did indeed have a broken back, the bones had fused, and there was absolutely nothing that could be done for her. Bill asked to see them and was shocked to hear they weren't there any longer. Although the clinic staff had urged her to stay there and let them care for her, she just wanted to go home. The priest said her husband placed her gently in a carrying bag, which he carefully slung over his shoulder, and walked home. Their two children tagged along behind him.

A cliff dwelling, for all its potential dangers, was sometimes the ancient Puebloan's home of choice after A.D. 1150. Why? This is an enduring and highly controversial mystery in Southwestern archaeology.

Definition

Our definition of a barrier to entry is: Any manmade or natural obstacle or combination of the two that must be overcome to enter a cliff dwelling. The obstacle controls entry and puts the intruder at risk. Access is limited to single file.

We define the cliff dwelling above as having a single, uncomplicated barrier to entry: This ruin sits out on the open ground, on bedrock. There is no cliff in front of it. But it is tucked up against a cliff — its back is against a wall. We classify this as a barrier to entry because 180 degrees of its exposure and vulnerability is blocked.

Height

We classify height as a barrier to entry because the cliff exposure makes access dangerous. The height barrier can range from not particularly difficult and simply funneling visitors to single file, to being virtually inaccessible, such as the one above. On the right, the 10th Annual *Hayden Survey of 1878.*

Choke Points: Man-Made

A choke point is an obstacle, man-made or natural, that controls access by funneling intruders to single file, sometimes bent over in a vulnerable position or even on hands and knees.

Left is a stone wall blocking the ledge. A doorway in the wall creates a choke point. Access is controlled by permitting only one person at a time to enter.

This ruin has double choke point walls, a wall behind a wall. It suggests that if one wall is breached, there is a second chance to block access behind the next wall.

129

Choke Points: Man-Made

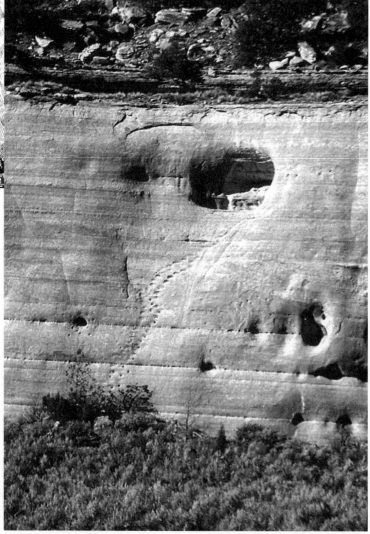

U.S. Geological Survey.

Hand-and-toe holds are an example of a combination of natural and man-made barriers to entry. They are extremely difficult to negotiate and put an intruder at great risk with little effort from the defenders. These were often used by the inhabitants in combination with ladders which are of course long gone now. Hand-and-toe holds can be seen from the northernmost reaches of the territory, all the way to Mexico.

The 10th Annual Hayden Survey, 1878.

As we mentioned earlier, climbing hand-and-toe-hold trails should never be attempted. First of all, they were designed by their makers to be dangerous and to keep intruders out. Most of them have eroded over time and are even more difficult now than they were then. Also, they must be negotiated correctly — some require starting with a certain foot. If begun with the wrong foot, the person will become stuck part way up unable to go up or down. They are even more difficult to descend, because you cannot see where to place your foot.

Choke Points: Man-Made

Ladder engravings from the 8th *Bureau of American Ethnology*, Victor Mindeleff.

This rock art panel shows a detailed image of a ladder. Photographer: Andrew Gulliford ©.

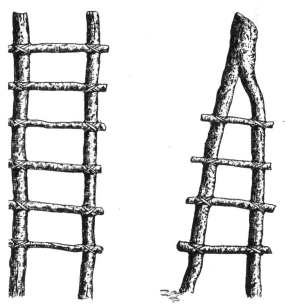

Ladders were another man-made choke point. Today it's rare to see the remains of a ladder in a cliff dwelling. But sometimes there are telltale clues to where there were once ladders at a site. At the top are pecked slots in the sandstone cliff edge at a cliff dwelling that once held and stabilized the ladder rails. Earlier we pointed out the pecked sockets that once secured the base of the ladder.

Choke Points: Natural

Ledges provided natural choke points and controlled access not only by single file, but also by putting the individual at risk.

On the left, the entry ledge to this cliff dwelling rolled off to the abyss, requiring a person to sidle along while slipping toward the edge.

The ledge below ran for a quarter of a mile and because of the overhang, the whole way had to be negotiated on hands and knees. The exposure was daunting and the wind kicked sand in our eyes keeping us dizzy and off balance its entire length.

Curtain Walls

We define a curtain wall as the outermost wall blocking the front of the cliff dwelling. The curtain wall provides the final barrier to entry. Access is controlled by one or more choke point entrances. Not all cliff dwellings have curtain walls, and many curtain walls have fallen away because of their location at the edge of the cliff, so that you'll only see the remains of it.

In this engraving from the the 10th Annual Hayden Survey, note how the ancient structures blend in with the surrounding landscape, they are almost, but not quite camoflaged. Also note the tower in upper center.

7

STRUCTURES: WHAT THE BUILDINGS TELL US

The tangle of gambel oak completely blocked the ledge; it snatched off our hats, tugged at our clothing and slapped us in the face. Again and again we brushed aside the clingy branches, and eventually we were able to step out of its reach and into the open. And there we saw the shadow of a building on the narrow ledge.

Although this structure was not grand, it still had a fascinating story to tell us. The small stone and adobe mud structure was of the landscape. That is, it did not stand out from its surroundings like monumental architecture does — instead, it was a coherent part of it. It was built of materials close at hand, in this case sandstone and adobe mud with sturdy piñon and juniper beams. It was as at home here on this ledge as a cliff swallow's nest. As such, this building, like all other pueblo architecture, is an excellent example of vernacular architecture.

Vernacular — or folk — architecture is often interpreted as ethnic architecture that has stood the test of time. It is the distinctive vernacular architecture that gives a location its sense of place and of time in human history. And since it was built by its owners for their own family use, it also speaks of a particular culture. Indeed, nothing evokes the spirit of the Southwest more than the pueblo structures that have endured for a millennium.

Although it was bitter cold the day we came across this structure, in the sun on the ledge it was almost warm. Indigenous architecture such as this has solved the problems of climate and topography through the generations. In this particular dwelling, the south-facing sandstone building would absorb

135

This doorway was converted into a vent for the hearth in ancient times. Remodeling is common at cliff dwellings.

the sunlight all day, which would then radiate warmth all night. This building would be warm in winter and would require less fuel to heat. Then in the summer, when the sun is higher in the sky, the sandstone overhang of the alcove would provide cool shade in which to live and work.

As we studied the building more closely, we could see that what had at one time been a doorway had been filled in with slightly different stone than was used in the original building. This told us that this structure had been remodeled not once, but several times. One of the hallmarks of vernacular architecture is buildings that have been remodeled many times. And of the possible rooms that are remodeled, rooms that were lived in (as opposed to storage rooms and ceremonial rooms) were remodeled more often than any other type of room.

We rarely visit cliff dwellings that do not show signs that some construction was under way — the ancient ones remodeled their homes as often and as enthusiastically as we do today. This is so true, in fact, that there is a correlation between how long the structure was inhabited and how many times it was remodeled. The longer a structure was occupied, the more likely there is to be remodeling. And sometimes at sites, a pile of uncut stones and a stack of timber sit somewhere nearby, patiently waiting a thousand years to be put to use.

Scholars of vernacular architecture have long pointed out that the basic layout of a culture's structures remains stable for generations, and this is beginning to be confirmed archaeologically. The cliff dwellers maintained a modicum of the building layout that they used when they still lived in small farmsteads scattered across the mesa tops and wide canyon bottoms. Recall that in the northern reaches of the Southwest the small farmsteads were called *unit pueblos,* a term coined by early archaeologist T. Mitchell Prudden. The unit pueblo has a line of ground-level stone rooms facing south and fronted by an early kiva or pithouse. When the ancestral Puebloans moved their homes to the cliffs, they kept the same arrangement as much as possible: a small, one-family structure containing perhaps one living room and several smaller "other" rooms. In the larger more complex ruins, this is suggested by a series of room clusters. Each cluster belonged to a related group of people, possibly a family or a clan.

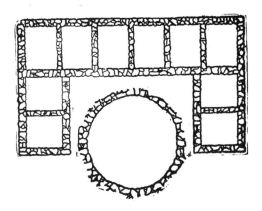

Recall the unit pueblo that the ancient people lived in before their move to the cliffs. From T. Mitchell Prudden's *On the Great American Plateau.*

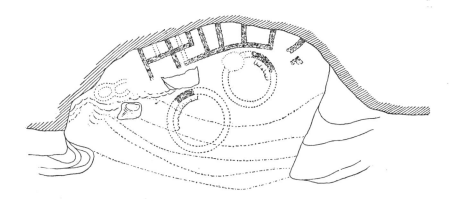

Left, whenever possible, the ancients maintained as much as they could of the original unit pueblo lay out. C. Mindeleff, 16th *Bureau of American Ethnology*

Note how the kivas are on the outside of the alcove, near the cliff edge, while the other rooms are behind them against the cave wall. Of course not all cliff ledges were deep enough to allow for this arrangement, we have seen many ruins that are strung along a narrow ledge. C. Mindeleff, *16th Bureau of American Ethnology.*

A cluster — or suite of rooms — consists of a living room, at least one storage room and several granaries. The living room opens out onto the plaza or courtyard, and the other rooms typically open into the living room. But these groupings of room clusters are seen only at the largest, most complex cliff dwellings, such as Mesa Verde National Park. The small cliff dwellings that we usually visit have just one living room and several storage rooms/granaries and a ceremonial room.

Building materials often change as conditions change and reflect what materials were available. In the northern part of the Greater American Southwest, sandstone in the shape of slabs was readily and widely available, and the buildings on the Colorado Plateau reflect this fact. In the southern parts of the Southwest, the building material that was most available was adobe mud, and the buildings there reflect this.

Below, even from a distance we could tell the tall doorway on the left was probably the living room.

Photographer: Andrew Gulliford ©

Vernacular architecture can also tell us something about the culture of the people who built the structures. Modern Puebloans tell us that buildings are built with prayers and offerings and are viewed as living entities. In *Hopi Dwellings: Architectural Change at Orayvi*, archaeologist Catherine Cameron states the Puebloan viewpoint this way: "The buildings are living things that come from the earth and return to the earth; they have a life cycle like any other living thing."

What does a Puebloan person see when he or she looks at a pueblo structure? To the modern Hopi, all things have a "house." For example, the sun has a house in the east that it arises from in the morning and a house in the west that it sets into in the evening. All animals have their houses, too. The corn has its house. Every person, every animal has its own place. So they see their buildings as a house for people.

The buildings mirror their environment — the flat tops of the tablelands, the red-to-buff color of the adobe mud. The terraced buildings reflect the sandstone geological benches. They also reflect some of the Puebloan beliefs about their place in this landscape. The buildings do not show an attempt to dominate or conquer the surroundings but instead reflect a sense of harmony or oneness with it. And generally, Pueblo individuals do not seek to stand out, but to be in harmony with the group instead.

Habitation Rooms

As we stood facing the cliff ruin, we noticed the largest doorway in the ruin was a rectangular doorway. The threshold was low, near the floor, and the lintel was high enough for easy daily access. This room was not originally intended to be closed from the outside like the others, and therefore, it is easy and straightforward to identify today.

Inside that doorway was a typical backcountry living room: the walls were heavily smoke-blackened, the floor had been leveled and the walls had been plastered.

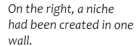

On the left, a peeled stick plastered into the wall looked like a coat hook to our modern eyes.

On the right, a niche had been created in one wall.

We carefully stuck our heads inside and before us saw a large room, probably the largest in the dwelling. And then we noticed the man-made walls were heavily fire-blackened — the dead giveaway that this was a habitation or living room. Stones outlined the hearth. Even if we could not actually see the hearth today, the sooty walls would have told us as much. We rarely see the fire pits today since they are usually buried under ankle-deep sand and dust on the floor.

The floor had been carefully leveled — laboriously pecked away with stone hammers on the high side, and filled in on the low, outside edge. These floors often had layers of adobe plaster covering them and were therefore smooth. The living room might be one of the few rooms in a cliff dwelling where the floors have been leveled.

As we looked more carefully, details came to our attention that further confirmed that this was indeed a living room. The walls were plastered. There was a niche to store things in. A rough imitation of a bench had been pecked from the cliff wall which made up the back wall of the dwelling. Short wooden pegs projected from the walls just below the primary roof beam, like coat hooks.

Of course the room was empty today. But if we were to step back in time, what would this room have looked like filled with people and things — filled with life? Ethnographer Victor Mindeleff wrote of the Pueblos in the 1880s: "In the corner . . . as one enters are two [large] ollas or water jars which are always kept filled. On the floor near the water jars is a canteen." Canteens were usually highly decorated. Scattered around the room – tucked in a niche, on the bench, stashed in a corner — were assorted pots. Archaeologists also find much pottery from other places that they call "tradeware." This may well have been prominently displayed. Somewhere in this room might have been a chamber pot. Spanish chroniclers reported the Zuni Pueblo was surprisingly clean for such a populated place — these chamber pots were emptied every morning away from the pueblo.

Bin

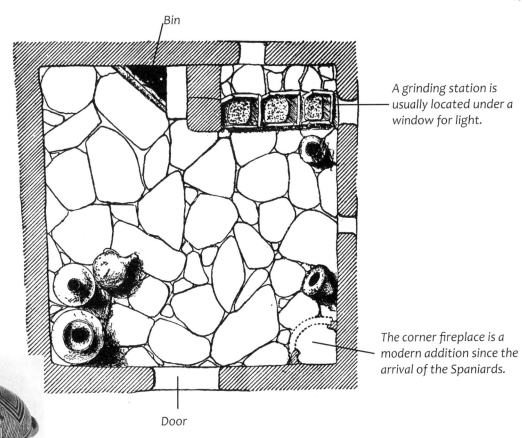

Early ethnographer Victor Mindeleff pictured a typical Hopi living room lay-out in the 1880s. Below, in the corner, are where the ollas (water jugs) were located. Keeping these ollas topped up with water was a full-time job for the maidens. From V. Mindeleff, 8th Bureau of American Ethnology.

A grinding station is usually located under a window for light.

The corner fireplace is a modern addition since the arrival of the Spaniards.

Door

Frank Hamilton Cushing described the Zuni governor's living room as being dark: "In the dim twilight of this place the uninitiated would have stumbled almost at every step upon its furnishings; for scattered over the floor, [hanging] from the rafters or against the walls were sieves made of coarsely woven yucca, meal trays, bread plaques, enormous cooking pots . . . pigmy water boilers with their round stone covers, polished baking stones blackened by a thousand heatings, bread bowls . . . numerous hardwood pokers charred to all degrees of shortness, and, finally, bundles of grease-wood suspended in the [roof] for drying — were some of the objects which would meet the eye as it grew accustomed to the place."

A typical, hypothetical ancestral Puebloan living room most likely had cattail mats in it. Early archaeologists often found pieces of this matting in the old dwellings, "much like the bed-mats of the modern pueblos," wrote Alfred V. Kidder in 1919. One of the main purposes of the living room was for sleeping. Nineteenth-century ethnographers reported that the entire family slept together, side by side in this living room. In more modern times the family slept on sheep skins, but in ancient times they slept on these cattail mats. They covered up with feather, rabbit or cotton blankets and had a wood block or a stone for a pillow.

Grinding tools were often located in the living room. This is where a woman would have spent most of her time. Roberts, Bureau of American Ethnology, Bulletin #111.

Most cliff dwellings we visit have those coat-hook-like wooden pegs high on the walls. No one knows what they hung from those hooks, but at Mug House in Mesa Verde National Park, early explorers found three or four highly decorated black-on-white mugs hanging by a yucca string from such a wooden peg. Besides sleeping with their cotton blankets and their feather and rabbit-skin robes, they wore them as outerwear on cold days. Nineteenth-century ethnographer Matilda Coxe Stevenson reported that these were hung from pegs and sometimes slung over poles suspended from the ceiling. Frank Hamilton Cushing reported that also hanging from these pegs were "quivers and bows, war-clubs, and boomerangs or 'rabbit sticks,' disks of haliotis shell, and other ornaments."

Sometimes there are grinding implements — a mano and metate — in this room as well. We have never encountered one in place in our travels, but archaeologists often discover them. Ethnographers report that these were usually placed about a foot and a half away from the wall so the woman could brace her feet against the wall and face the room as she ground the corn. Besides sleeping, living rooms were used for cooking and as a place to retreat during inclement weather. But most of one's time would be spent in the courtyard. More on this later.

So what was it like to live in a place such as this? The sounds that would come to our ears would be the sound of corn being ground on the mano and metate. Journalist Charles Francis Saunders in his book *Indians of the Terraced Houses,* written at the turn of the last century, described the sound as being a "hum." A woman would have to grind corn perhaps four or five hours a day, so this hum would be the music of home to a cliff dweller. The sounds of turkeys — their yelps, clucks, cackles, purrs, rattles and gobbles — would have been common sounds in the cliff dwellings. There might also have been a barking dog or two.

Saunders also described in the pueblos the rich smell of corn being parched. Thanks to archaeologist Victoria Atkins of the Bureau of Land Management at the Anasazi Heritage Center in Dolores, Colorado, we obtained some Hopi freshly parched corn. We would describe the aroma as being a cross between popcorn and peanuts. In the northern Southwest, the sharp, tangy smell of juniper fires would be a smell reminiscent of home to a cliff dweller or a pueblo dweller.

Sleeping at Zuni, 1879

Frank Hamilton Cushing, "My Adventures in Zuni"

On the evening of the second day he [his Zuni host] beckoned me to follow, as he led the way into the mud-plastered little room . . . All trappings had been removed, and the floor had been freshly plastered . . . Two sheepskins and my few belongings, a jar of water and a wooden poker, were all the furnishings. "There," said he, "now you have a little house, what more [could you possibly] want? Here, take these two blankets — they are all you can have. If you get cold, *think* you are warm, as the Zuni does. You must sleep in the cold and on a hard bed: that will harden your meat . . . I want to make a Zuni of you."

I suffered immeasurably that night. The cold was intense, and the pain from my hard bed excruciating. Although the next morning, with mental reservation, I told [my host] I had passed a good night . . . I resigned myself . . . and suffered throughout the long nights of many weeks rather than complain or show any unwillingness to have my "meat hardened."

In Mexico and the southwestern part of the region, doorways often have a small vent hole above.

Some living rooms of cliff dwellings in the southernmost region of the American Southwest and northern Mexico have a distinctive rectangular, square or oval hole above the doorway. This is thought to have been for a vent for the smoke. Two rangers at Walnut Canyon National Monument in Arizona spent the night in one of these cliff dwellings to test this theory. They hung a heavy blanket over the doorway and lit a fire. The vent hole above the doorway dispersed the smoke very effectively and they spent a comfortable night.

Occasionally we encounter ruins with no living room at all in the cluster of buildings. Typically these are small ruins, although we have come across even large, multiroom structures that have no apparent living rooms. Usually these don't have a kiva, either. This suggests that the cliff dwelling was used for storage.

How many people typically inhabited a cliff dwelling? This has been a source of contention among the archaeological community. Formulas have been created based on the total number of rooms, but none has been well accepted. But one cross-cultural, worldwide number that is often cited for a typical extended family household runs about five or six individuals. Worldwide, each woman has her own hearth. In Europe at the time of the cliff dwellings, taxes were levied and a census taken based on the number of hearths in a town, the most reliable means they had at the time for determining population numbers. So a good rule-of-thumb number would be about five or six individuals per room with a hearth in it, or blackened interior room walls if the hearth is not visible.

Early archaeologists identified at least five or six basic types of distinguishable rooms or spaces in cliff abodes: living rooms, storage rooms, granaries, courtyards and ceremonial rooms or kivas. Kivas or ceremonial rooms will be discussed separately. Grinding rooms, sometimes called mealing rooms, are rare, and if they are encountered it's in the northern region. Each of these rooms has certain characteristics that can distinguish one from the other with a little study. In the 1960s archaeologist Jeffrey Dean defined the architectural features for the prehistoric Kayenta people. Most recently Larry Nordby defined architectural features for Mesa Verde people. Both updated the architectural observations offered by early archaeologists.

HEARTHS

Hearths come in many sizes and types. On the far left is a round hearth. Near left is a D-shaped hearth against a wall. Below it is a square, slab-lined hearth typical of the northern province of the American Southwest. It is also against a wall.

The far left image photographer: Ron Horn.

A ll over the world, hearths may well have been the most important part of the home a millennium ago. This was the domain of the firekeeper. Worldwide, each woman would have her own hearth. In Europe a thousand years ago, the only way to achieve a census was to count the hearths; this formed the basis of their tax system. In the American Southwest, counting hearths is the most accepted way for archaeologists to calculate ancient populations. A ballpark guestimate of population size is five or six individuals per living room with a hearth in it.

This hearth is typical of the hearths in northern Mexico. They were on a raised platform, usually in the middle of the room. Many, like this one, also had a post to support the roof. Some have just the adobe platform with no post hole. This hearth is unrestored in the backcountry of Mexico.

Revisiting this photograph again, we can see that to the right of the one long doorway, there are two window-like openings. These are actually doorways. These small doorways often are for storage. When we looked inside, we found none of the walls of those two rooms were smoked, a giveaway to storage rooms. Photographer: Andrew Gulliford ©.

Note the wooden peg in the wall.

Also note there are no openings or loopholes other than the door.

This storage room has a two-tone plaster design on the outside called a dado. It is unusual for plaster to have survived for 800 years. The other store room, on the left, is unfinished — you can see the stack of wood and stones in front of it to complete it. Storage rooms have no vents or loopholes in them that could allow rodents in.

Storage Rooms

Near or connecting to the living room is nearly always at least one storage room. The storage room is a large room, though usually not as large as the living room. Storage rooms have *no smoked walls.* In fact, storage rooms are the largest rooms that do not have blackened walls. For every living room, there might typically be one storage room and sometimes as many as four.

Some storage room walls are plastered and a few go so far as to have gorgeous geometric designs on them. Sometimes these highly decorated rooms are found on the second floor; others are found next to a kiva. Why some storage rooms are highly decorated and others are not is a mystery. Did they house something special — ceremonial or ritual paraphernalia, perhaps?

Storage-room and granary doorways are usually smaller than living room doorways or public access doorways. For the purpose of this book, we define a storage room doorway as one that shows no signs of having been sealed with adobe mud — that is, it has no adobe collar around the opening or any traces of adobe mud that once sealed the door. However, be aware that after hundreds of years the weather and elements could have removed any signs of an adobe seal. Also, the threshold of a storage-room doorway is higher than a living room or public access doorway.

Sometimes there is a willow device outside the doorway on the wall that was intended to hold the door closed. The willow was looped and set into the stone wall on either side of the doorway; then a stick would be laced through

On the right is the same storage room with the door in place.

the loops to hold the slab in place. These devices are particularly evident at Mesa Verde National Park.

What did the interior of a storage room look like? To our twenty-first century urban-American eyes this room looks like a pantry, and it probably functioned like one in ancient times. It was intended for short-term storage, for in-and-out use daily.

In modern Pueblos, storage rooms are neat and tidy. The different colors and types of corn are carefully stored separately. Today's large corncobs are typically stacked like cordwood along one side of the storage room. But corncobs of the cliff dwelling era were smaller than those of today, and it would have been difficult if not impossible to stack them in this way. However it was actually stored, the corn in this room was intended to be used soon.

There were wooden pegs on the walls of this room as well as the living room, and roots and dried plants would dangle from them or ceiling beams. Seed corn would be given the most beautiful seed pots, covered securely with lids. This room would have no windows, vents or loopholes. A careful look at its construction would show that it was more tightly built than the living room. Although the walls might be unfinished and rough on the inside, there would be no gaps that could allow rodents or insects inside. The floors might be only partially leveled and slope. This room might well have a bench or a shelf around the perimeter or along one wall.

Our practical sense tells us that all manner of necessary household things would be stored here: In old photographs we have seen basket trays with

The doorways of storage rooms are typically larger than granaries, but smaller than habitation rooms. They were generally not meant to be sealed. The peeled stick that forms the "dropped lintel" in the doorway on the left, is there to support the slab door, as in the photograph on the right.

ground corn meal piled high and covered with a cloth and carefully placed on a shelf in a storage room. Shelled corn may have been stored here in big covered pots or baskets. Besides corn, they stored piñon nuts, gourds and cactus pads. Archaeologist Alfred Kidder found a ball of yucca string a hundred yards long neatly wound up and stuffed in a pottery bowl, so perhaps this is where this type of string would have been stored. Could this

On the left, a well-constructed storage room interior.

Below, Pots such as these would have inhabited this storage room. They would have held foodstuff such as shucked corn or beans. The large pots often had lids on them; in this case the lids were stone slabs. From Bureau of American Ethnology *#65, Kidder and Guernsey.*

These granaries are nearly camouflaged against the cliff wall. An accident, or purposefully done?

be where they stored their tools for making pottery, dyes and brushes? Don Talayesva wrote that one thing that was stored in here was a ceramic pot containing stale urine that was used for making dyes. In the south along Tonto Creek, archaeologists found a room that had been filled with agave plants, judging from all the pollen there. The Hopi people of today still consider agave hearts a delicacy.

Granaries

The most ubiquitous buildings are granaries. They are everywhere: tucked under overhangs, plastered to sheer cliff walls, and sometimes camouflaged on a cliff face. Often there are no other dwellings associated with them; today they appear alone and abandoned to time. At other times they appear in cliff dwelling settings but situated high on a tiny ledge, well above the living level.

Granaries can be quite small structures, although there are plenty of huge examples. Like vaults, these structures were intended as secure containers for a family's most valuable possessions — that which they had slaved over for months and without which their families would go hungry — their food. Granaries were *sealed* — intended for long-term storage. Once that sandstone slab door was closed, it was sealed with adobe mud and was intended to stay sealed until it was time to empty the granary. Of all the cliff dwelling structures we encounter in the backcountry, granaries are the most common.

For the purposes of this book we differentiate granaries from store rooms by the remnants of a sealed doorway. Granary doorways typically have an

On the left, note the adobe "collar" around the slab door of this granary to seal the structure shut. It was not intended for in-and-out daily use; it was meant to stay closed until ready for use and then emptied.

On the right is a granary from the Kayenta region. These ancient people constructed a step or shelf at the door of a granary. Note the dropped lintel for the door to rest against.

adobe "collar" around the door, the remains of adobe mud still evident that originally sealed the stone slab door across the opening. Sometimes the stone slab door still rests nearby, shaped to fit the doorway perfectly. Granary doorways are high off the ground level and small. This doorway often has a *dropped lintel,* a peeled stick inserted an inch or two below the actual lintel, intended to support the stone slab door that rests against it.

The sill of a granary doorway among the Kayenta ruins is often large and shelf-like, extends outward and can be as high as three feet from the floor level. We don't know what its original purpose was. Perhaps the high sill allowed the granary to be filled higher — a low sill on the door would have allowed the contents to spill out while it was being filled.

The interior of a granary, like the one on the right, will sometimes still have a scatter of corncobs on the floor. Can you see the wooden pegs imbedded in the wall in this granary interior?

In Mexico the ancients constructed different types of granaries. This is Cueva de Olla. Above, note how well it fits into the landscape. Below, the living rooms and storage are at the back of the cave, behind the granary.

A man stands in front of three mushroom-shaped granaries. From: Carl Lumholtz, Unkonwn Mexico.

Granaries were tightly built so that no rodents, bugs or water could get in and ruin the corn. The original builders ignored attractive finishes on the inside of granaries, so the inside walls are coarse and the floor uneven. However, granaries are often still dry and tight even today. Like storage rooms, there are no vents, loopholes or any other openings in the walls besides the doorway. And also like storage rooms, there is no sooting on the man-made walls.

In Mexico, we saw a spectacular cave with a misnamed structure — *Cueva de Olla* (Cave of the Water Jug). This onion-shaped structure sits on a pedestal base and in all is perhaps twelve feet high, and stands proudly at the front of the cave overlooking the river valley. When we carefully peeked inside, there we saw the telltale remains of corncobs. This had been a granary! Other granaries in the area also have fantastic sculpted shapes. Some were shaped like mushrooms. These granaries are made of adobe mud with a grass filler as a binder, much like rebar in cement. Originally they were sealed on top.

Although the sculpture-shaped granary is usually gone today, archaeologists often find the pedestal bases. And early explorer Carl Lumholtz claimed in his turn-of-the-last-century book, *Unknown Mexico*, that these pedestal-based granaries extend all the way to South America.

Some granaries do not have a doorway on the side but open from the top instead. We call these *bins* when they were intended to be filled from the top.

It is not uncommon to find a scattering of corncobs still present in a granary, and this can be a valuable clue to the function of an otherwise unidentifiable room.

Granaries and storage rooms can easily be confused. There is a lot of overlap, but for the purposes of this book, these definitions work for us in small, remote back-country cliff dwellings.

Milling Stations

Between the cliff wall and the living room was a rare find — a milling station.

Photographer: Ron Horn

We struggled all day to reach a remote cliff dwelling. After scrambling up the slot entrance we spotted a single habitation room that was extremely well preserved. Obviously it had seen very little visitation in the last eight hundred years. The cliff wall, a storage room and the living room formed a small courtyard area. And next to the living room wall was the remains of a single milling station. Vertical slabs inserted into the ground protruded upward in

154

a rectangle shape. These would have cradled the grinding stones that they used to grind up the corn into meal. It was at this spot an ancient Puebloan woman would have spent most of her time — on her hands and knees, grinding corn.

Milling bins are exciting to find because we rarely see them at sites and because their presence is the only evidence that this spot is where milling took place at this site. Grinding stones are portable and could be moved not only by the ancient inhabitants, but also by later visitors to the site.

Milling could occur almost anywhere in a cliff dwelling. Living rooms typically had a milling station of some kind in them. Courtyards were popular places to grind corn. Some of the larger, more-populous cliff dwellings even had a special room for grinding. The key requirements were protection from the wind and the need for light.

The wind at this cliff dwelling was horrendous. We carefully placed our feet on the narrow ledge and leaned into the gusts so as not to be blown off the face of the cliff. We inched past the remains of several rooms where there was not enough rubble left to be able to identify what types of rooms they might have been. Then we noticed a room set off by itself, with what appeared to be a large window in the front. This was unusual since windows really aren't common among cliff dwellings. What might appear to be windows are, on closer inspection, actually doors.

As we leaned over the window sill we noticed inside all was still and the wind was kept at bay. After studying it for a moment we decided this might well have been a grinding room. Why have a separate grinding room? Oftentimes the mealing bins are outside in the courtyard. Then we turned into the stiff wind again and it seemed obvious: the wind. In the courtyard it would be impossible to grind very fine cornmeal for piki bread in a wind like this. Your work would be blown away before it was even finished being ground.

We occasionally see rooms we think are grinding rooms as defined by archaeologist Jeffrey Dean. Not all cliff dwellings have them, or at least have a room that we would identify as one. Usually they are among the Kayenta Anasazi culture. A grinding room typically has a storage room or two connecting to it, or at least nearby.

Mealing rooms will almost always have a window. In some we have tentatively identified, this is more of a partial wall — the wall does not extend all the way to the cave ceiling. And the window tends to be wide and long, much larger than the openings we see in other rooms.

Typically the grinding room would have had a bin for three metates — the base stone of the grinding stones. The bin is outlined by upright slabs set into the floor, separating the three compartments. One of three metates of different levels of coarseness would be placed in each of these bins, progressing from coarse to medium to fine meal. Archaeologists sometimes find a pecking stone next to the metates or grinding bins – apparently this was for keeping the grinding surface rough.

Courtyards

As we rounded the point on a wide, grass-tufted cliff ledge, we nearly stumbled over a tiny cliff dwelling. Enthralled by our find, we stopped to explore this little gem. It was nearly complete: a small, blackened living room with two even smaller storage rooms off to its side in a tiny alcove. The only room it was missing was a kiva. And then as we were just getting ready to leave, we spotted a half-circle of melon-sized stones in front of the unit. The

This backcountry cliff dwelling courtyard is anchored by three living rooms, two granaries, one storage room (not seen) and is enclosed by a curtain wall. These rooms have been identified by archaeologist William Bloomer in his 1989 thesis. Most of an ancestral Puebloan's life would have been played out in this plaza or courtyard — cooking, making stone tools, sometimes grinding corn into meal, visiting with friends and relatives.

unworked stones outlined a semi-circle perhaps twelve feet or so in diameter on the slickrock in front of the ruin. It could have been a natural occurrence. But the more we studied the tiny group of buildings, we decided that it probably wasn't an accident. No, this was probably their courtyard area. In a larger, more populated cliff dwelling, their courtyard would have been outlined by buildings. But this dwelling was so small the residents suggested the presence of an enclosed courtyard by placing a semi-circle of stones in front.

As was mentioned earlier, each family group had a suite of rooms that were sometimes interconnecting, but at least adjacent. These typically opened onto a private courtyard area; part of this courtyard was comprised of the roof of their kiva. Archaeologists call these *room clusters*. The heart of the room cluster was the courtyard. The courtyard was the "center place" of the structure — their world radiated out from this like ripples on a pond. As an ancestral Puebloan, you would have spent the vast majority of your time in the courtyard. It was in the courtyard that all the day-to-day activities took place, so it is not uncommon to find grinding bins, hearths and other indications of daily life in the courtyard area. The people of the cliff dwellings lived mostly an outdoor life and retreated to their rooms only in bad weather.

The architecture endures, protected by the cave environment and the dry desert climate. As such it is an artifact — a window not only into the past, but also into a culture. For the discerning eye, it has a story to tell.

T-Shaped Doorways

One of the most visible symbols of the Greater American Southwest is the T-shaped doorway. This is a doorway that has the form of the letter *T:* The upper part of the doorway is wider than the narrower lower part rather than the usual rectangle shape we are familiar with. Because it is a door shape that is unique to the Greater American Southwest it is an excellent example of vernacular architecture. That is, the T-shaped doorway image is strongly associated with the American Southwest and as such evokes the essence and spirit of the Southwest.

The origins of the T-door are shrouded by the mists of time. Among the Mayan the symbol *T* was known as *ik* and represented the breath and wind. It was at Chichen Itza in Mexico that builders incorporated the *T* image into architecture, but they employed the *T* symbol

just in windows and on the carvings on the stone columns. The *T* symbol was not employed in doorways. The classical Chichen Itza culture collapsed about A.D. 1000. The actual T-door that we are familiar with today appears first at Chaco Canyon, New Mexico, by circa A.D. 1020, according to archaeologist Stephen Lekson in his book *The Chaco Meridian*.

The T-door concept accompanied Chacoans when they left Chaco Canyon circa A.D. 1120—1150 and moved north to Aztec, New Mexico, and then to Mesa Verde, Colorado. The unique sign of the *T* appeared in other artifacts as well as their doors, including a cut-out design on the handle of a mug and other artifacts. The T-door grew in popularity during the time of the cliff dwellings, demonstrated by the fact that the unique doorway appeared more and more in structures as the

T-Shaped Doorways

This is one interpretation of the Mayan sign for ik. There were actually many versions of it.

ancient people embarked on their Great Migration, finally reaching its heyday in Paquimé in northern Mexico. There, at Casas Grandes, T-doors represent about half of all doorways. The T-shape also appears as vents, in niches and as an altar shape. After the fall of Paquimé in A.D. 1450 the T-door seemed to be no longer in fashion, and it is rare to see examples dating after A.D. 1450, although they do exist.

For decades archaeologists have sought a practical explanation for the T-shaped doorway. It has been suggested that it was easier to enter the T-door while carrying a burden. Others have put forth that it was a quick way to enter a room by placing one's hands on the stone sides of the doorway and then swinging one's legs through. Some have postulated that perhaps there was better air flow and light through a T-door.

Some sort of symbolism has also been suggested, as opposed to a practical reason. Lekson

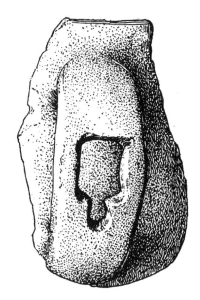

A mug sherd found at Spruce Tree House in Mesa Verde National Park Bureau of American Ethnology #41. Early archaeologist Jesse Fewkes found another one at Awatobi in Arizona in 1895.

pointed out the doorways were noticable, sometimes from a substantial distance. And they typically were an entrance to a public area like a courtyard or plaza, or to a habitation room. He and others see a possible symbolic meaning to the doors.

From our experiences in remote backcountry sites we, too, have noticed the T-door/habitation room or ceremonial room connection. They are not associated with storage rooms or granaries.

For us today, the T-door is a symbol of the era of this book, the time of upheaval, the time of the Great Migration, the time of the cliff dwellings.

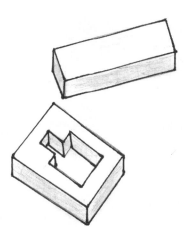

*On the left is a reproduction of the **T** altar stone as it was found at Paquimé next to its pedestal. It was carved from green feldspar and is approximately two feet by two and a half feet.*

T-Doors

T-Doors come in all sizes and in many variations. This one is in Canyon de Chelly, and was documented by Victor Mindeleff in 1891. From the 8th *Bureau of American Ethnology.*

This one is a classic from Aztec National Monument, New Mexico, that reflects its Chaco influence.

T-doors are often the first thing you see when nearing a cliff dwelling. This is a huge T-door in Gila National Monument, New Mexico.

This large T-door was recorded on the Hopi Mesas in Arizona by Victor Mindeleff, from the 8th *Bureau of American Ethnology.*

T-Doors

Even this tiny ruin in southeast Utah had a T-door entrance to this habitation room.

Mesa Verde National Park in Colorado has many T-doors in its cliff dwellings. The upper part narrows on this one.

This doorway in southeast Utah was access to a public area such as a courtyard, hallway or entry point.

Note the notched corners on this T-door. We discovered this one in southest Utah, it was the access to a public area.

Mexico T-Doors

T-doors in Mexico often have an overhead vent. Pictured here are some in the Sierra Madres, Mexico, but we have seen them as far north as Walnut Canyon, Arizona, near Flagstaff. The Mexico T-doors also lead to habitation rooms or ceremonial rooms.

All these T-doors lead to habitation/ceremonial/public areas. The elegant T-door below right was sculptured by its ancient creators.

Half T-Doors

This variation of the T-door can be seen occasionally throughout the entire region from Colorado and Utah on the north, through Mexico in the south. However, in our research we have found little about half T-doors.

Victor Mindeleff documented this half T-door at Hopi in the 8th *Bureau of American Ethnology*.

Tonto National Monument, Arizona.

This half T-door in southeast Utah leads to a habitation room.

Half T-doors also appear in the Sierra Madres, Mexico. This doorway leads to a habitation room.

163

Off-Set T-Doors

We call this an Off-Set T-door because the arms are of different widths. They are rare, we have only encountered them a few times. Victor Mindeleff, 8th Bureau of American Ethnology.

This Off-Set T-door is in Southeast Utah, and it leads from a kiva to a habitation room.

Double T-Doors

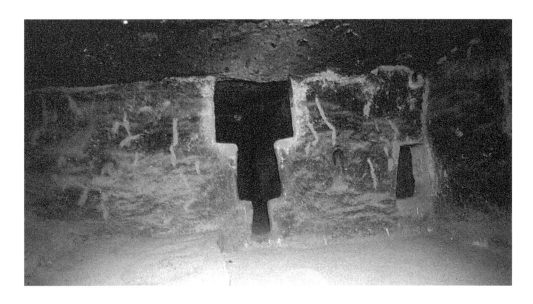

This fascinating variation of a T-door we call a Double T-Door because there appears to be two T-doors — one on top of another. Note the smoke-blackened walls surrounding it. This is in the Sierra Madres of Mexico.

The Double T-door is rare, we have only seen a few of them, and have never seen them referred to in the literature. We have not seen them anywhere else except Mexico.

Huge T-Doors

The huge T-door on the left is surrounded by smaller, living room-sized T-doors. The photograph above was taken in the 1890s by Carl Lumholtz for his book, Unknown Mexico.

The enormous T-door on the left of the above old photograph led to public access. When we first visited this ruin in 1986, that T-door was no longer there.

On the right is a large T-door (but not as large as the one above) that leads to a public courtyard. This ruin is located in the Sierra Madres, northern Mexico. For scale, pictured here is Jaime Dozal.

Construction Materials

Construction materials reflect what was near at hand — as is true for all vernacular architecture. On the lower right, tab-shaped sandstone was readily available and was used extensively in buildings on the Colorado Plateau. Above, in Mexico and in the southern part of the region, pure, formed adobe was the material of choice. Below, *jacal* or mud and wattle is common.

Living Room Interiors on the Colorado Plateau

You will encounter much variation and individuality in all the rooms you see. There are plenty of times we will never know what an ambiguous room was. These clues are Rule of Thumb and Ballpark guestimates and are not exacting, so don't despair if a ruin is not decipherable. But we have found these clues to be of use more often than not.

Soot on Man-made Walls

Natural or Cave Wall

Bench or Shelf

Leveled Floor

When we encountered this half T-door we wondered if it could possibly be a habitation room. Our suspicions were confirmed when we looked inside.

Clues to rooms that were lived in:

- The doorway is often larger than other rooms doors in the immediate vicinity. T-shaped doorways are common in living rooms.

- Soot is on the *man-made* walls. The blackening on the natural cliff walls could be from ancient times or could occur naturally. Sooting on the man-made walls is a giveaway to a living area. There are exceptions, however. Keep in mind that early explorers might have camped in a non-living room and the walls are smoked from that incident. We have found that the walls are *lightly* sooted in this case, whereas in ancient times the rooms were heavily used and resulted in *heavy* sooting.

- Living rooms are generally the largest rooms in the complex.

- A hearth or firepit is present, but often not visible.

- There are vent holes for smoke.

- The floors are flattened or leveled and sometimes plastered.

- One or more wooden pegs are imbedded in the walls.

- Sometimes there is a bench or a niche.

Ethnographic Living Room Interior

Early ethnographers recorded how the Pueblo people lived in the late nineteenth century. This picture of the inside of a living room is from the Stevenson, 23rd Bureau of American Ethnology.

Elsie Parsons, in her book, *Pueblo Indian Religion,* described life in a pueblo household:

"The house floor is clay, well smoothed down . . . This room is a grinding or baking room as well as a general living room and sleeping room . . . Ordinarily the whole household sleeps in the same room, more or less alongside . . . The pelts and blankets for sleeping pallets are taken down from the roof poles and wall seats, and spread out all at the same time . . . Household mates may sit up late into the night talking with visitors, while others may be asleep."

Note the bench encircling the room and the niche holding a pot.

Also note the pegs and poles holding the blankets and other bedding.

Living Room Interior Below the Mogollon Rim

Above, a doorway to a living room and a hatch to another living room, both occur throughout the region. Left is a nineteenth-century Zuni hatch from the *8th Bureau of American Ethnology*, V. Mindeleff. They are amazingly similar.

The living rooms below the rim have many similar features to living rooms on the plateau, as discussed on the previous pages. But in our experience, they are larger than the living rooms on the plateau, as in the picture on the right. Also we have not seen benches there.

Living Room Interior in Mexico

When we spotted the T-door, we wondered if it was a living room or public access or ceremonial room. When we peeked in we could see it was a living room.

Below, the room had much in common with Paquimé: There was a platform, which you don't see in the north, but is common at Paquimé. No one knows exactly what it was used for. In the foreground is a raised hearth, this one without the post. The inset picture is a venturi window.

On the right there are two porthole-type openings. The one on the left is counter-sunk like those in Paquimé. Archaeologist Charles Di Peso called this a venturi window. DiPeso reported that these windows sometimes contained a plug. Paquimé had a sophisticated ventilation system that resulted in air flowing through the entire structure. It also caused soot to be deposited in most rooms — the storage rooms are sooted as well as the living rooms. However, the sooting is not as heavy in the storage rooms as in the living rooms.

Note the wooden pegs imbedded in the adobe mud high on the wall.

Above is an example of a typical storage room above the Mogollon Rim. Storage rooms can look a lot like a living room, but without the soot on the walls. In fact, storage rooms are the largest rooms in the complex without sooting on the walls.

Note the raised threshold.

Clues to a storage room:

- No soot is evident on the *man-made* walls or ceiling.

- Floors are not usually leveled.

- The doorway is smaller than a living room doorway, but larger than a granary doorway. The room was intended for in-and-out use daily, so the doorway will be easy to get in and out of.

- No windows or loopholes are present.

- Wooden pegs are imbedded in the wall, usually under the roof beams. Sometimes there is a hole at that location indicating a wooden peg was there at one time, but is gone now.

Ethnographic Storage Room Interior

This image of a storage room interior is from the 23rd Bureau of American Ethnology, Stevenson.

Above is an illustration of a Puebloan storage room about 1900. Early ethnographers reported seeing stored in these rooms: Roots and dried plants would be hanging from pegs or stuck between the timbers. Seed corn would be stored in beautiful seed pots with lids. Ears of corn would be stacked in a corner like cord wood, or perhaps in a separate room. Large pots would hold grains, and what could not be hung up might find a home in a niche. Sometimes ceremonial devices were also stored here — things like a ritual feather box, pieces of dance constumes. Most pueblo store rooms of today are neat and tidy and each year at harvest would be freshly replastered.

From Elsie Parsons, *Pueblo Indian Religion.*

Storage Rooms Below the Mongollon Rim and Mexico

Doorway to Storage Room

In this Sierra Ancha region living room, a doorway leads to a storage room. That storage room is small and unsooted; the floors are unleveled and rough.

Below is a living room in Mexico; the doorway in the center right leads to a storage room. The inset photograph shows what is inside that doorway: a large room, partially smoked from the ventilation system. This storage room is at the back of the cave, as are most that we have seen in Mexico. Its floor is uneven and rough. Other living rooms open into this same storage room.

Typical Colorado Plateau Granaries

What you will see most of the time on your backcountry travels will be granaries. They are everywhere: They can be small and high on a ledge or tucked against the back cliff wall, away from moisture. Or they can be large and in commanding locations.

Some are large and can be seen from quite a distance away.

Photographer: Peg Hoffman.

Some are nearly camouflaged and you have to strain to see them.

Colorado Plateau Granary Doorways

Granaries are usually the smallest structures in a cliff dwelling complex, however, there are exceptions. Doorways are typically the smallest in the cliff dwelling, some with a "raised threshold" — a high step up to the threshold. Perhaps this was to keep rodents out and/or to allow it to be filled higher.

Clues for a Granary:

- There is typcially an adobe "collar" surrounding the doorway, apparently to seal the door slab.

- The door is obviously meant to be closed from the outside.

- No windows or loopholes are present.

- The floor slopes and is rough, not leveled.

- No sooting is apparent.

- Often this is a small-sized room, certainly no one could stand up in it or live in it.

- Occasionally we find pegs on the walls for hanging things.

- Sometimes there is still a scatter of corncobs on the floor.

Above is an example of a Kayenta granary. These granaries of the Four Corners region usually have a stone step in front. Sometimes this resembles more of a shelf. Below is an excellent example of an adobe collar.

Granary Interiors

The natural cave roof and floors are incorporated in to the structures.

Photographer: Peg Hoffman.

This is a "classic" example of a granary interior. The room is small, too small for a person to have ever lived in or even to have stood upright in. A peg for hanging things is evident; there are no loopholes or port holes, only a small, carefully sealed doorway. The walls are thick and solid. And if we still had any doubts about this being a granary, there were still corncobs on the floor after all these years to give us a clue as to its function.

As are storage rooms, granaries are sometimes still neat and tidy inside, on the right.

Photographer: Peg Hoffman.

Interior Granaries Below the Mogollon Rim and in Mexico

We call these small interior granaries "bins" because they open from the top. Victor Mindeleff wrote that these were kept covered and that corn and beans were stored there. This example is from Hopi in the late nineteenth century.

Below is an example of a triangular-shaped bin, circled. From the 8th Bureau of American Ethnology, V. Mindeleff.

We found similar bins in the cliff ruins in Mexico. We can see they were also kept covered because we can see the outline of the cover in the soot on the wall behind it.

Below, this deteriorated wall in Mexico shows how some of these bins were constructed. Archaeologist Emil Haury showed that they were constructed in a similar fashion in the Sierra Anchas.

Exterior Granaries in Mexico

These fascinating granaries filled from a hole in the top, which was covered with a stone slab. This etching is from Unknown Mexico *by Carl Lumholtz.*

The adobe rings on the left originally would have looked similar to the tall intact granaries above. This is all that remains — their pedestals. The image above also shows some of the pedestals without their impressive tops, on the lower right quadrant of the picture.

This is mostly what we see today — just the pedestal. Some complete specimens do exist, but they are rare.

Granary Pedestals in Mexico

Above, two different granary pedestals. The one on the left shows it in human scale. The one on the right shows a pedestal and the base of the granary globe, fallen.

Below, the base of the granary globe that is still attached to the pedestal. Looking closely you can see the granary globe and pedestal were originally made from adobe with a grass-binder, similar to rebar in cement.

On the right is a close up of the pedestal with the part of the granary globe attached. If you carefully look you can see a wooden peg that helped support the globe base.

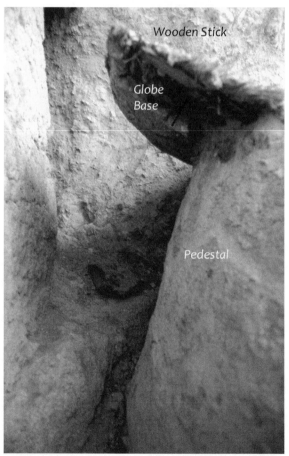

Wooden Stick

Globe Base

Pedestal

Courtyards

Above is a classic example of a small couryard from a backcountry cliff dwelling. It has a curtain wall with cut-outs high on the wall for illumination and venting. The courtyard is anchored by one living room, behind the half T-door. At the opposite end of the courtyard, behind the camera, is a storage room.

This is the type of cliff dwelling we often see in the backcountry today: A small courtyard, with a number of rooms opening onto it.

Archaeologist Jeffrey S. Dean analyzed the architectural attributes for Betatakin and Kiet Siel in 1969. For a deeper understanding of the architecture of cliff dwellings, we recommend his paper: *Chronological Analysis of Tsegi Phase Sites in Northeastern Arizona.*

Courtyards

This photograph is from the book by Larry V. Nordby, and is used with his permission.

Above is Courtyard J in Cliff Palace at Mesa Verde National Park. It is an excellent example of a large, complex cliff dwelling with many rooms. The courtyard would have originally included the roof of the kiva, making a large open area. The living rooms marked here were originally granaries that were later converted to living rooms, hence the small doors. Cliff Palace is made up of many courtyards such as this one, with rooms opening out onto each of them.

Archaeologist Larry V. Nordby has done some of the most recent work on Mesa Verde architecture. We recommend his book: *Prelude to Tapestries in Stone: Understanding Cliff Palace Architecture.*

Refuge Sites

We have encountered backcountry sites that did not fit the definition for rooms discussed in this book. These places have sometimes been called fort-like structures. Our friend Andrew Gulliford suggested the name "refuge site" instead. We like that name. It reminded us of an incident that happened back in the early 1970s in a very remote part of Mexico. We had descended into a broad valley surrounded by cliffs where there were perhaps a half a dozen Tarahumara homes — some were in the cliffs, some were on the valley floor. The moment we entered the valley in the Land Rover, the vehicle was spotted by the inhabitants and the entire valley immediately emptied. We caught fleeting glimpses through the trees of people hurrying somewhere. It seemed they just disappeared into the cliffs and canyons. As we drove through the valley, we saw campfires burning with pots of food still cooking, but no one was there attending them. Their houses stood open and empty. Dogs barked. Livestock wandered around, unattended. The Tarahumara people did not return to their homes while we passed through the valley.

Was there some safe place they retreated to until the perceived danger was gone?

Photograph by Andrew Gulliford ©.

We decided to go ahead and introduce this architectural feature in this book, even though the idea is still under development.

Clues to Refuge Sites:

- There is a curtain wall with choke point entrance and loopholes.

- Behind the wall is a large empty room, no sooting, no habitation attributes — no storage, no granaries, and no ceremonial attributes.

- There is no roof, nor any trace of one.

- Occasionally there is a rock art shield above it.

183

Ghost Walls

Sometimes rooms and structures have been lost to time and all that remains are clues that a room or a building might have been here in the long ago past. These are popularly known as *ghost walls*. Take the photograph above from Bandelier National Monument, for example. Lines of beam socket holes are pecked into the cliff face outline where rooms and structures used to be. Note the stone ruins at the bottom of the above picture — these are one story tall. But the beam socket holes show that the structure was once many stories high.

On the left is another type of ghost wall. Here a smoke-blackened square is all that remains to tell us that once there had been a room or structure here. Muddy rivulets have washed across the ghost wall, but have not completely obliterated it. Since the ghost wall is smoke-blackened, we can guess that the vanished room was once a habitation room.

184

Ghost Walls

Above, a mural of pendant triangles hang from the adobe remains of a previous ceiling/floor. Sometimes the ghost wall consists of bits of adobe clinging to the natural cave wall, showing an outline of where a room once was. In both cases, we can guess the ancient vanished room was once a storage room or granary because it is not sooted. Below, this ancient room — thought to be a kiva — shows both smoke blackening and a line of beam socket holes giving us a clear picture of where the roof once was.

A ceremony is underway in this kiva interior. This image is reproduced from a chromolithograph of an 1892 painting by Julian Scott. Sagstetter collection.

8

KIVAS AND CEREMONIAL ROOMS

We lay down in the tall grass and drew out our binoculars. It was just as we thought — two long-legged burrowing owls were standing outside their burrow looking back at us. These were babies, owlets curious about this new world.

We are fascinated by these small owls because they are unique among owls. First, they are the only owls that are diurnal — that is, active during the daytime, making them easy to watch. They are also the only owls that live in colonies instead of nesting alone with a mate, meaning you will often see a group of them rather than just one. They are also the only owls that live underground; they share underground burrows with their cousins the prairie dogs and rattlesnakes. But most fascinating of all, it's as though they have mastered three worlds: the world of the sky, the earth's surface, and the underworld beneath the surface. We must have watched them for nearly an hour, enjoying their explorations before moving on.

Later, as we approached the cliff dwelling we sought, we spotted a large, circular outline in the red dirt. We looked closer. In the center was a slab-lined hatchway , and we recognized it immediately as a subterranean kiva. These ceremonial rooms still exist among the Pueblo tribes of today and are the center of their spiritual lives. This kiva was special: Although it had been vacant for perhaps eight hundred years, it still had its roof.

We often encounter the remains of these round rooms in our backcountry explorations on the Colorado Plateau. Most ruins, no matter how small, will have a kiva if the buildings were inhabited year-round. But the kivas

The kiva we discovered that day. The center support beams were added recently because the roof was beginning to sag. Below, note the benches and plastering.

we typically encounter are roofless because of their age; a kiva with a roof is extremely rare, as one can imagine.

We walked around the perimeter of the kiva structure, not wanting to step on the ancient roof to get to the hatch and perhaps damage this fragile artifact of long ago.

It was then we discovered an entryway facing outward and overlooking the cliff edge. Had it been built this way? Perhaps it originally had a Mesa Verde-type of keyhole that had fallen away — yet another reason why this kiva was special. Or perhaps this opening was just the result of erosion. It was hard to tell.

A kiva is a ceremonial structure — a spiritual place — that today represents the cosmos to Puebloan people. So with awe and reverence, we peeked around the edge of the opening and peered inside. The interior was even more well-preserved than the outside: The walls were still neatly and simply plastered in a monochrome russet red. Although it is extremely rare,

A typical Mesa Verde-style kiva at Mesa Verde National Park.

some kivas sport two-tone plastering, and some even have geometric designs around the inside perimeter. Later kivas might have murals painted on the walls, but we have only seen a possible mural on a ceremonial room in the cliff dwellings of northern Mexico.

This was nearly a classic Mesa Verde style kiva, common north of the San Juan River: It was round with six pilasters along the perimeter of the room supporting the roof. These square pillars project slightly from the surface of the wall as supports. Between the pilasters were rectangular benches. A niche occupied the far wall. During ceremonies the niche would house sacred fetishes, important to the ritual being performed.

The floor was deeply covered with sand, so we were unable to see if there was a *sipapu* (pronounced see-PAH-poo). The sipapu is a hole in the floor that represents among modern Puebloans where their ancestors emerged from the underworld that features in their legends. The Pueblo underworld is not the fire and brimstone sort of place of some religions. Their underworld is much like the world above that we see. The sipapu is usually kept covered except when it is used in rituals. Not all kivas have a sipapu, but they are common to these structures.

We also didn't see a *deflector,* a slab of sandstone standing vertically, or sometimes a knee-high wall used to direct the air flow so as not to disrupt the fire. A deflector was a clever substitute for a chimney. A ventilator shaft drew fresh air into the room; the deflector directed the fresh air around the perimeter of the room and the smoke up through the hatch. We also couldn't make out the outline of a hearth that typically can be found in the floor. Mesa Verde-type kivas are typically aligned roughly south to north measured from the vent through the deflector, the hearth and the sipapu. Sometimes the alignment is amazingly accurate considering the compass was not a part of the technology available to the builders.

All the architectural floor details in the kiva we found that day would have to wait until archaeologists could carefully and scientifically reveal their secrets.

Kivas sometimes occur together with a tower, especially at the later ruins. Such was the case at this particular ruin: A square tower stood guard, overlooking this kiva. It stood two or three stories high, another indication of its Mesa Verde link. We checked for a tunnel that would lead from the kiva to the tower, but this particular kiva did not have the tunnel connection. Archaeologists do not know for certain the original intent for the tower/kiva connection. But to our modern eyes it looked as though it could have a defensive component. While the men were in their kiva performing ceremonies, they were vulnerable to attack.

The ceiling was black with smoke, an indication this kiva had seen many ceremonies in its day. The ceiling of the kiva represents the sky to modern Pueblo people. Above us, the hatch dimly lit the dark room. Even the hatch is important to Puebloan rituals; the skies are watched through the hatch and the movements of the constellations are used to time the rituals. More on this later.

The beams of the kiva ceiling were smoke-blackened —a sign that it had seen much use in its day.

As we stood there we tried to picture what went on here a millennium ago. No one can know for sure, of course, but chances are it might have resembled what goes on in Puebloan kivas today.

Here they gathered to perform the rituals necessary to ensure the survival of the Pueblo world. Each kiva is typically the property of a clan. In the winter this semi-subterranean room would be a warm and cozy retreat. Today the kivas are usually considered the domain of men, but archaeologists have found evidence of household activities in the kivas of Mesa Verde. It appears the members of the clan would retreat to their kiva during the winter. Here the men would card cotton, spin cotton into yarn, weave cloth, and indeed, some ancient kivas have the remains of loom anchors in the floors, just as modern kivas do.

Whose were the hands that built this special place? Among the Pueblo people today, building a kiva is the job of a clan; perhaps there were similarities a millennium ago. Nineteenth-century anthropologist Victor Mindeleff visited the Zuni pueblo in the autumn of 1881. He wrote a volume about the process of building a kiva. These steps are the same whether for a residence or ceremonial room.

The excavation would have been done beforehand in readiness for construction to begin. Also cottonwood and pine trees for roof beams would have been felled and collected in a pile. Stones would have been gathered and roughly *dressed* by breaking them into a handy size. All this would be stockpiled at the site in readiness for construction to begin.

When construction is to begin, first the Kiva Chief sprinkles corn meal on the ground along the perimeter of the future walls as he sings in a soft voice: "Si-ai, a-hai, a-hai, si-ai, a-hai," which is known as "The House Song." Mindeleff asked the elders what these words meant, but the meaning has been lost to time. The chief also prays the wall "will take good roothold." He places *pahos* (prayer sticks or prayer feathers) at the corners of the future building. Then the chief selects stout corner stones from the stockpiled stones, and places them on top of the pahos. The walls are then built.

Pueblo people of the late nineteenth century place the beams for a new structure. From the 23rd Bureau of American Ethnology, *Stevenson.*

Some Pueblo people build above-ground, rectangular kivas, such as this one. Note the benches around the perimeter of the room., the hearth in the middle of the floor and the loom anchors along the sides of the room. This engraving is from the 8th Bureau of American Ethnology, V. Mindeleff.

The floors are laid with flagstone or plastered with adobe. In the center of the floor, under the roof hatch, a shallow pit about a foot across is made for a fireplace. Sometimes it is slab-lined; sometimes it is coated with a thick rim of adobe. It can be square or round, or even D-shaped. Sometimes today the sipapu is created by drilling a hole in a plank in the floor and is covered with a wooden plug flush with the plank. But in one ancient kiva we saw a sipapu cover made of fired clay, and we have heard they are sometimes of stone. The sipapu is the most sacred part of the kiva; some elders told Mindeleff the kiva was in fact built to house the sipapu. During ceremonies fetishes surround it.

There are also planks imbedded in the floor along the side walls that have pairs of holes in them. These serve as loom anchors for weaving the beautiful cotton cloth the Pueblo people have produced for centuries. The ancient kivas we see in the backcountry sometimes have loom anchors in the floors.

Below is an example of a wooden sipapu with a plug. From the 8th Bureau of American Ethnology, V. Mindeleff.

Then the women of the clan take over and plaster the walls of the kiva, just as they do for residences. In the future, they will also re-plaster the walls when necessary.

A ladder is propped from the center of the floor to the roof hatch. During ceremonies the ladder can be removed for privacy. But day to day, the kiva will be entered and left by way of the ladder which leans across the hearth, so every time a man enters or leaves, he is being purified by the sacred smoke from the hearth. He is also reliving the Puebloans' symbolic emergence from the underworld.

When the kiva is complete the Kiva Chief "feeds the kiva." Mindeleff described this as the chief placing some corn meal mixed with a little *piki* bread crumbs on a roof beam along with a paho. Then he softly murmurs his fervent wish that the "roof may never fall and that sickness and other evils may never enter the kiva." As we stood in the ancient kiva we had found that day, it was so — the roof of this kiva still stood after nearly a thousand years. Once the Kiva Chief has fed the kiva, it's time for celebration! The women prepare a feast. Then all night they sing their sacred songs to the rhythm of a drum. Last of all, the Kiva Chief names this kiva.

The kiva we found that day was typical except for being in very good shape. But every now and then we stumble across one that is special in some particular way, as we did on one winter afternoon a decade ago. This cliff dwelling was strung along a ledge like rough-cut beads in a Native American necklace. One rectangular building was larger and in better shape than the others in this group. As we looked closer we could see a hatch in the roof. Could it be that we had discovered a rectangular kiva? Among modern day Pueblo people, the rectangular kiva is not unusual. The Hopi have them and so do the Zuni.

As we studied it with binoculars, we could actually make out a pole protruding from the hatch. Our breath caught in our throats, could it possibly be a ladder? As we mentioned above, finding a kiva with a roof is uncommon enough — but for a ladder to have survived as well is almost unheard-of! We have only seen an original ladder in a museum.

But our excitement drained right out of us when we saw the route to get to this kiva. A crack split the ledge and separated us from the kiva. It was maybe six or seven feet across, and an overhang in the cliff above us kept us on our hands and knees. As we peered over the edge, a blast of wind pummeled us. It was hundreds of feet down to the canyon bottom. We stretched, but there was no way we could reach across the chasm and find a handhold. We wouldn't be able to reach the kiva without some serious technical climbing equipment, which is prohibited in some places.

It was such a special kiva — so near, yet so far away. The ancient people had indeed protected it well.

We sat down in the sandy red dirt of the ledge and pondered our options. In the end we decided to attempt to approach the kiva from the other side

Above is the rectangular kiva we discovered that day. Amazingly a ladder still protruded from the hatch in the roof. Below is a kiva hatch from the late nineteenth century, a ladder extending up to the sky. From the 8th Bureau of American Ethnology, V. Mindeleff.

— finding the right ledge and coming around the point, a distance of quite a few miles of scrambling along the ledge, timber bashing the overgrowth. And there was no guarantee that the ledge wouldn't pinch out and our efforts would be in vain.

Determined, the next day we tackled the trek. We found the ledge on the backside of the mesa top with little trouble and struggled all the way to the point of the mesa, and then slowly worked our way around and back toward the kiva. Just about the time we were exulting in the fact the ledge did indeed go and did not pinch out, we encountered our first choke point.

This choke point was a narrow ledge with a low overhang that required us to crawl on our hands and knees. The rock ceiling was so low we had to remove our backpacks and push them along in front of us for a distance of maybe ten feet. This effectively limited the amount of equipment an intruder could bring with him to the kiva.

Then we encountered an exposed choke point where the slickrock sloped off sharply toward the abyss. A person trying to gain access to the dwelling would be very vulnerable; a casual push by a single defender could protect the dwelling.

Altogether there were six choke points we had to navigate — Six on the way in and then again on the way out. The last point was another low overhang, but this one also sloped outward and around a bend. It was so low we couldn't traverse it on our hands and knees; we had to crab along on our stomachs. And when we struggled to our feet, there it was: the rectangular kiva. We had made it!

The kiva was certainly unique. The rectangular building was tucked under the overhang of the cliff wall and wedged behind a boulder. The pole protruding from the roof hatch was definitely a ladder, we could now see. We walked the perimeter of the building and found a hole in the backside that had eroded away. That meant we could enter it without damaging the roof or the precious ladder.

Inside, we found a high ceiling — kivas were often the largest building in a cluster. The ceiling was soot covered, and the walls were carefully plastered in a monochromatic russet color. Against the south wall were neatly plastered pilasters. This is a trait of Mesa Verde-type kivas. It was above ground, a Kayenta feature, so this kiva had traits of both Mesa Verde and Kayenta.

But the most fascinating thing was the ladder. Now that we were up close we could see it was fashioned from a tree that had been stripped of its bark and buried into the floor of the kiva. Most of the branches had been lopped off,

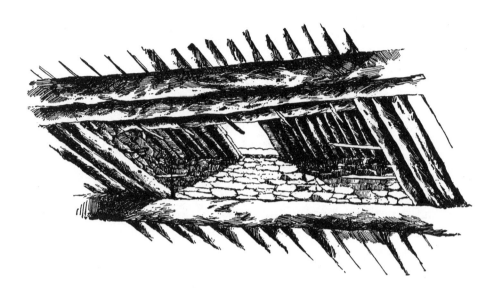

At the top, an engraving of a kiva hatch from the late nineteenth centure, 8th *Bureau of American Ethnology*, V. Mindeleff. Note how the construction of the hatch on the top resembles the hatch on the bottom, on the rectangular kiva we discovered that day.

The ladder is placed over the fire so that a person entering or leaving is purified by the smoke.
23rd *Bureau of American Ethnology*, Stevenson.

We see a similar arrangement in the ancient backcountry kiva ruins we visit.

leaving a knob in place to assist in climbing up it. When we looked closer, we could see that the missing branches had been removed with a stone tool — we could see the peck marks of the stone axe. These peck marks were worn and shiny from people climbing up and down on them. We peered even closer still at the ladder/tree, and it appeared solid. In front of the ladder/tree was a deflector.

Kivas were eventually replaced in some places with a plaza. The plazas were larger than kivas, and it is thought today that they could accommodate more participants and viewers who sat on the rooftops to watch the pageantry.

In Mexico at Paquimé there are many large plazas scattered throughout the ediface. But cliff dwellings by their very confined nature could not accommodate a big plaza and instead had decorated ceremonial rooms.

THE IMPORTANCE OF BIRDS

A Taos youth and his pet eagle in 1883. From The Continent Maga-zine, *"A Harvest with the Taos Indians."*

Birds and feathers are one of the most enduring symbols of the Puebloan people. And nowhere would this be more apparent than in the kivas.

Birds, and more specifically feathers, had always been an important feature of the ancient Puebloans ceremonies: They were on altars, masks, headdresses, prayer sticks and rattles. It is thought the feathers flew their prayers to the cloud people, who brought rain.

Bird effigy pots — sometimes they are also referred to as "duck pots." These are from the 10th Annual Hayden Survey *and are nineteenth century.*

Many different interpretations of Knife Wing exist. The below pair of Knife Wings face the viewer under terraced rain clouds. From the 33rd Bureau of American Ethnology, Fewkes.

Even in the earlier Basketmaker times birds had been represented on pottery designs, in pot shapes — as in a "duck pot" — and in rock art.

But after the fall of Chaco Canyon circa A.D. 1150, the use of birds and feathers in ceremonial settings exploded. Now they were everywhere — on whistles, gourds, road markers. They were depicted on rock art and in pottery designs more often than before. Feathers were woven into clothing. Birds also became a common clan sign. One widespread feather motif is the plumed serpent (sometimes also referred to as the feathered snake), a symbol that diffused to the north from Mexico.

According to ethnographer Elsie Parsons, the Zuni referred to birds as little servants, and as messenger scouts, and were dispatched to find lost Corn Maidens or any stray girl.

The most common feather used was probably the turkey feather, which might be the main reason they raised turkeys — for their feathers. Macaws were also a favorite bird and feather motif. At Paquimé in northern Mexico the ancient people raised parrots, and parrots were found in the northern Southwest as well. The most powerful feather was the eagle tail feather, which has a white body with a distinctive black stair-step design on it. Eagle feathers came late to the Puebloans, popular just before the arrival of the Spaniards. Their representations are unmistakable because the ancients depicted them meticulously.

During the Pueblo IV Period (beyond A.D. 1300) the figure of Knife Wing began to appear in rock art and pottery along the Rio Grande. Knife Wing is the representation of a bird of prey, usually depicted facing the viewer with wings outstretched. The wing tips end in sharp knife-like points. His talons are usually prominent and so is his sharp beak.

In kivas birds were often depicted on kiva murals. One mural at the ruined Hopi pueblo town of Awat'ovi (ah-WAT-oh-vee) in northern

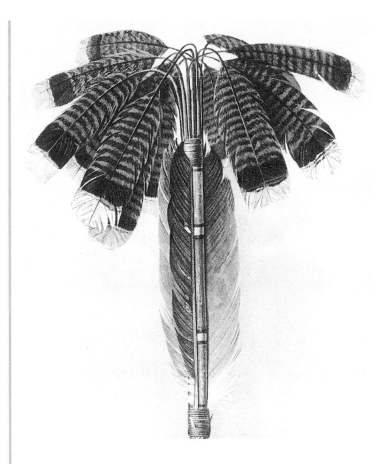

After the fall of Chaco, birds and feathers became powerful symbols to the ancient Puebloans. Feathers adorn this sword, not shown. From the 23rd Bureau of American Ethnology, *Stevenson.*

Arizona depicts warriors around the perimeter of the room. Behind each one is a bird — a different type of bird shadowing each warrior.

It would be difficult to think of a symbol more important to the Puebloans than birds and feathers.

Round Kivas

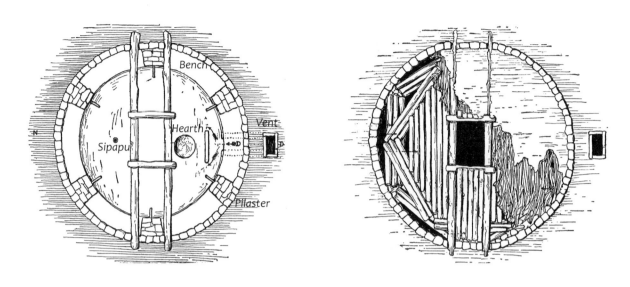

Above, left, a sketch of a round, subterranean, Mesa Verde-type of kiva, without its roof. On the right, the same Mesa Verde type kiva showing its roof. The above etchings are from the *Bureau of American Ethnology, Bulletin #41*, Fewkes. Below, a round, subterranean Mesa Verde type kiva in the backcountry. Also note below, the faint remains of a geometric design painted just above the floor level.

Rectangular Kivas

Rectangular kivas or ceremonial rooms can be found throughout the region. Some of the Pueblo people of today still have round kivas along the Rio Grande. But the large pueblos had large plazas. Above from: *8th Annual Bureau of American Ethnology*, V. Mindeleff.

Mexico Ceremonial Rooms

This large T-door led to a courtyard. Off the courtyard were two tall double T-doors which led into the room pictured below. The walls were covered with art and there were bins in the corners. Doors led to living rooms. Locals called this a "church." We would call it a possible ceremonial room.

A Puebloan farmer tends his corn. This photograph is thought to have been taken by William H. Jackson in the 1890s. Sagstetter collection.

9

Farming: Corn Is Life

Since the ancient days I have planted.
Since the time of emergence I have planted.
— Puebloan Song.

We hiked across the mesa top seeking a cliff dwelling glued to the cliff face under the far end escarpment. As we entered a clearing, the distinctive song of the bluebird filled the air. Puebloans of today call bluebirds the Rain Bird because their song can be heard just before a rain. Because of this, they are considered sacred to them. As we crossed the clearing we surprised the birds — up they went, their song filling the air. We watched them climb higher and higher into the sky until they seemed to disappear into the pale overcast of the sky.

Later, as we stood on the mesa edge, we could see for miles: the deep green of the mesa tops, torn by ragged chasms. In this semi-arid place, the rain is negligible. The winds are so strong they can shred tender plants in an instant. What isn't shredded is buried in loose sand, smothering young plants and even obliterating springs and seeps. The wind sandblasts every single thing in its reach, sneaking past our most ingenious defenses, including our sealed, double plastic bags, and still it becomes a gritty presence in our delicate electronic devices anyway.

The sun blisters everything hit by its rays: Plants are withered. And at night, the heat is replaced by cold — sometimes the canyon bottoms are so much cooler than the mesa tops that ice can form in water until quite late in spring. Torrential rainfall counterbalances the occasional drought. And the soil! What isn't sand is heavy, dense, hard-to-till clay. It's surprising that anything, even cactus, can grow here.

No doubt about it, farming here would be a marginal, risky business. Yet ancient people somehow coaxed corn from this land for perhaps as many as 4,000 years!

207

A trinchera, or check dam, in Mexico in the 1890s. From Carl Lumholtz's Unknown Mexico.

Today in Mexico, the remains of a trinchera.

We were so engrossed in the view from the mesa edge that we hadn't noticed it had started to rain.

If you were an ancestral Puebloan man, farming would be your mission. It would be your responsibility to wrestle crops — the life's blood of your family — from this balky, uncooperative place. It must have been a humbling experience. You were betting not only your life, but also those of your family, that you would succeed in harvesting enough of a crop to last your family a year. It was an awesome challenge.

As a practical man, you would successfully farm in such an inhospitable place by hedging your bets. At the time of the cliff dwellings, ancestral Puebloan farmers had developed a series of techniques that would assure a harvest most of the time, no matter what happened with the weather.

One technique was to plant crops in a variety of settings. Some plots were on the mesa tops — as it turns out, it is a little warmer here. If the season was a cool one, your corn crop planted on the mesa top might survive. But you would also plant on the canyon bottoms in case the season was a hot, dry one. You might at least get a crop from the plot on the canyon floor if a drought occurred. Then you would plant on every swale or rivulet that ran off the mesa top. You would set up *trincheras*, or check dams, that are terraced off the steep sides of the mesa at the places where the water runs off. Check dams act as baffles for the runoff and help prevent erosion as well as water your crops. This way every drop of water that happened to fall on the mesa would end up watering at least some of your crops. We stumble across the remains of these trincheras in cliff dwelling country today, and they still seem to work after all this time. Today we often find indigenous plants thriving in those old check dam terraces.

Besides this technique, you would also have in your arsenal different types of corn that had been developed over the centuries. Some would mature early. Some late. Some were resistant to low temperatures and had a chance of maturing even in a cool year. Some were resistant to drought and might mature even in a very dry year. You would plant all these different types of corn, in all the differing locations, in hopes that at least some would survive and mature no matter what conditions Mother Nature threw at you. All these different types of seed corn were carefully separated by color and stored in different areas in your granaries and store rooms.

Above and below, the remains of check dams from 800 years ago in Mesa Verde National Park today.

Your final hedging technique would have been to plant far more than you needed for one year. When the Spaniards arrived in the year A.D. 1540, they were told by the Pueblo people that every year they planted enough of a crop to last seven years. This is probably why we see so many structures devoted to storage in our backcountry explorations.

These were the variables that ancestral Puebloans would have had some control over. For all the other variables, they would beseech the spirits. With feather paho offerings and prayers while they planted and tended their crops, they beat back the odds. The Puebloan people of today believe if their hearts are pure, if their thoughts are happy, if they make their prayer offerings, the gods will reward them with a bountiful harvest. And it must be so: The Pueblo people have wrestled a living from these lands for more than four millennia.

We were hiking up a canyon bottom when we spotted a small cliff dwelling tucked into the jagged sandstone wall above us. It wasn't much: just a single, tiny, stone structure on a high ledge overlooking the canyon bottom. We knew it was probably just a granary but scrambled up to it anyway, even though it was hardly an impressive find. The doorway was also tiny, and as we took turns peeking inside we saw a smattering of tiny corncobs scattered on the

ANCIENT TRINCHERAS?

We were hiking in southeast Utah when we stumbled across these mysterious ancient constructions. Someone many years ago, had placed upright sandstone slabs into the sandy dirt. They were located at key run-off points around the mesa top. The slabs were positioned in a Y-shape, with the stone that was the leg of the Y bracing the two slabs in the V-shape above it.

As we walked the mesa top we spotted these devices in several places. In the area inside the V, indigenous plants like piñon, juniper and sagebrush thrived. Could they be an ancient water control feature of some kind? Maybe even a unique form of trinchera?

Above and below are two of them we saw that day that were not hidden from the camera by all the growth. Since then we have encountered them again, but only in southeast Utah. We have never seen them anywhere else in the Greater American Southwest.

floor. Each cob was no longer than your pinky finger. And when we picked up an ancient cob and gently rolled it over in our fingers, we counted eight rows of indentations that cradled the original corn kernels. *Maiz de Ocho!* (*Ocho* is Spanish for the number eight.) We then returned the cob to its original resting place. We often find these tiny, ancient corncobs scattered in and around cliff dwellings today, and it never ceases to enchant us. Whenever we find a tiny Maiz de Ocho corn cob, it always conjures up a story that goes back thousands of years and thousands of miles to southern Mexico.

Above is a Maiz de Ocho *corncob. We find them scattered all around cliff dwellings on the Colorado Plateau. They are usually smaller than your pinky finger.*

When you look at a mature corn plant today, what you are really looking at is a giant blade of grass. Maize developed from what was originally a tropical grass, *teosinte*. It still grows in southern Mexico today. This teosinte plant is a grassy plant with many stems instead of just the one large stem that we see on maize today. On each of these stems are small clusters of kernels — more like tiny spindles than cobs — that are encased in very hard shells. So hard in fact that they were meant to pass through the digestive system of an animal and out the other end and still be able to germinate. Each of these stems has tassels at its top, just like corn does today. And it has the sweet taste and the ability to "pop" like corn does today. It also can be ground up into a flour and baked, just as corn can be.

The earliest undisputed date for the domestication of corn is 4,000 B.C. However, in the November 14, 2003, issue of *Science* magazine, geneticists moved that date back as far as 9,000 years before the present. These scientists believe that in the Balsas Valley of southern Mexico, humans genetically altered teosinte into something a little more usable, a little more convenient to humans than teosinte, and began the first attempts at farming maize. That humans genetically altered teosinte into something similar to modern corn and did it so many thousands of years ago is mind-boggling to consider. And the idea of farming it spread.

Archaeologists discovered that by 4,700 years ago, residents of the Tehuacan Valley in southern Mexico were growing and using a small ear of "pop" maize that had only six to nine kernels per cob. And just as importantly, they had invented stone milling tools — the mano and metate — to grind it into flour. Maize became the basis for a farming lifestyle in the Americas.

From these humble beginnings as a tropical grass, *Zea Mays* — as it's called scientifically — has become one of the three staple grains that feed the world: Rice and wheat are the other two. Maize ranks as one of man's greatest accomplishments; today it is the most versatile of all grains. It can grow in the semi-arid conditions of the American Southwest, or it can grow in Peru on the shores of Lake Titicaca at 12,000 feet above sea level. It can grow in places too dry for rice or too wet for wheat. Nearly twice as much corn can be harvested from an acre of farmland as can wheat.

Maize, and the idea of farming it, spread north from its origins in southern Mexico to the American Southwest. According to archaeologist Jeffrey Dean, modern pollen analysis has placed it in the Sonoran Desert and on the southern Colorado Plateau in the Zuni area rather suddenly around 4,200 years ago. It was probably also present in other Southwestern areas as well. Little evidence exists for what followed for about a thousand years. But by 3,200 years ago intensive farming, including ditch irrigation, was present in these areas.

One of the earliest types of corn to be farmed on the Colorado Plateau was called *chapalote*. This was not terribly productive and had only a few kernels per cob, and the kernels were smaller than what we see today. The big change came with Maize de Ocho. Although it had a smaller cob than chapalote and had fewer rows of kernels, the kernels were larger and meatier than the old chapalote maize kernels. Maize de Ocho produced greater yields than earlier versions of corn and was better suited to the arid climate. This new type of maize helped make a sedentary farming lifestyle more feasible for the early people of the Southwest. And every time we see these small, eight-rowed corncobs in the backcountry today, we are reminded of the story of maize and its incredible journey to today.

The Hopi developed a type of corn that was uniquely suited to their particular location. Early explorers (who should have known better) traveling to Hopi land reported seeing fields of corn plants that were small and "stunted" compared to what they had seen in the Midwest. Because this corn was not "as high as an elephant's eye" as in the song from the musical *Oklahoma*, they wrote disparaging remarks about this Indian corn.

The Hopi farm in what are basically sand dunes. It would not be possible to grow *anything* there except for the fact that there is an aquifer about 12 to 15 feet beneath the surface. The Hopi developed a type of corn that produces roots 12 to 15 feet long and taps into that aquifer. The low-growing, bushy plants are better adapted to the windy, sandblasting conditions that prevail in their land. A tall plant would be shredded by the blowing sand and flattened by the strong winds that sweep the area. And the Hopi have lived on this land since about the 1400s, so they had to have developed this strain of corn by about A.D. 1400. Today modern Hopi corn has twelve rows of kernels.

As an ancestral Puebloan farmer, your cornfields would be marked by a row of stones. The modern Pueblo people today still mark their fields in this way, and the corner markers will typically have the clan sign engraved on it. Archaeologists have found these lines of stones marking ancient fields, but we have never personally seen any of them in our backcountry travels.

Maize needs about 120 growing days to mature. If the weather is cool and/or dry it will need more time. In some parts of the American Southwest like north of the San Juan River, the number of days between frosts are as few as 130. So there is not much room for error on the planting date.

When the time came to plant your crops, you would have piled up the dirt in little hills about six to eight feet apart. (Planting far apart prevents competition between plants for the moisture and any disease might not spread to the entire plot.) Then using your planting stick, you'd bore down into the hill ten inches or more. This would help the roots reach the deep moisture below the wind-swept surface. Into the hole you'd drop perhaps five or six seed kernels, in hopes that at least one would germinate. The following year, you would create dirt hills between the hills from the last year, thus "resting" the soil every other year — an early form of crop rotation. Archaeologists have experimented with planting in many different ways and

Planting with a planting stick. Everyone helps, even the children play a part. From Century Magazine, Frank H. Cushing, 1883.

have had the greatest yields when they planted in this ancient way.

On the same hill you would also plant some squash and beans. Beans, as a legume, helps to replace the nitrogen in the soil consumed by the corn, thus helping the farmland to not become depleted. Corn by itself can supply enough calories for a person to live on, but it does not have a complete protein in it. Children in particular need protein to be healthy. But corn does have a certain amino-acid, a building-block of protein, in it. Beans have the needed remainder amino-acid required to create a complete protein and together with corn can provide as much protein as is in a glass of milk. So beans and corn together can provide a nourishing diet.

Beans came much later than corn onto the scene. Until the people had invented pottery in which to cook dried beans, there would have been no way to cook them. Beans also store well.

These three plants, corn, beans and squash — sometimes called the Three Sisters — formed the foundation of the diet in the Americas before Spanish contact. However, in some places in the southernmost region of the American Southwest they were also able to grow cotton and tobacco.

For the first few weeks after planting your crops, you wouldn't have to watch them too closely. Any loss to pests you would merely replant. But these replacement plants you'd soak first in water overnight to encourage them to germinate. After a certain point-of-no-return, when the new plants had no chance to develop before the frost, you'd watch your fields very carefully. You might even build a simple "field house" overlooking your fields where you could stand guard over next year's food supply. Here you'd maybe even stay for the rest of the growing season.

Harvest is a time for celebration! Modern Zuni people save the most perfect ears of each color of corn to be the seed corn for the next year. These corn kernels are removed from the cobs and are stored in a ceramic seed jar with a lid. Some of these seed jars are beautifully decorated.

After the harvest, the corn must be dried before it can be stored; otherwise it would sit in the granaries and rot or mildew. Archival nineteenth-century photographs show the terraced houses with corn spread on every conceivable inch of the rooftops and courtyards — hanging from the protruding vigas along the roofline, dangling from peeled stick wooden pegs — drying in the hot sun, a riot of color. These cobs of drying corn had to be turned often to insure thorough drying.

Juanita Tiger Kavina relates in her book *Hopi Cookery*, "all the old corn must be removed from the storage bins and the bins cleaned and plastered for the new corn. The old corn will not be thrown away, but will be placed in the storage area last so it will be used before the new corn, a system of supply rotation that has always been practiced by the Hopi."

Cornmeal appears in most every Puebloan ceremony. In fact, as much cornmeal is used for weddings and ceremonies as is consumed by the family. Most all of the corn plant was used. The corncobs could be burned as fuel. And historically, Pueblo peoples during times of hunger cooked and prepared corncobs (with great difficulty) until they were rendered more or less edible. So any time you see the scatters of cobs at a cliff dwelling, you can surmise that this was a place of "plenty." The people of this particular dwelling did not have to eat all those cobs or burn them for fuel.

B ut at some point the harvests would become smaller and smaller, perhaps after twenty years or so. And since no one in the world was yet aware of the benefits of fertilizer, it was time to move on, to migrate to new farmlands. It must have seemed as though the spirits had forsaken them.

Note the rooftop of the building in the front center — corn is spread out drying. 8th Bureau of American Ethnology, V. Mindeleff.

215

This would be a situation that might occur once in every lifetime. So how did a Puebloan farmer discern good new farmlands? How did he locate fertile land in this desert environment?

Modern Native American Southwestern farmers look for certain plants today. Sunflowers are a good indicator of fertile lands with enough moisture present for growing crops. Rabbitbrush is the marker that Hopis look for. Below the Mogollon Rim, farming is along waterways — either floodwater farming in and along washes or by irrigation. The also employ run-off farming techniques with extensive check dams or terraces.

Modern Native American farmers also look for ironwood on the slopes of streams that tells them this area is frost-free and winter crops might be able to grow here. Tasting the soil is a good way to check for saltiness. Healthy stands of mesquite and palo verde trees are indicators of good soil and plenty of moisture beneath the dry surface.

Along washes they attempt to control the water flow with brush "fences." This helps keep unwanted water from inundating their fields. In more vulnerable spots they might even pile up heaps of stones to help deflect the water and prevent it from undermining the soil. They also use brush fences to slow the water down in the channel and spread it onto their fields. One Papago young man recalled having to run to his parents' fields whenever they heard the clap of distant thunder — even in the middle of the night — to set up and repair their brush fences so the water would either be kept off their fields or directed onto the fields to water them.

Full-scale irrigation was and is labor intensive and beyond the scope of a single family. It requires a rather large labor pool of workers to build and maintain the channels. But short ditches are sometimes dug by individuals.

A newcomer might have to spend a year just observing his chosen waterway to see how the water flows and at what time of the year. But eventually he would establish himself as a farmer again.

Today all that might be visible to the discerning eye is the remains of trincheras, piles of stones, irrigation canals, and perhaps the stones that lined the ancient fields. But eight hundred years ago there may have been much more happening in these places. The ancient brush fences and perhaps stands of trees along the edge of the fields or the edge of the channels, would leave no trace today. All we are seeing are the most enduring remains that did not disintegrate with time.

And when you are lucky enough to see a humble corncob, what you are actually seeing is the entire story of corn and how it made it possible for the ancient people to live and thrive here.

WALLED GARDENS

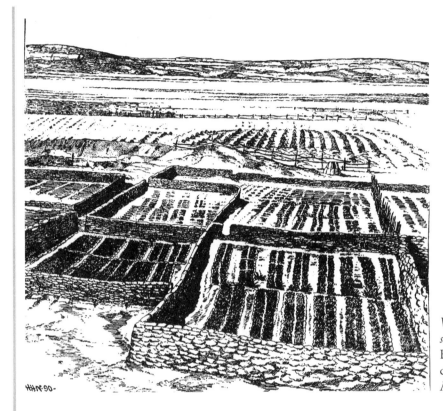

Walled gardens shown in the 8th Bureau of American Ethnology, V. Mindeleff.

Archaeologist Ruth Lambert discovered the remains of an unusual structure in Arizona, near Flagstaff. It was away from the pueblo living area, on a sunny slope overlooking the cliffs. No function she could imagine for the structure seemed to fit it. Eventually she asked a Pueblo man if he could identify the structure. His response: a walled garden. Particularly the Zuni constructed gardens surrounded with an adobe wall. Inside the wall, the area was partitioned by additional walls in a grid fashion, somewhat like waffles — hence they are sometimes called waffle gardens. Each square of the grid contained up to four plants. The walls protected the young, tender plants from being sand-blasted by the wind, and the walls helped contain water better, like syrup on a waffle, making it more accessible to the plants. They also absorbed the heat of the day and released it at night, thereby stretching the growing season a little.

Some Pueblo groups also employed cobble gardens. In this garden, stones the size of grapefruit were spaced about the garden. This helped control erosion. On cold nights, heat that had been absorbed by these stones during the day was released, thereby extending the growing season. Also, the stone cobbles prevented evaporation, leaving more moisture for the plants to absorb.

This haunting image overlooks a cliff ruin in southeast Utah. It is usually interpreted as a shield.
Photographer: Vaughn Hadenfeldt, Far Out Expeditions.

10

Rock Art: The Writing on the Walls

Spider Grandmother spoke. She said: "You will go on long migrations. You will build villages and abandon them for new migrations. Wherever you stop to rest, leave your marks on the rocks and cliffs so that others will know who was there before them."

— *Harold Courlander,* The Fourth World of the Hopis.

We had hiked many miles down a southwestern canyon and now were starting to get tired. As we rounded a bend a cliff dwelling came into view in the distance, high above the canyon floor. Above it, as though it were hovering, was a white circle painted on the cliff face. Two empty eyes stared back at us, seemingly challenging our presence there. We stared at the apparition: It was meant to be seen, and from a distance. It was as though it was somehow meant for us and it made us feel uncomfortable. Since that first trip to this area decades ago we have found out that these disks above some cliff dwellings are often interpreted as shields.

If there is one type of rock art element that conjures up reminiscences of cliff dwellings, it would be shields. According to rock art expert and author Polly Schaaftsma, these round rock art elements exploded in popularity during the PIII cliff dwelling era (A.D.1150–1300). Often they are white with designs in different colors.

We couldn't help but think there was a message here. What were the ancient people saying to passersby like us? We felt frustrated and longed to know exactly what it meant.

It has taken us four decades, but we have come to the conclusion that we can get a *glimpse* of what it might have meant, but first we have to develop a certain mindset in order to appreciate that glimpse.

Rock art appears all over the world — in the Americas, Europe, Australia, Africa, even among the Inuit. Antarctica is the only place it does not occur. It spans all cultures, and it spans an amazing range of time. The cave paintings in Europe are thought to be 30,000 years old.

In the American Southwest, rock art can be found most anywhere: near structures and ancient campsites, near water, along ancient trails. It can be found on flat surfaces like boulders or cliff faces that are nice and smooth. Some rock art is huge and in an obvious place, like it was meant to be seen, such as the shield we saw that day in the canyon wall. Other rock art is small and in an out-of-the-way hidden spot, as though it was not meant for prying eyes.

Rock art is generally assumed to be the domain of men, just as worldwide pottery is thought to be the domain of women. Around the world rock art has been associated with ceremonial rites, and some of the fantastic beings we see depicted on the cliff walls today reinforce that assumption.

The rock art of the American Southwest was not made by aliens in UFOs, not by the lost tribes of Israel, not by ancient European Ogam writers. There really is no doubt that it was made by the ancient peoples of the Southwest. One has only to check out their pottery designs and kiva murals, all of which replicate the same design elements and make it obvious who produced the nearby rock art.

Rock art is an extremely controversial subject — even the name "rock art" is disputed. Is this "art" or are these messages — a form of ancient picture writing? This question has been hotly debated for decades. And complicating the issue, the term "rock art" itself originated far away with the ancient cave pictures in Europe. However, modern Pueblo people tell us these pictures on stone are not simply decorative. They insist that they are messages from the past. So for us, this answers the debate: They are ancient messages on stone. And anyway, writing often begins in this way, with pictures that are later stylized and eventually become standardized, so that others may "read" them.

Add to this controversy the fact that rock art is notoriously difficult to date. It can't be dated like other ancient artifacts can be, so for decades archaeologists avoided putting too much emphasis

On the left is a human figure usually considered to be Basketmaker, that is, older than the cliff dwellings. First of all he is depicted with atlatls (the sticks with circles on the ends). Atlatls had been replaced by bows and arrows by the time of the cliff dwellings.
Photographer: Vaughn Hadenfeldt, Far Out Expeditions.

on its study until recently. Today rock art is usually dated by its association with nearby sites that have been scientifically dated.

Another technique that has been used for dating rock art is by considering the specific artifacts that human-like figures are shown carrying or using in the art. The most obvious example is a person riding on the back of a horse. This dates the rock art to after the arrival of the Spanish since horses were not present in the Americas at the time of the Spanish *entrada*. For another example, is the human figure depicted on the cliff face portrayed carrying a spear or *atlatl* (spear thrower)? The atlatl was replaced with bows and arrows. And of the bows, was it a simple bow, or was it a re-curved bow? The re-curved bow replaced the simple bow. So the atlatl is older than the bow and arrow and the simple bow is older than the re-curved bow. The use of weapon images in a piece of rock art suggests its relative age and is an example of *relative* dating.

Relative dating means determining one element is older than another without any attempt to firmly date it. For example, often we see ancient rock art superimposed over other ancient rock art. The implication is the rock art that is beneath another is older than what was superimposed on top of it. You can often see the difference in the patination in the rock art figures; the older designs are darker, the younger designs are less dark. We can look at this as similar to stratigraphy: The youngest examples are on top, the oldest examples are on the bottom. But it doesn't tell us what year either was most likely created.

This hunting scene may be a transitional scene. The stick figures are engaged in an activity and seem later, but they are hunting with atlatls which are older. Photographer: Vaughn Hadenfeldt, Far Out Expeditions.

The figure on the far left is thought to be a Basketmaker rock art figure. He faces the viewer and has a trapezoidal body with small appendages. Note he is wearing an elaborate headress, necklace and a fringed blanket. Above are figures thought to be later — they are stick figures engaged in an activity.
Photographer (both photographs): Vaughn Hadenfeldt, Far Out Expeditions.

It is also possible to get a rough date for rock art using style and/or subject matter as an indicator. For example, over time rock art depictions changed. In the Four Corners region, the Basketmakers — predecessors to the Anasazi — depicted the human figure facing the viewer straight-on and static. They portrayed humans with a trapezoidal body with tiny appendages. Often this trapezoidal body shape displayed blankets or clothing and jewelry, and sometimes strange headdresses. By about A.D. 800, humans were often depicted in profile and engaged in some activity. They were more like stick figures and were no longer portrayed as a trapezoidal shape.

Certain new elements appeared at different times. For example, shield figures increased exponentially at the time of the cliff dwellings. The cross or plus sign became popular along the Rio Grande in New Mexico after the ancient Puebloans migrated to the region after A.D. 1300.

There are two types of rock art: *pictographs* and *petroglyphs*. Pictographs have been painted upon the surface of the stone. The ancient people used many different kinds of paint or colored clay and had numerous colors available to them. Paint brushes were made by chewing stringy yucca leaves, although sometimes they used their hands and fingers. Sometimes even their feet were used for footprints.

The term "petroglyph" comes from the Greek word *petro* for stone, and *glyph* for carving. A petroglyph is pecked into the stone wall using a stone. Sometimes archaeologists have found the pecking stone that is thought to have created the work at the foot of the cliff where it was presumably abandoned a millennium ago. A cliff face that was coated in what is popularly called *desert varnish* was a favorite place to peck petroglyphs. Desert varnish is a dark patina on the stone composed of hydrous iron and manganese oxides. It can be brown or black, or sometimes even orange. If it is particularly thick and the conditions are right, it can be quite shiny, hence the popular name. When this patina is chipped away as the image is created, the new creation is lighter than the dark desert varnish background.

Here the dark desert varnish has been pecked away with a stone tool leaving an image that is lighter than the surrounding rock.

If the pecking stone is used directly on the surface, it leaves a rough, rather crude design. The pecking stone by itself cannot achieve thin, graceful lines. But fine lines can be created with a pecking stone and an intermediate tool like a piece of antler, bone or a stone drill or awl. By tapping on the antler or awl, an artistic line could be created. And most men would have these devices at hand much of the time. Occasionally archaeologists have found tiny scraps of paint still clinging to a petroglyph that suggests the petroglyph was originally painted as well as pecked.

Of all the rock art that survives today, petroglyphs by far outnumber pictographs. Did the painted pictographs at one time number equally with petroglyphs but were washed away over time while the carved stone images survived? Were many of the petroglyphs also painted with bright colors? Is it possible that these cliff walls in the American Southwest were once alive with colorful pictures? As of this writing, no one can say.

What Does It All Mean?

There in front of us a strange world of supernatural beings was depicted on the cliff face. Huge human-like figures stared back at us with blank eyes. There were humans with bird heads or with contraptions sprouting from their heads. No question about it, this was a different world from ours today.

A world where cloud people in the sky send the rains.
A world where birds are messengers to the heavens.

A world where horned and feathered serpents dwell in springs and seeps.
A world where animals can share their extraordinary powers (the strength of the bear, the agility of a mountain sheep, the hunting prowess of a puma) with man, under certain conditions.
A world where by donning the mask and costume of a spirit, a person could become that spirit.

As Winston Hurst and Jonathan Till write in "Mesa Verdean Sacred Landscapes" in the book *The Mesa Verde World*, many Pueblo people still today "believe that images have the power to affect nature, that art invokes reality, that art *can make things happen*. Creating art, therefore, is a potentially powerful and sometimes dangerous act." And for that reason rock art has been considered the realm of the shaman, the man who has the power to undertake such a dangerous, powerful act. For example, take the scenes that are called "hunting magic." These scenes depict a single hunter or several successfully bagging a deer or bighorn sheep. It is thought that the shaman was attempting to "make this happen" and make it "real" by depicting it on the rock face.

In fact, some of the strange beings we see depicted on the cliff faces are thought to be the results of a shaman's visions. At times the shaman would undertake vision-quest-type voyages — journeys of his spirit — for his people. Sometimes these were brought on by sleep deprivation until he began to hallucinate or sometimes with the help of peyote. It was thought there were spirit helpers to guide him on this journey — birds were often considered to be spirit helpers, and it is believed this is why they were portrayed so often in the rock art. For example, when there is a human-like figure with a duck for a head, or a duck on top of his head, this is thought to be a depiction of a shaman's trance. Or sometimes it has been observed that a duck is attached to the head of a rock art figure by a meandering line. Some experts would infer this to mean the duck was his spirit helper.

Below is a hunting magic rock art scene depicted in the pages of Bureau of American Ethnology #65, Kidder and Guernsey. It is thought that art could "make it happen."

Another use for rock art is in sun watching. The Southwest abounds with petroglyphs of spirals that are pierced or framed by a sun ray dagger design or other device at certain key times of the year. More on this later.

But there are plenty of other types of rock art that do not fit in this category. Some appear to be more like tally marks — a census of who lived or visited here and recorded by handprints. Others seem to be more akin to boundary markers or ownership markers.

Birds, in this case, ducks, attached to the head of a person figure, are usually interpreted as a shaman having a vision. Photographer: Vaughn Hadenfeldt, Far Out Expeditions.

However, we are told we might be barred from fully understanding these ancient messages. A person who has been trained in the Western thought process of the ancient Greeks, basically Aristotle's logic and way of organizing material, might never truly understand what the rock art means. We might be able to identify the image — for example a bighorn sheep — but we might not ever be able to attach a meaning to it. Liz and Peter Welsh express it best in their book, *Rock Art of the Southwest*. They point out that five hundred years from now someone might look at a twenty-first century drawing of a star-spangled elephant or donkey and recognize the animal, but would miss the political implications. Knowing that implication can change the meaning of the animal's context.

Part of the problem is that symbols were never standardized, and as such, each design element was personal. On occasion the symbols were what has been called a mnemonic device — that is, something to pique one's memory. An example from archaeologist Florence Ellis is tying a string around your finger to remind yourself to pick up a loaf of bread on your way home from work. The string reminds *you* of the bread, but someone else would not know the connection. And on another day the string might be there to remind you to buy milk instead. It's personal. During modern times a member of a certain Plains tribe used a buckskin with symbols on it to designate each winter over several decades. One year there might be a picture of an elk, a reminder that that was the year Chief Grey Elk died. Another might be a symbol for snow, meaning to the person that that was the year there was

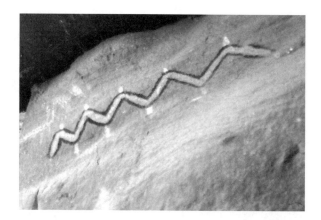

The plumed serpent is another motif popular in Mexico that found its way north. The white marks at every zig and zag are usually interpreted as feathers. Some snakes have a horn depicted on the head area.

The cross or plus sign is thought to signify the morning star in Mexico. But it is often found in the Greater American Southwest. Photographer: Andrew Gulliford ©.

The bulls-eye, or concentric circle design was a rock are element that diffused north from Mexico.

much more snow than usual. And so on. But no one else — even in his own tribe — would be able to fathom the meanings of the symbols.

So it may have been for at least some of the symbols on the cliffs: They were personal, not standardized.

The closest rock art elements come to being standardized is when the symbols were borrowed from Mexico, such as the horned and/or plumed serpent, the cross, the bulls–eye symbol (or concentric circles) and the representation for *Tlaloc*, the Aztec rain god. These symbols were well known to the ancient people in Mexico, and their meanings in that context are more or less understood. But even these are in question when they are found in the American Southwest. As ideas and symbols diffuse, sometimes folks adopt the symbol but prefer to attach their own meaning to it. So sometimes design elements mean one thing at the point of origin but something much different out on the fringes of that civilization.

Today archaeologists have taken members of different Pueblo tribes — the descendants of the ancestral Puebloans — to rock art panels and asked them to translate the symbols. They received many different opinions as to what the rock art meant. If it is true the meaning of the symbols changed as they diffused across the landscape and to different groups, that could explain why there are so many different interpretations today. The different interpretations could also occur over time: As time went on the meanings of certain symbols subtly changed or became more complex, just as they do in our own culture today. But by understanding the original meaning of the symbols that are known to have originated in Mexico, we at least have a starting point.

Handprints are the most common rock art element worldwide. Above are positive handprints. On the left are negative handprints.

As we entered the alcove containing the cliff dwelling, we were struck by the handprints on the wall above the dwelling. There appeared to be scores of them. Some appeared to be prints of adults, some were smaller and appeared to be of children. Some were in black and some in red. Some had designs on the palm. Some handprints were in negative images.

Of all the rock art worldwide, the handprint is the most common element. It appears on all continents (except Antarctica) and far outnumbers all other rock art. It can be a "positive" image where a person dips his or her hand in paint or liquid clay, and then applies it to the surface of the rock. Or it can be a "negative" image where the person places his hand on the surface and then spits paint or liquid clay over the surface of the rock so that when he removes his hand, a negative image of his hand remains. It can be what Polly Schaafsma calls a *patterned handprint;* that is, after the palm is covered with wet paint or clay, a pattern is carved into it, and then the wet hand is applied to the cliff. The most typical pattern we have seen is of a spiral motif in the palm area.

On the left, a patterned handprint with a spiral pattern in the palm area.

Long spidery fingers on handprints such as on the near left were created by dragging paint-wetted fingers down the rock before applying the palm. Photographer: Peg Hoffman.

227

Sometimes rock art seems to be meant to be seen from a distance, as above.

Sometimes we have seen handprints with overly long fingers where the person apparently dragged his paint-wetted fingers down the rock face for several inches before he pressed his hand down. This left a handprint with long, spidery fingers.

Ethnographers have noted that the handprint has been used in some circumstances as a signature or an identifying mark. When young girls finished replastering a kiva, they might "sign" their work with a handprint on one of the beams. In other instances, when someone had prayed and left gifts for a deity at a shrine, the person would leave a handprint so the spirit would know who had done this for them and know who to reward. And a shaman occasionally signed or signed-off with his handprint when he has completed a ceremony. So at least sometimes the handprint functioned as a signature of sorts.

Archaeologists know that modern Puebloans often mark the boundaries of their cornfields with stones that have their clan symbol marked on them. And lo and behold, when they visit the ancient sites archaeologists have found stones marking out the boundaries of cornfields or villages with clan symbols on them. So it is assumed that at least some of the time, clan symbols were used to mark boundaries.

Along this vein, sometimes we have been to cliff dwellings that have a huge clan symbol emblazoned on the cliff face in front, centered, as though it were meant to be seen and seen from afar. Our *bahana* minds interpret this to be an announcement along the lines of: "We are the scorpion clan, we live here."

Don Talayesva in his book *Sun Chief* told of a time when he went on a difficult rite of passage to the place the Hopi go to get salt, deep in the remote parts of the Grand Canyon. It is a dangerous journey and is undertaken each generation by a group of young men. When they arrived at the edge of the Grand Canyon they found a boulder with many clan symbols pecked on the surface, from other young men who had taken this journey before them. Generations of clan symbols. Don and his companions all "signed" the boulder with their own clan symbol. Archaeologists have found this boulder with all the clan signs on it and have found others in other places that appear to have had a similar function. So apparently some of the rock art was intended as a tally of some kind.

We might never know *exactly* what rock art means — particularly those of us with a Western mindset. Even the descendants of these ancient people struggle to understand precisely what these symbols mean. Our friend, Joe Pachak, an expert on rock art, suggested that if we wanted a better understanding of the meaning of rock art, we should read about the Puebloan culture. And we have found this to be true. The more we have come to know some of the symbols that are important to these people, the more we recognize in the symbols we see emblazoned on the rock walls. Just what we have presented here has increased our delight in the rock art immeasurably. We are allowed a glimpse into its meaning, and we understand it better than we did before, even if our understanding remains imperfect.

Types of Rock Art

Rock art is either painted on the rock (pictograph) or chipped or pecked into the rock (petroglyphs). Of the two types, petroglyphs are far more numerous than are pictographs. Among petroglyphs, there are is also incised petroglyphs which are cut into the rock. We see incised petroglyphs less often than the others.

This above rock art is a pictograph panel — it is painted on.

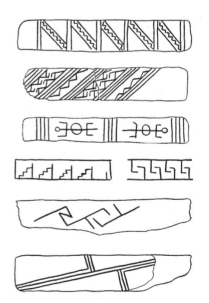

On the left are examples of incised stones. Incised designs are cut in with a sharp tool and create a linear design. These have been found mostly in buildings and on thresholds. From: Bureau of American Ethnology #65, Kidder and Guernsey. On the right, a petroglyph pecked into a cliff wall in southwestern Colorado.

Handprints

All over the world, handprints are the most common rock art element — this is what you will see most often. There are four different types of handprints.

Negative handprints.

Positive handprints.

Above is a petroglyph of handprints with elongated fingers. Photographer: Vaughn Hadenfeldt, Far Out Expeditions.

On the left is a patterned handprint. After wetting his hand with paint, the ancient person drew a design in the palm area, removing the paint there, and then pressed his hand down on the stone. The palm design here is a spiral, which is the most common palm design.

Spiral

The spiral was a Mayan symbol for the sun, but could also symbolize water. Among many Puebloan people of today it can be a migration symbol as well as a sun symbol. The Zuni people told early ethnographer Matilda Coxe Stevenson the spiral was the symbol for themselves. The spiral can scroll from the left or from the right. Among the Hopi of today, the direction of the scroll indicates a different meaning. Besides a circular spiral, it can also be a square spiral or even a triangular spiral. Or it can be concentric circles like the bull's eye design as we discussed before. The symbol for the state of New Mexico is based on the Zia Pueblo's sun sign. The various scroll types are some of the most common rock art elements you will see. The scroll was also the most popular design of the Hohokam people in the southern part of the region.

Shields

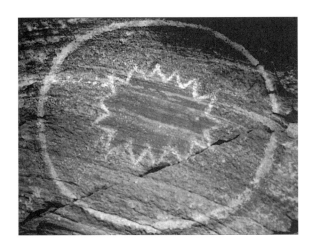

Shields are one rock art design that are usually associated with cliff dwellings and sometimes can be seen overlooking the ancient structures in the cliffs. They can be either pictographs or petroglyphs. According rock art expert Polly Schaafsma, they are typically white with colored designs on the interior.

All of these shield photographs are by Vaughn Hadenfeldt, Far Out Expeditions.

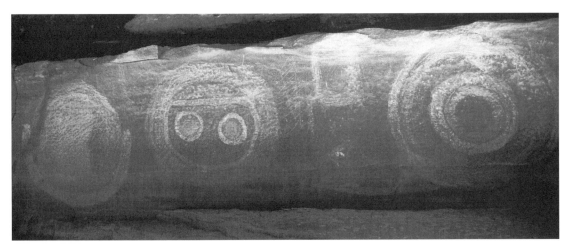

Flute Player

On the middle left a flute-player plays to plants and animals. Associated with the scene is an atlatl dart, on the far right. Therefore, this petroglyph panel probably dates to before the era of cliff dwellings. Photographer: Vaughn Hadenfeldt, Far Out Expeditions.

The flute player is one of the most common images you will see on the cliff walls in the American Southwest. Sometimes he is depicted with a humpback and/or a phallus. Today he is often called Kokopelli, however, early archaeologists like Kidder always referred to him as the flute player. According to Ekkehart Malotki in his book, *Kokopelli: The making of an Icon,* the name Kokopelli is a misnomer.

Malotki has pointed out that the flute player in the American Southwest developed north of the Hopi mesas by at least A.D. 800. The number of depictions of the flute player increase substantially by A.D. 1000. This flute-player is usually interpreted as the symbol of the flute clan.

When the Hopi today see the flute player on the cliff walls, they call him *maahu*, the cicada. This insect fills the canyons with music every August and creates the warmth that ripens their crops. They have a story about how the cicada saved snakes from a bitter cold death by bringing to them the warmth of the sun. And occasionally we will see rock art flute players associated with snakes and sun images. The cicada is the second most important insect to the Hopi, after the spider. They even eat the cicada when times are lean and the storage rooms are empty before the crops have ripened.

Flute Player

The flute player was sometimes depicted as an insect, an animal or even a shaman with a bird on his head. After A.D. 1400 the flute player was rarely the subject of rock art and he seemed to fall out of favor or go out of style. Coincidentally, this era between A.D. 1000 – 1400 roughly coincides with the cliff dwelling era we discuss in this book.

The kachina cult may have begun as early as circa A.D. 1300. One of the kachinas that evolved is called Kookopölö, Hopi for the robber fly that has a hump and is very lusty. Thus it is associated with fertility of humans and plants. Kookopölö is portrayed at dances today with a hump and a phallus, but *never* has a flute.

It may be that when early visitors to the pueblos saw the kachina Kookopölö at dances they became confused and misinterpreted him as the rock art symbol. Then by mispronouncing the name, Kokopelli was born.

So when you see the flute player image on the cliff walls, you should remind yourself that he is *not* Kookopölö the kachina. Nor is he Kokopelli. He is the flute player or maahu, the cicada.

Some of the flute players on the right are shown reclining, one has an antenna and no hump. The others have humps and no antenna. The flute player on the bottom right is in full regalia: He has a flute, hump and is shown phallic. He was discovered near a cliff dwelling, so we assume he is from the cliff dwelling era. From: Bureau of American Ethnology, #65, Kidder and Guernsey.

Stepped Elements

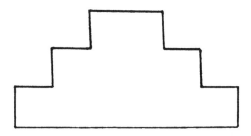

The Pueblo people of today call these stepped designs *cloud terraces*. They symbolize clouds, specifically rain clouds. The cloud terrace image is ubiqitous among the modern Puebloans as well as the ancients, you will be able to spot this symbol again and again. On the above left is a typical cloud terrace. On the right, is what we call a half-terrace. Cloud terraces can be in an outline form, or color filled. They can also be opposed or opposite each other, such as the colored and opposed half-terraces on the near right.

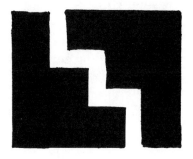

Note in this design and in the one below, that the negative space becomes an important part of the design.

Four-Pointed Star

Sometimes called a "plus-sign," the four-pointed star is thought to symbolize the morning star among the Maya. The morning star is important to the Puebloans in timing ceremonies. This star sign is outlined.

Photographer: Andrew Gulliford ©.

236

Horned and/or Feathered Serpent

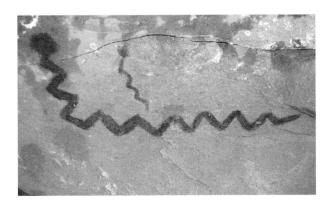

Photographer: Vaughn Hadenfeldt, Far Out Expeditions

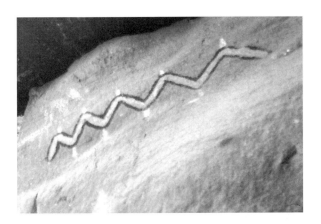

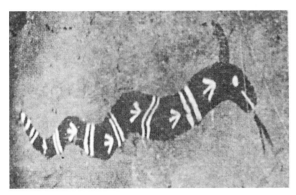

From: *American Indians: The First American Families.* A horned snake on a kiva wall.

On the right is a 19th century example of a horned snake. The square design in the coil created by his tail is a stylized representation of a shrine. From: *Bureau of American Ethnology, # 33,* Fewkes.

Snakes are another symbol that diffused north from Mexico. Mayans recognized the snake as a water symbol, and associated it with caves and springs. They called him *Quetzalcoatl.* Among Pueblo people today the snake is sometimes called Avanyu.

In the late 1880s artist Julian Scott was sent by the U.S. government census bureau to record the Pueblo people. He returned again and again was was eventually inducted into the Hopi's Antelope Society. He stated about snakes: "The 'snake deity' is the 'water god' of the *Moquis* [Hopi] . . . To the Moquis' mind lightning is the snake's tail striking the clouds and thunder the report of the blow; rain is the effect."

With the close relationship between snakes and lightning, it's no wonder that lightning rock art can be mistaken for a snake: The difference is a snake will usually have a head, but not always.

On the left center is a feathered snake. The white marks at each zig and zag are usually interpreted as feathers.

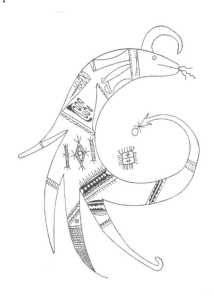

Square within a Square

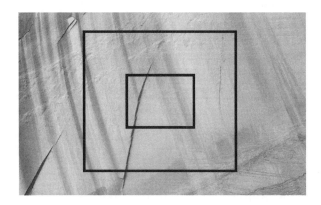

The symbol of a square within a square is often interpreted as a sipapu, the sacred place on the kiva floor where some of the Pueblo people believe they emerged from their third world into this world.

Fringed Line

These long lines with pendant lines hanging from them are often called fringed lines or rakes. It is a common element and you will encounter it often in your backcountry travels. The fringe is thought to symbolize rain.

Sandal Prints

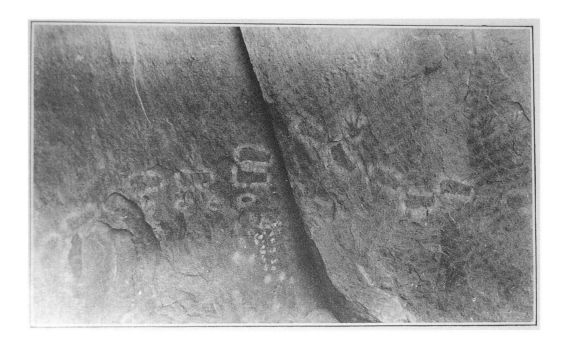

Archaeologists A.V. Kidder and Samuel Guernsey discovered the above rock art panel at the turn-of-the-last-century. They are called sandal prints and are a common rock art design that you will encounter often in your travels. A story emerged for them from the above panel: "The imaginary individual is shown by his tracks to have walked to a little projection in the vertical wall, to have jumped down from it, landing with both feet together, and then to have continued his journey." *Bureau of American Ethnology*, #65.

Above is a petroglyph version of a sandal print. This sandal print is far more common than the pictograph sandal prints above it.

Animal Tracks

In the hunt scene above, sandal prints appear to follow the hoof prints of a bighorn sheep, then they stop and then start again. Next to it, a barefoot print approaches another bighorn sheep. This rock art panel was reproduced in *Bureau of American Ethnology*, #65 by Kidder and Guernsey.

On the left is usually interpreted as a turkey track painted in red. Since turkeys were so important to the ancient Pueblo people, we find turkey tracks often. We have seen them as far north as southeast Utah and as far south as the Sierra Madres in Mexico. Sometimes they are pictographs, sometimes they are petroglyphs.

This X track is thought to represent the track of a roadrunner. The roadrunner is called the "liar" because you can't tell which direction he is traveling from his track.

Meandering Line

The wandering line under the human-like figures is often called a meander. Was it intended to imply a story here? Was it intended to show connectedness? Or is it a map? We don't know. But this, too, is a common element that you will encounter many times on your journeys. The meanders below were documented in the *Bureau of American Ethnology, #65*.

Quartered Designs

The number four is important to the Puebloans of today, and it is common to find designs that are quartered. This is true of pottery as well. Among some of the Puebloans this indicates the four cardinal directions, north, south, east and west. For some Pueblo cultures the world of today is their fourth world.

Lizard Men

Both these lizard men are from the Bureau of American Ethnology #65.

Are these elements lizards or are they men? No one can know for sure, so they are usually referred to as "lizard men." Lizard men can be seen scaling cliff faces in rock art panels all over the Greater American Southwest in large numbers. Worldwide, when a figure is portrayed upside-down, it signifies death, as in the figure on the right. The same is true if it is an animal that is portrayed upside-down.

Moons

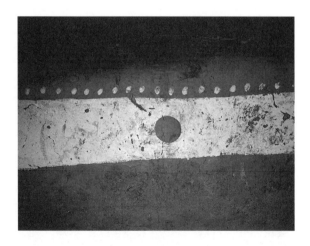

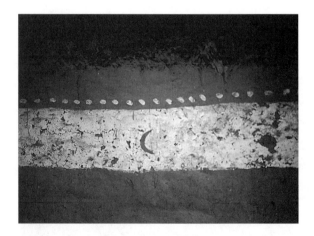

These two moons come from the same backcountry cliff dwelling. The design is a mural in an interior room. The moon sign is less common than the sun sign, but we have encountered them in our backcountry treks.

Tlaloc

Tlaloc is a rock art figure that diffused north from Mexico. The main identifying feature of Tlaloc is his huge goggle eyes. They can be round or squared and typically take up as much as half the entire figure. The lower half of the figure usually features geometric designs. There are many differing versions of Tlaloc, the giveaway is the eyes.

Rock art symbols of Tlaloc are a common sight in the desert Mogollon region of southern New Mexico. Among the Mayan the eyes are made up of two coiled snakes and he is associated with water.

Corn

The handle of this ladle has a grid pattern with a dot in each cell. This design is thought to symbolize corn. You will encounter it often not only in rock art but in pottery as well.

Bighorn Sheep

On the left is an example of a western bighorn sheep with a crescent-shaped body and huge horns. Above is a Jornada version of a bighorn sheep. The body is a rectangle filled with geometric designs.

Bighorn sheep are one of the most common rock art subjects of the ancients. Were these elusive animals difficult to hunt? Were the ancient cliff dwellers impressed by their agility on the cliffs?

Among the ruins in the western part of the region, bighorn sheep rock art will usually have a crescent-shaped body with much emphasis on the horns. These are extravagant and over-sized. The legs are stiff and straight. More often than not, the rock art is done as petroglyphs. Typically their hooves are shown in profile to look just like their hoof prints.

In southern New Mexico is the desert Jornada (hor NADA) style. This style is related to the Mimbres and the desert Mogollon. The Jornada-style bighorn sheep has a body like a box car which is decorated with a textile-like geometric design, almost as though the animal is wearing a blanket. Often they appear to be laughing. The giveaway to the Jornada style is the bent legs. The desert Jornada style is also on their pottery.

Above are different versions of western bighorns — some are depicted with long graceful necks, some have none at all. From: *Bureau of American Ethnology*, #65, Kidder and Guernsey.

Processional Figures

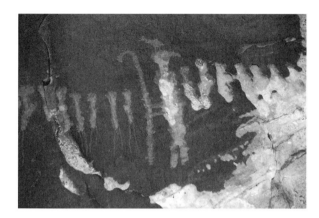

Scattered among the canyons of the Greater American Southwest are lines of people pecked into the rock walls. Are they walking or perhaps even migrating? Or are they participating in a ceremony of some kind? No one can know for sure. Even the era they represent is uncertain, since it is nearly impossible to date rock art. They may be from an earlier era than the cliff dwellings, but that's not a sure bet. Note in the center of each photograph, a figure carries a crook-necked staff, a sign of importance. Also note the figure on the left has a bird on its head, a symbol for a shaman. Photographer of both of the above pcitures: Ron Horn.

Hohokam

The giveaway to identifying Hohokam rock art is the animals typically have a bulging stomach, as though they are pregnant. As is true for the rest of the Greater American Southwest, spirals are also an common element. But sets of frets and interlocking scrolls are seen often as well.

The setting sun illuminates a few pieces from the extensive ancestral Puebloan pottery collection at the Edge of the Cedars Museum in Blanding, Utah.

11

POTTERY

An impassive cliff dwelling overlooked a perpendicular drop of hundreds of feet and tantalized us. Strung along the ledge below us were eight or so attached structures that were in pristine condition. Two buildings still sported exterior two-toned adobe plaster. They looked as though the inhabitants had left only yesterday instead of eight hundred years ago. We itched to be able to explore this site's secrets.

But how to get to it? The overhanging canyon rim we stood upon formed a perilous barrier — the ledge was a formidable 25 feet or so below us. It looked impossible. Undaunted, we set about scouting the rim looking for a way down anyway.

After awhile we came across a wide crack breaching the solid sandstone rimrock. Nature had wedged stones in the crack — like stair treads part of the way down — which put us halfway to the right level for the cliff dwelling. However, the remainder proved to be a much more difficult obstacle and we experimented for most of the morning trying to get down to the next ledge. It was during this time that we asked the question: Was *this* the way the ancient inhabitants came and went? They would have needed to get up to the mesa top to tend their fields daily, and for many other activities. Was this the way?

Just then we spotted a tiny sherd of pottery, no bigger than the nail on your pinky finger. Enchanted, we held the tiny fragment in our hands and studied it. As small as the triangle of ancient white pottery was, we could see a partial painted black line down one broken edge. It had been a black-on-white ceramic container of some sort. But even a tiny sherd such as this sometimes has a wonderful story to tell.

Today, it told us that this was indeed the route that we sought. This was the way the ancients had come and gone eight hundred years ago, although they had probably used a ladder at this difficult spot. And someone all those many years ago had faltered in this difficult place and accidentally dropped a pot here, shattering it.

A whole pot may break easily, but the pieces that remain, such as this tiny one, are nearly indestructible by nature. Potsherds can survive rain and sandblasting winds. Time is almost incapable of destroying them. As such, potsherds are a boon to archaeologists.

If an archaeologist specializing in ceramics were here today, he or she would be able to tell wonderful stories from this tiny sherd of pottery. She would be able to tell whether this pot was created here at this cliff dwelling or had come from a long way away. She would be able to tell us not only where this pot had originated, but also what era in time this pot represented. She would be able to tell us what kind of paint had been used to make the designs on it and what kind of additives had been used in the clay to make the pot stronger and less prone to breakage. Archaeologists can also tell if a bowl was used often by faint scratches on the inside of it. And they find pots that have been mended — that is, small holes drilled into either side of a break, and then yucca twine threaded through the holes and the bowl tied back together again. Sometimes they were even made watertight again by applying pine tar to the crack.

Each sherd of pottery has a story to tell, if one can only decipher it. The black and white sherds below are pictured in the 10th Annual Hayden Survey.

Dendrochronology (tree ring dating) is the most accurate way to date a site,

but ceramics are probably number two. Someone trained in ceramics can date a site to within 20 years.

In all cultures, pottery generally comes with sedentary life — at the end of the hunter/gatherer era and at the beginning of agriculture. Baskets are a far more efficient container for nomadic hunter/gatherers: They are light and easy to transport, and are not breakable like pots are. And with a coating of pine tar over it, a basket can be made watertight. Cooking was even done in them indirectly — by dropping heated stones into the water-filled basket, again and again, until the water boiled.

Above is a pottery lid or stopper for a jar. The ancients used a variety of things to cover pots, including stone slabs. From: Bureau of American Ethnology, #41, Fewkes.

But there are limitations with baskets. Although baskets can be used for cooking, cooking in them is clumsy and time-consuming. It also uses up a lot of wood to heat things indirectly in this manner. But for nomads, their portability trumped all other concerns.

Once agriculture became the dominant way of life, baskets were less essential. Their strongest point — their portability — was now less important. What farmers needed was storage — and lots of it. Storage in baskets leaves the contents vulnerable to insects, rodents and water. Pottery solved all those problems, as well as effectively storing either liquids or dried things. Pottery could also be stoppered. And it was more efficient for cooking. Now a pot could be placed directly over the open flame of the fire pit and heated — a much faster way to cook and one that consumed much less fuel. And this way of cooking was also more versatile; now stews and other long-cooking dishes were feasible.

In the Greater American Southwest the idea of pottery — and maybe even the techniques for creating it — more than likely came up from the south, from Mexico and Mesoamerica. In the American Southwest, the Hohokam people of southern Arizona began making pottery first, long before the people of the Colorado Plateau or the Mogollon people. It is thought that the farming of beans might have played a role in the development of pottery: Dried beans require hours of cooking, not feasible in a basket. Beans came to the Colorado Plateau about A.D. 500, and that is about the time that pottery began being made there. And just as the ancients had to develop new ways of farming and new types of corn up on the Colorado Plateau, they also had to develop new ways of making pottery as well.

Students of archaeology are taught as a "rule of thumb" that brown pottery is generally representative of the Hohokam and Mogollon people below the Mogollon Rim. And that gray pottery is usually representative of the Anasazi, the people of the Colorado Plateau. The Mogollon and Hohokam

THE ROLE OF OLLAS

Maidens at the well. From: 23rd Bureau of American Ethnology, Stevenson.

The large ollas in the corner of the living rooms were kept full of water, a job that fell to the maidens. A large olla typically held several gallons — some as much as seven or eight gallons. This full big olla represented trip after trip with a smaller olla, carried on a young woman's head, down the ladders to the spring and then, when heavily filled — back up the ladders on her head to the waiting corner olla. Julian Scott noted that the women carried the heavy pots one to two miles, sometimes as much as three miles. Cushing remarked that "all through the day there was an unceasing carrying of the water — the women passing and repassing through the streets on the way to and from the springs." Undoubtedly the large corner ollas were kept covered to keep the precious water from evaporating and to keep the dogs out of it and the children from playing in it.

Ethnographically this scenario has been true in modern times, but was it true a thousand years ago? Certainly archaeologists have found many sherds of large ollas as well as the smaller carrying kind of olla. Then an archaeologist noticed under a microscope a film coating the inside of an ancient large olla potsherd. He tested it and found it was salts left from standing water — ancient stored water. It appears the ancients used their ollas just as their modern descendants have.

When we see a potsherd at a backcountry ruin or in a museum setting, it always conjures up a story to us of all the human labor that went into the fetching of the water and the making of the many pots to store it. And reminds us why it was considered impolite for guests to ask for water.

people were able to use alluvial clays, that is, clay that had collected on the bottoms of canyons and waterways, and had settled there. This clay needed no supplements to make it ready for firing. Nature provided it complete and ready to go off the stream bottoms. This clay has iron in it and so is usually brown after firing, and the pots made from it are called *brownware*.

Not so on the Colorado Plateau. There was little alluvial clay up on the Colorado Plateau and the clay typically had little or no iron in it. When fired in an atmosphere with little oxygen in it, a gray pot is the result. So the pots of the people of the Colorado Plateau are generally called *grayware*.

Basically, the ancient people of the Colorado Plateau had to re-invent the making of pottery for their particular environment. The ancient people there had to discover different types of clays to use in pottery, and the clays required the addition of *temper* — a stabilizing agent like sand or ground-up rocks (or later even ground-up old pot sherds) — to provide a buffer against rapid changes in temperature. Otherwise, the clay's natural tendency to shrink and expand too rapidly during drying, firing and cooking would cause the vessel to break. If you look carefully at a broken edge of a potsherd, you can see what the ancients used as temper, and this fact can help to date a piece of pottery and locate where it was made. By the time of the cliff dwellings, pulverized pot sherds were the typical temper.

Worldwide, making pottery is usually the domain of women. So it was in the Greater American Southwest. We like to think that this is because it is a woman's tool for cooking and for storage, and that is why she would make the pottery. After all, men made their own arrowheads and other tools.

What this means is that it was more than likely women who experimented and developed the techniques for making pottery. It was they who re-invented the making of pottery on the Colorado Plateau. A great accomplishment indeed!

Once Anasazi women began making pottery, they quickly became *very* good at it. In the records of the second Spanish conquistador expedition to contact the Puebloan people in A.D. 1581, it was noted that the pottery of the Puebloan people was quite good, better than pottery of New Spain (Mexico). Even today these ancient pots of the American Southwest are considered art.

The production of pottery was staggering and amazing to consider. Each area had its own distinctive pottery, and the designs evolved over time. Pots were transported far and wide, so archaeologists often find pots that are "out of context." They call these pots that are from far away *tradeware*. Were these tradeware pots considered valuable to the inhabitants? Archaeologist Kathryn Kamp tested this question by counting the number of long-distance pots that

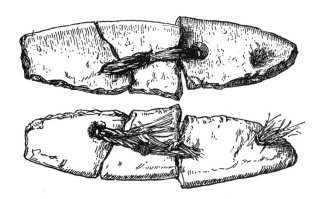

This broken pottery has been painstakingly pieced together again by drilling holes into the pieces in ancient times. The person then threaded yucca string through the holes and tied the pieces back together. With a generous application of pine tar this pot would still be usable. Archaeologist Kathryn Kamp discovered most repaired pieces were tradeware. From: Bureau of American Ethnology, #41, Fewkes.

had been painstakingly repaired, and comparing it to the number of local pots that had been repaired. She found the percentage of tradeware pots that had been mended was much greater than the number of repaired local pots. She concluded that the tradeware pottery must have been considered valuable to the ancient inhabitants for them to go to the trouble of mending them.

When we first began exploring the Southwest 40 years ago, whole areas in the backcountry seemed to be paved in potsherds. You literally had to watch your step not to tread on them. Not so anymore. It is becoming more and more unusual to see potsherds today, yet another reason to leave what you find exactly where it is. We left the tiny black-on-white potsherd we found that day exactly where we found it, so it could continue to tell its story to future explorers.

The Making of Pottery

In the1880s, early ethnographers James and Matilda Stevenson studied the Zuni people and their customs. On one unforgettable day, they accompanied a Zuni woman, We'wha, to collect clay for making pots:

> [We'wha] visited the shrine at the base of the mother rock and tearing off a bit of her blanket deposited it in one of the tiny pits in the rock as an offering to the mother rock. When she drew near to the clay bed she indicated to Mr[.] Stevenson that he must remain behind, as men never approached the spot. Proceeding a short distance the party reached a point where We'wha requested the writer to remain perfectly quiet and not talk, saying: "Should we talk, my pottery would crack in the baking, and unless I pray constantly the clay will not appear to me." She applied the hoe vigorously to the hard soil, all the while murmuring prayers to Mother Earth. Nine-tenths of the clay was rejected, every lump being tested between the fingers as to its texture. After gathering about 150 pounds in a blanket, which she carried on her back, with the ends of the blanket tied around her

forehead, We'wha descended the steep mesa, apparently unconscious of the weight."

The collection of the clay was only the first step in a lengthy procedure to create a pot. Pottery making was "expensive," that is, it required much time, much labor and a lot of fuel to make it. And yet, vast quantities were produced.

After the clay was collected, it had to be ground up on grinding stones until it was the consistency of powder. Any impurities discovered in this process would be carefully removed or the pot might crack or break during firing. Added to the clay powder would be some kind of temper; it could be sand or ground-up rock. We'wha used old potsherds that were pulverized into the same consistency as the clay. Matilda Stevenson noted that potsherds had been "carefully hoarded for this purpose."

Then water was added to this until it held together in a ball that was elastic and malleable. Kneading it like bread dough women forced out all the air pockets — again, so it would not break or crack during firing.

The ancients never "threw" clay or used anything like a wheel for pottery making. They used the coil method. The clay ball was formed into a long "rope" shape, and a length of this clay rope was wrapped around a base until the general shape of the vessel was achieved. Then using their index and

Left, making pottery circa 1883. From: Cushing, The Century Magazine.

Now famous Tewa potter Nampeyo creates pottery in her second-story-terrace courtyard circa 1920. Her niece, also a potter, stated: "I often dream about designs and sometimes I remember them, and then I always use them . . . I always use different designs." (Bunzel)

From: *American Indians: First Families of the Southwest.*

middle finger they pinched the new coil to the one beneath it in order to anchor them together. Then, using a scraper tool like a potsherd or dried piece of gourd, the coils were smoothed out until they were obliterated and the sides of the pot appeared smooth. The Hohokam used a "paddle and anvil" instead of a scraper to smooth the sides of the pot. The anvil was a smooth piece of stone like a river rock, and the paddle was a flat piece of wood.

Lastly, the rim was finished. The different ways the rim could be done were also cultural markers. If there were to be handles on the piece, this is when they would be attached.

Then the unfinished pot would be set aside to dry out thoroughly. In order to achieve a crisp white background on decorated pots instead of the natural gray or brown, the bowl was first covered with *slip*. Slip is a thin emulsion of liquid clay; in the case of white slip, it was an emulsion of white kaolin clay. This was wiped or painted on the bowl.

Only when it was completely dry could the pottery maker begin to paint a design on the vessel with yucca brushes. The designs they painted were from their own thoughts and dreams, according to Pueblo potters quoted in *The Pueblo Potter: A Study of Creative Imagination in Primitive Art* by Ruth Bunzel.

The paint used was either organic — that is, made from a plant like Rocky Mountain bee weed — or mineral, which was pulverized iron or manganese. If you look closely at an ancient potsherd today, you can still discern which type of paint was used. The organic paint was absorbed into the clay of the pot and left the design slightly fuzzy, not unlike the Flow-Blue china you see sometimes in antique stores today. Mineral paint, however, was not absorbed into the clay and left a clean, hard edge that can be seen yet today, and indeed, its raised edge can sometimes even be felt by rubbing your fingers ever so gently down the decorated face of the pot.

Paint made from Rocky Mountain bee weed looks brown when first painted on but turns black when fired. Sometimes there are errors in firing and the designs on the pots retain their brown color.

Firing a pot in 1883. A blanket is being used to block the wind to prevent flare-ups — calm air is the ideal. Cushing, The Century Magazine.

Finally, the piece would be fired. Effectively firing pottery required years of experience. Sometimes you can see black smudges or clouds on a piece of ancient pottery. These are caused from problems in the firing of the piece and are called *misfires*. Other problems arose in the firing as well. If there was too much oxygen in the firing process, it could cause mineral paint to be brownish in color. Or if it was too hot, it could burn the organic paint designs off the pot.

Corrugated pottery was usually used for cooking and occasionally storage. From: 10th Annual Hayden Survey.

About A.D. 900, a century and a half before some of the Anasazi moved into the cliff dwellings, they developed a new kind of pottery called *corrugated* by archaeologists today. These pots left the coils of clay unobliterated — that is, they did not smooth out the sides of the pot. These pots were used exclusively for cooking and perhaps some storage. The corrugated pots were superb cooking ware in that the corrugation created greater surface area and were able to heat faster and with better heat distribution. The corrugation may have also been easier to handle. Only the Anasazi and the Mogollon made corrugated ware; the Hohokam did not. Today corrugated potsherds are often found still coated with soot from the ancient fires. At cliff dwelling sites that have any potsherds, most sherds will be corrugated.

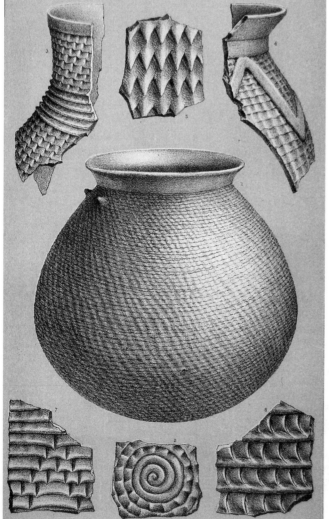

To our modern eyes, the area outlined in stones looked like a slightly oversized grave. The lines of stones were perhaps seven or eight feet long and about three to three and a half feet wide. Although it looked like a grave to us, this was not the way the ancients buried their dead. And the placement was all wrong; it was situated at a slight cant, toward a small drainage. We studied it, frankly curious. There was a cliff dwelling nearby on the opposite edge of the bluff. But what were they doing here? We wondered about this spot for quite awhile. Clearly it was man-made, but

what was it? We learned from Norman Oppelt's book, *Earth, Water, Fire,* that what we saw that day was probably an ancient kiln for firing pottery. This was not an enclosed kiln as is used today; instead it would have been open.

Firing a pot required a lot of fuel, so much so that it was easier to carry the unfired pottery to where the trees were than to carry the firewood to the pottery-making station. Anasazi potters preferred juniper wood for firing pottery because it wasn't as smoky as other fires. But sometimes even corncobs were used. Later on in their migrations, the ancient people discovered coal in Arizona on what we refer to today as the Hopi Mesas. They used coal for cooking and heating, but also for firing pottery. Coal-fired pottery is different from wood-fired pottery. The coal-fired pottery almost has the appearance of porcelain, and the background color is more of a yellow than white.

To make a firing kiln, ancient women would have excavated a shallow depression in the sandy soil. Sometimes these are long and narrow, almost like a trench, and sometimes they tend towards round or rectangular in shape. It would be dug at a slight slant to allow the smoke to escape. After pre-firing the pit, stones would have been placed to line the bottom of the depression. Then around the sides were placed unmortared vertical sandstone slabs that tipped outward. These vertical sandstone slabs are the stones we saw that day and are the giveaway to an ancient kiln. The pottery would have been arranged on the bed of stones and firewood placed on top.

Most pots did not have a flat bottom as we would expect today. They had rounded bottoms, and in order for them to sit on a floor or on a shelf, they had to rest on a woven yucca ring, or pot rest. When they were carried on a woman's head, they also needed one of these yucca pot rests.

Whenever we are lucky enough to spot a sherd of ancient pottery like the tiny one we saw that day at the cliff dwelling, we are awed by the

An ancient rectangular kiln in southeast Utah, we have seen round and oval kilns as well. The stones surrounding it slant outward.

257

Ancient yucca pot rests discovered by early archaeologist Earl Morris. 33rd Bureau of American Ethnology, 1911.

story of creation that even a tiny sherd has to tell an observant person, all the prayers and efforts that went into its manufacture: The discovery of the clay deposit. The hauling of heavy loads of clay back to the dwelling. Grinding the clay on metates. Creating the pots and other containers. Collecting the paint materials, then making the paint and making the yucca brushes. Painting the pottery with intricate and exquisite designs. Toting the unfinished pots to where there were trees. Digging a firing trench. Then hauling the pots back to the potter's home. And finally, on occasion someone carrying the delicate (and heavy) end products to faraway places — sometimes hundreds of miles away.

But we are most intrigued by what these potters may have been expressing on the pottery. As we scrutinize a potsherd closely, are we witnessing their ancient thoughts and dreams as modern Puebloan potters tell us? And for a brief moment in time we can almost connect with them across the abyss of time.

Typical Household Pottery Array

In the midst of the Technicolor world of the desert Southwest, most of the ancient people chose to create black and white pottery until about A.D.1300. Identifying pottery is a job for experts and can take many years of study to master and so is beyond the scope of this book. Following we present an *introduction* to the subject with a few basic principles that hopefully will enhance your appreciation of the ancient pottery. And as a starting point for your studies if you should decide you want to know more. Just mastering this small amount of information has greatly enhanced our visits to museums.

Ancient Puebloans made a wide variety of pottery for household use. Above are just a few examples of what a typical household might have on hand at any given time. From: *10th Annual Hayden Survey.*

Pottery Function

The above two examples are from the 4th *Bureau of American Ethnology*, Holmes.

Cooking Vessels

The most common potsherds found at a site are those for cooking. During the time of cliff dwellings this was done in corrugated ware. These pots were unpainted. Sometimes corrugated pots and sherds still have ancient soot on them. If there are potsherds at an ancient dwelling, most of what you will see will be corrugated ware.

Corrugated ware was made in a wide variety of sizes ranging from small to enormous.

There are different types of corrugations, most were plain such as the one above left. But sometimes the corrugations were interplayed for a sort of decoration, such as the pot on the upper right. Some have small handles or lugs on their shoulders, possibly for ease of moving them, as in the top left example. On the right, a bird claw decorates a sherd from a corrugated jar.

Bureau of American Ethnology #51, Fewkes.

Some corrugated pottery may have seen duty as storage in storage rooms and granaries.

Pottery Function

A black-on-white olla, the base of this olla is concave. 33rd *Bureau of American Ethnology*, Fewkes.

A canteen with the ancient yucca cord still attached. Early archaeologists discovered this canteen at Spruce Tree House in Mesa Verde National Park. From: *Bureau of American Ethnology*, #41, Fewkes.

Water Vessels

Ollas are water jugs and they come in all sizes. Some were large enough to hold six or eight gallons and were probably intended for temporary storage of water. These ollas would have a large mouth, suitable for scooping out the water. Other ollas were smaller and held perhaps a few quarts and were apparently intended to carry water to and from the well or spring. These would have a constricted mouth so the water would not slosh out as it was being carried, to aid in decanting the water and so they could be stoppered. Water vessels are usually highly decorated in design elements related to water.

Canteens were also water containers, but small. They might have held a quart or two of water. They had a very small neck and also handles or lugs on them for holding yucca string for carrying it. A corncob was used to stopper it.

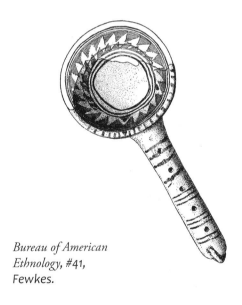

Bureau of American Ethnology, #41, Fewkes.

Ladles were used as scoops for water and for food. They were made in a number of different sizes and are usually highly decorated. They always had a handle on them. Sometimes today you can still see a beveled edge on the side of the cup where it was dragged along a rough surface to scoop up water or food.

261

Pottery Function

Serving bowls could be small for indiviuals, or large for serving groups. *Bureau of American Ethnology, #51, Fewkes.*

Ancient mugs are usually highly decorated., included the handles. *Bureau of American Ethnology, #51, Fewkes.*

Serving Vessels

Serving bowls are usually highly decorated. How large the bowls are may be a window into how many people were fed at this location. Serving bowls sometimes show wear from use in that scratches can be seen on the bottom of the inside. The Mimbres people of southern New Mexico often buried corpses with a serving bowl inverted over their face. They punched a hole in the bowl, called a *kill hole*, so the bowl could accompany the person to the other world. Some modern Puebloan people relate that the hole allows the bowl's spirit the ability to come and go.

Ancient mugs are about the size as coffee mugs today. They are usually associated with Mesa Verde and are rarely seen elsewhere in the American Southwest. They are highly decorated, including the handles.

This interesting pitcher has an example of an effigy handle — the handle depicts an animal. From: *Bureau of American Ethnology, #111, Roberts.*

Pitchers have a smaller neck than body and are usually decorated. They generally have a handle.

Pottery Function

These corrugated pots had been covered with thin slabs of sandstone. From: *Bureau of American Ethnology #65, Kidder and Guernsey.*

Above is a highly decorated seed pot. It would have held seeds for the next planting season. From: *Bureau of American Ethnology #111, Roberts.*

From: *Bureau of American Ethnology, #65, Kidder and Guernsey.*

Storage

Early archaeologists sometimes found large pots similar to ollas in storage rooms still closed with a thin sandstone slab that was sealed with mud, see above. Inside there was still corn after all this time, so large pots such as those above served their job as storage well.

Seed jars stored the precious seed corn for the next crop. Seed jars are ovoid in shape — that is, the width was greater than the height. These pots rarely had a rim around the small opening. Seed jars are usually highly decorated.

The seed pot on the bottom left was red, and was "half full of squash seeds and kernels of corn, most perfectly preserved and appearing as fresh as if harvested within the year," wrote archaelologist A.V. Kidder in 1919. He added: "The little red jar had clearly been overlooked at the time of the abandonment."

263

Design Elements

You will recognize some of the symbols on pottery are also portrayed in rock art. And as with rock art, pottery symbols are not standardized in the Puebloan world. Symbols that mean one thing to one person or group may have an entirely different meaning in to another, which can be difficult for those of us born and educated in the Western World to accept. But following are a few reoccurring symbols that are more accepted than others and that you are most likely to see.

10th Annual Hayden Survey.

Framing Lines

Lines that completely encircle the pottery vessel and do not have a break or gap in them are often called *framing lines*. Examples of this are above and on the right — the area just below the rim is outlined by a series of lines. All the lines are closed with no gaps in them. Framing lines can be wide or narrow or a combination of both. The lines can also have pendants like barbs hanging from them.

In the top example, the whole bowl has been extrapolated from a large sherd, on the right-hand side of the bowl. If you see any pottery at all at a site, it will likely be sherds, so we will show you sherds as often as possible in this discussion on pottery design elements.

From: *Bureau of American Ethnology*, Bulletin #41, Fewkes.

264

Design Elements

Life Lines

A life line is different from a framing line in that it has a break or gap in it, as in the magnificent nineteenth-century example above. The wide central line as well as the outermost encircling line both have gaps in them and are incomplete. The wide central life line is encircled by three thin framing lines, which are complete. For another example of a life line, see the Knife Wing pot on page 200. J. W. Fewkes called the bowl pictured here a butterfly design. From: *33rd Bureau of American Ethnology*.

Modern Puebloan potters told ethnographer Elsie Parsons the life line symbolizes the end of the pot's life. She was told by them: "The Zuni potter who closes the circle or 'road' around her pot feels that her own life road will end, and she will die."

Design Elements

Bureau of American Ethnology, #65, Kidder and Guernsey.

Bureau of American Ethnology #41, Fewkes.

Hatchures

Thin parallel lines called hatchures like those on the left are also a common element found on pottery. Above is an example of a hatchured design.

Hatchure designs were popular during the Chaco phase, shortly before the cliff dwelling era. Below is a typical Chaco type of design. Later, hatchures were adopted into other pottery designs.

Hatchuring can also be crossed with another set of hatchuring — called cross-hatching, like in the center of the diamond design above. *Bureau of American Ethnology, #41, Fewkes.*

Design Elements

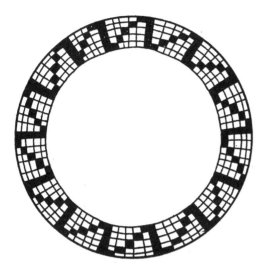

Bureau of American Ethnology, #111, Roberts.

Bureau of American Ethnology, #111, Roberts.

Checkerboards

Checkerboards were another popular design element hundreds of years ago in the American Southwest. On the above right note that there are dots in some of the grids on the left side of the bowl.

On the right are examples of squares and diamonds with dots in the centers. Checkerboards or squares with dots in them are thought to represent corn.

Bureau of American Ethnology, #65, Kidder and Guernsey.

Design Elements

Cloud Terraces

Just as with rock art, stepped or stairstep elements are a common pottery design. It is thought they represent clouds, and hence the name, cloud terraces. This design is thought to have originated in ancient Basketmaker times when the people of that age couldn't make their design elements rounded. Many designs probably originated on baskets first.

The cloud terrace design appears in pottery way to the south in Mexico as well as far to the north in the Mesa Verde province.

Cloud Terraces can be whole or halved, and are often interplayed with other elements. They can be opposed, with the negative space between the two elements creating yet another element of its own.

The three potsherds above each show examples of half-terraces that are opposed to each other. The negative space between them forms a separate element: a white zigzag line. From: 10th Annual *Hayden Survey.*

Design Elements

Dots

Dots are thought to symbolize rain. They can be freestanding, such as those above. Or they can be attached to a line, like those on the below left. From: All these pictures are from: *Bureau of American Ethnology #111*, Roberts.

The bowl below has dots on the bottom. Could they symbolize rain? Or do they refer to something else? The sides are adorned with four panels of checkerboards.

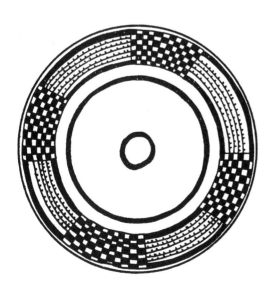

Design Elements

Spirals

Scrolls or spirals were a popular design element on pottery in ancient times, just as it was a most common rock art symbol. The scroll can be a sun symbol, or it can also be the symbol for the Pueblo people themselves.

The spirals can be squared, as in the one above. Or they can be rounded, which is most commonly seen. The two pots below show triangular spirals.

The above bowl and the one on the lower right are both from: *Bureau of American Ethnology*, #111, Roberts.

From: *Bureau of American Ethnology* #65, Kidder and Guernsey.

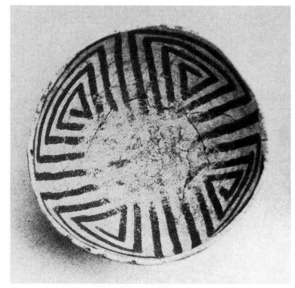

Note all the wear on the bottom of this pot. Roberts

270

Design Elements

Friendship Design

One of the most common elements you will encounter on ancient Southwestern pottery is interlocking scrolls, or the friendship design. The friendship scrolls can be a central theme to the pot, or they can be secondary and in the background. But we are surprised how often the friendship design is present.

Below is a bowl interior where the friendship design is the central element and covers the entire interior.

Above left, from *Bureau of American Ethnology #65, Kidder and Guernsey.*
Above and Below right, from: *10th Annual Hayden Survey.*
Below left from: *Bureau of American Ethnology, #65, Kidder and Guernsey.*

The negative space is often an important element in the friendship design.

Banded Designs

During the early years of cliff dwellings, especially in the northern reaches of the territory, it was popular to create what is now called "banded" designs. This is where the potter drew a wide band around the pot and decorated inside the lines . The rest of the pot was left relatively undecorated. Besides bowls, ladles also often had banded designs. On the left is from: *Bureau of American Ethnology, #111,* Roberts.

Below is an example of a banded design from the Mesa Verde area. Note the dots around the rim. This pot is typical of a classic Mesa Verde style pot: black-on-white banded design with dots around the rim. From: 33rd *Bureau of American Ethnology,* Morris.

Polychromes

The word polychrome means "many colors" and that is how pottery changed with the Great Migration. Instead of black-on-white pottery, the ancient people began making pottery that had at least three different colors. The two ancient pots above are from Carl Lumholtz' book *Unknown Mexico*. The pot on the above left has half cloud terraces opposed with friendship designs. Both pots are black and red on a yellow/buff background.

The polychrome bowl on the right has a buff-colored background with a reddish-brown design, that is outlined in black. Note the scratch marks on the bottom of the interior of the bowl — it was used many times. When the Hopi began using coal to fire their pottery, white became a more yellow color. This pot was photographed at the Edge of the Cedars Museum in Blanding, Utah. It sits on an ancient yucca pot rest.

In the pot above you can see a horned (and maybe feathered) snake, or Quetzalcoatl. In his body are corn designs interspersed with checkerboards. A bird is above him. Beneath the snake on the right is a cloud terrace. There are also framing lines above and below. Both of the above pots are from Casas Grandes or Paquimé.

*Ancient grinding tools rest outside the doorway of a cliff dwelling.
These tools were considered "expensive" because they required much
time and effort to make, yet they were left behind when the residents
moved on.*

12

STONE TOOLS

We inched our way up the base of the mesa. Just as our noses cleared the mesa edge, there in a sandy pocket sat a round stone about the size of a soft ball. It rested in a spot that had probably cradled it for a thousand years, near the edge of the mesa. The reddish-brown stone was shiny, like jasper, and the surface was roughly faceted.

What we were looking at might have been what is called a *core* by archaeologists. This is the raw material for chipped stone tools like arrowheads. Since each man made his own tools, any ancient Puebloan man worth his salt would have carried one of these with him most of the time. With a core at hand, he had the ability to create any tool he needed at the drop of a hat. Need more arrows? With a single blow, you could chip off a chunk of rock and quickly shape it into an arrowhead. Need a knife? Just a single blow could knock off a chip the size of a potato chip with a razor sharp edge. This tool was extremely versatile and could be used for any number of chores: as a scraper, peeler of sticks, or a knife. In fact, if you were to look in your modern toolbox, most of the tools that you rely on there could be fashioned by a competent *flintknapper* — a person who makes stone tools — from a stone core such as the one we saw that day. The difference between the ancient tools and modern ones is the ancient tools were made of stone, were hand-powered and they were made from scratch. In other words, that stone core took the place of a hardware store for the ancient peoples.

Chipped stone tools begin to appear in the archaeological record about 100,000 to 200,000 years ago. Somewhere back in time our human ancestors discovered that certain types of rock fractured in predictable ways. They also

Above is the probable core we discovered that day. It appears to have been used up and then discarded. The facets are eroded, but still visible.

found that some stone made better tools than others. If this stone was chipped in special ways, it could result in high quality tools. Stone tools have been used all over the world. Through the eons humans became masters at creating stone tools — Folsom points and Clovis points come to mind, for example. These projectile points are considered works of art even today. And it's only been recently that modern-day flintknappers have been able to reproduce these exquisite points.

Just because tools are made of metal today doesn't mean that stone tools were necessarily inferior. Some stone tools can be quite good. Some Russian surgeons actually preferred obsidian scalpels even recently because they found them to be sharper than their stainless steel counterparts. Indeed, the shiny, black stone known as obsidian is considered the very best stone for tools; the sharp edge of obsidian can be an impressive one molecule thick.

In the days of hunter-gatherers in this hemisphere, the best stone was sought out and traded across great distances. Arrowheads have been found in Washington state that were made of stone from an ancient quarry in Texas. In ancient times these tools were kept in a safe place. They were treated with respect and were sharpened and reused again and again. Archaeologists refer to this as being *curated*. In short, they were treated as though they were valuable.

But by the time of the emerging Puebloans, people were moving away from a hunter-gatherer lifestyle and becoming farmers. Exquisite stone tools were no longer a necessity for survival. The tools and what they were made of changed.

If you were an ancestral Puebloan farmer in need of some new tools, you probably already had a favorite spot to get the stone. It would be near your farmstead, on your way to or from your regular chores. So, sandwiched between your other duties, you would make a stop at this informal quarry site.

Old tools were frequently reused. Above are two fragments of a trough metate reused in wall construction. Other tools were reused as well. Arrowheads were reworked into drills. Large arrowheads or dartpoints were remade into smaller arrowheads.

This quarry site would consist of an outcropping of a stone such as flint, chert, chalcedony, jasper, agate or even petrified wood. Quartzite was one of the most popular choices for stone tools, not because it was superior, but because it was the most available. Obsidian and flint were considered the finest stone for tools because when struck they chipped off into large, round flakes with a ripple in them that tapered to a feathered edge. Superior stone such as this is easy to work and makes exquisite tools.

Finding the best stone does not appear to have been a major concern for ancient Puebloan flintknappers, even though it was available in various parts of the Southwest. Instead, you would choose the nearest site, even if the stone were not of the highest quality.

At the site, you might collect some of the rocks scattered around the informal quarry site. Or you'd use your handheld hammerstone or a hafted stone maul to knock off a promising chunk or two of the outcrop. You might whack this detached piece a few times to give it a more ball shape, mostly to lessen the weight. This core was the raw material you needed to make new tools, and you would take it back to your home.

Later, perhaps in the courtyard in front of your cliff home or in the cool shade of your *ramada* during the evening or time between your other duties, you might fetch this core and make a tool from it. For this more delicate work, you might use an intermediate tool, like a piece of wood or antler, between the core and the hammerstone. Tapping on this intermediate tool, you'd flesh out a blank for a tool. Say it was to be an arrowhead. After tapping on this intermediate tool, you'd end up with a piece of stone that had the basic look of an arrowhead. Then you'd use the antler or piece of wood directly on the roughly shaped arrowhead, and carefully chip off more of the stone in finer and finer pieces until it was a perfect, finely proportioned arrowhead.

Being an expert at this, you could knock out an arrowhead in just a few minutes. Some tools, such as a scraper/knife that was merely a flake of rock, might only take a single blow on the core to produce a suitable, usable flake of stone. Elegant tools like a Clovis point might have taken the ancient hunter/gatherer 150 blows to create.

By the time of the cliff dwellings, the days were gone when a person would spend a great deal of time traveling to obtain the finest stone for tools. No more did he spend time creating an elegant tool and then even more time sharpening it as it dulled. Instead, he now produced perfectly serviceable tools from lesser quality stone with just a whack or two. Granted it wasn't necessarily a *pretty* tool. And if this stone wasn't the best quality, its source was generally nearby and required less effort to procure it. However, they still traded for the good stuff on occasion. After using the tool once or twice he simply discarded it. We see these discards often in the backcountry of the American Southwest today.

It is something we can identify with today: *disposables*. With disposable tools one doesn't have to worry about *losing* a valuable tool, hesitate lending it to a neighbor or deal with the kids running off with an expensive, hard to replace item. Nor does he have to spend time repairing an expensive tool or sharpening it. After using it once or twice he just tossed it aside and quickly fashioned a new one. Although early Puebloans were capable of producing a more elegant and "expensive" tool, they had discovered the convenience of disposable items — like people of today choosing to use a Kleenex tissue instead of an embroidered, lace-edged, fine linen handkerchief.

Not all tools were projectile points or knives, of course. What tools might an ancient Puebloan conceivably have in his hypothetical toolbox? We were surprised how many tools were made from stone. In fact, the variety of different tools used then approaches what a typical homeowner might have today, only these were of stone and were hand-powered. Of course there were the knives and scrapers mentioned above. But he would also have drills and hammerstones, some without handles, some with handles. Axes were an important tool that an Anasazi household could not be without. There were also adzes for dressing wood and stone anvils as a base for their work, stone awls for punching holes and saws with serrated edges.

AN ANCIENT TOOLBOX

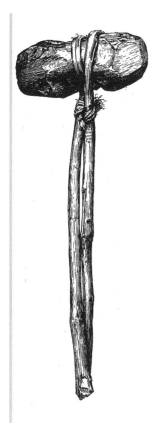

From: *Bureau of American Ethnology #41, Fewkes.*

From: 10th *Annual Hayden Survey.*

An axe was an important tool to the ancients. They can be large or small as in the illustration, left, from *Bureau of American Ethnology, #41, Fewkes.* Axeheads are sharp on one end and blunt on the other. On the right are wooden beams protruding from a wall. If you look closely you can see they look rough and tapered, to our eyes almost as though they had been chewed off by a beaver. When an axe dulled, it might be reworked into a hammerstone.

On the left is a drill. It was reworked from an old arrowhead, leaving the "ears" projecting from the sides. The "ears" were used to lash the base of the drill to a stick. Then the stick was twirled back and forth in the hands, achieving the same motion as a modern electric drill.

Above is a hammerstone. It was handheld. A hammerstone can be recognized by percussion marks on one or both ends. On this one the end is broken.

On the left is an arrow-shaft straightener. The shaft of the arrow was rubbed against this grooved stone to make it smooth and more aerodynamic. *Bureau of American Ethnology #111, Roberts.*

The two arrowheads on the left are corner notched, that is, the notches used to tie the arrowhead to the shaft are on the corners of the point. The two arrowheads in the center are called side notched, because the notches are on the sides of the point. On the far right is a basal notched arrowhead because the base of the point is used to attach the point to the shaft. From: Bureau of American Ethnology, #65, Kidder and Guernsey.

Flaked Stone Tools

There are two types of stone tools – those that are shaped by chipping and those that are shaped by grinding them away. Chipped tools include arrowheads, scrapers and knives, and drills and adzes.

Archaeologists call arrowheads "points" because it is often hard to tell what the chipped stone originally was or was attached to, if anything. It might well have been an arrowhead, or it could have been a spear-thrower (atlatl) point. What appears to be a point today might actually have been broken from a knife or some other tool.

The largest points are typically the oldest and thought to be atlatl dart points. Most of the time the stone point was attached to a shaft by the notches on the point; this notching was usually on the corners or the sides of the point. A few others were notchless and were hafted with pitch and not tied.

Arrowheads tended to became smaller over time. At one site archaeologists discovered a fascinating bundle of tiny arrow points that were each about one centimeter in length, almost like finding miniatures or toys. Collectors call these small points "bird points," but they probably weren't used for birds. In the right hands these small arrow points were as deadly as bullets are today. Not all the points were the small bird points, however; one of them was what collectors call the Pueblo Point. These large showy points were late in ancient Puebloan times.

It is something else we can identify with today: Smaller technology becoming the most sophisticated — such as today's computers, radios and such that become smaller and more powerful over time. Archaeologists have wondered about the significance of arrowheads becoming smaller during that era.

One theory is that game also became smaller over time, that the larger prey had vacated the area. Other archaeologists suggest that the smaller arrowheads were lighter and more aerodynamic than the older, larger arrowheads and atlatl dart points. In fact, the smaller arrowheads have been shown to have greater range than the larger points. These smaller points took less stone to make, and could even be created from a flake from some old discarded stone tool.

As time progressed, the amount of debris left from having made a new tool became less and less. In other words, there were fewer leftover chips lying around after making a new tool. They made fewer "formal" tools like knives and would use a sharp flake instead.

Today modern Puebloans greatly admire the old stone tools of their ancestors: It is thought they contain special magic. So a modern Puebloan man might want to fashion a special tool out of an ancient tool or flake that he happens to find.

Ground Stone Tools

We were exhausted. Having pushed our limits climbing a cliff to enter a dwelling, we now paid the price of hurrying before the sun set to avoid having to walk and find our way to the vehicle in the dark. As we wearily topped a low hill we practically tripped over a *mano* and *metate* (meh-TAH-tee) just sitting there on the sand. Manos and metates are simple grinding stones for processing corn into meal. A ray of the setting sun illuminated them through the piñon and juniper trees, and instantly we were revived.

A trough metate similar to the one we saw that day. This one is on display at Aztec National Monument in New Mexico.

Finding these household tools in such an unusual place told us a story: that there had once been a home here in this wild, windswept place and that nearby would have been farmlands. The home was gone now; all that remained were the mano and metate that had been kept swept clean of sand by the winds. Although we had to hurry on that day, the sense of place and time conveyed by those simple grinding tools have remained with us ever since.

Mano is Spanish for "hand." The *metate* is the heavy base stone, and the word is a corruption of an Aztec word. The metate we saw that day was what is called a "trough" type of metate. This type of metate was very good at grinding corn and not much else.

The mano, the hand tool, is typically hard sandstone — about the size of a blackboard eraser.

A basin metate is on a boulder with abrading marks to the right. Basin metates are round because the material being worked was moved in a circular fashion. During cliff dwelling times basin metates were used to grind up paint and wild seeds.

The earliest manos were small, one-handed units. As time passed the manos became larger and heavier two-handed units. A typical sandstone mano could be found in nature and did not require much if any shaping. Unless the mano is in context with a metate, it can be difficult to spot in the field today. The underside on the mano stone is typically much smoother than the upper side from the constant friction.

The metate, the base stone of the grinding stones, had to be created from a raw piece of sandstone. It took a great deal of effort to make a metate, and they were used and used and not discarded casually like other stone tools. Archaeologists have found a few metates so exhausted they were paper-thin to the point they had holes worn in them. A good metate might last many years; sometimes they were handed down from mother to daughter.

There are three types of metates. The earliest metate was basin shaped and is often found on a boulder or other rock feature. This round indentation was used primarily for wild seeds and nuts. Basically, it was a mortar and pestle arrangement that was state of the art during the times the ancient ones were still reliant on hunting and gathering. The basin metate was a good all-round tool: It did a reasonable job of crushing, mashing and grinding a variety of seeds and other materials. These can sometimes be seen at later sites, but they were probably

A trough metate had a deep groove worn in the middle. The mano was used in a back and forth fashion, instead of in a circular motion like the basin metate. From: #33rd Bureau of American Ethnology, Morris.

Above is a line of slab metates on display at Mesa Verde National Park. By the cliff dwelling era slab metates were the most popular type of metate, although we have come across a few trough metates at cliff dwellings.

used for the wild grasses and seeds that supplemented the ancients' harvested foods or for preparing dyes for pottery and such.

As time progressed and the ancient people became more reliant on farming, the manos and metates became larger and heavier. Now the manos were large, two-handed affairs, heavier than before. Metates were larger, too, with more surface area for grinding and a trough carved through the middle of the stone, open at one end. These grinding tools are the most efficient for grinding corn and reflect the growing importance of harvested food in their diet. Now the sheer weight of the mano and metate could do much of the grinding work. Good examples of this type of mano and metate can be seen at the Aztec Ruins National Monument near Farmington, New Mexico. The trough metates did a great job of grinding corn but were not so good at grinding wild seeds and other materials, like the basin metate was.

By the time of the cliff dwellings, slab metates had mostly replaced trough types. Slab metates consisted of a flat slab of sandstone perhaps a foot and a half in length, which was used with a mano. These are harder to recognize than the other types — in fact we might have missed spotting many of them. Those we have seen in the past have had the mano present with them.

If you were an ancient Puebloan in need of a trough metate, you would first search for a likely bedrock outcropping and break off a large piece of rock from it. Then right there at the quarry site, you would peck it into its basic shape and size and remove the excess weight. Now it was ready to carry home where you would continue to shape it by chipping away smaller and smaller flakes. Finally you would smooth it. A new trough metate represented a large investment of time and energy to make. Therefore, it would have been considered "expensive" and would have been used to the point of exhaustion.

Old metates were often reused. Sometimes we see them broken in several pieces and the pieces reused as building materials.

It was a simple cliff dwelling, only a few rooms, probably the home for a single extended family. In front of the rooms, around the courtyard, were dozens of smooth grooves ground into the sandstone cliff face. Some of the

Abrading marks on a sandstone boulder at a cliff dwelling site. We see these marks at most cliff dwellings we visit.

grooves were as big around as a pencil; others were wide, about as wide as a man's hand, and at least an inch or two deep. As we mentioned earlier, these are abrading marks — the wide, hand-sized marks probably sharpened axes. Here they also ground grooves in stones for hafted hammers or mauls.

These abrading marks are very common at cliff dwelling sites. We see them in nearly every ruin we visit. They are on boulders, on slickrock outcroppings and even on the cliff face. They are the telltale remains of a ground tool being made.

The ancient ones were wizards with stone. With a rock and a piece of antler they could create a whole toolbox of tools, enough to build and maintain a house, enough to operate a farm. They made tools that could make fires, tools for milling corn and wild grains. And then, with the aid of their prayers and songs, they made stones that could actually fly — in the form of arrowheads and spear points — to the heart of their prey.

William H. Jackson photographed these stairs carved into the face of a cliff at Chaco Canyon, New Mexico. Today these stairs are known as "Jackson's staircase." From: *10th Annual Hayden Survey Report of 1878.*

13

Hııhììmu*

*A Hopi word meaning a variety, a number of different things. This chapter discusses a number of different topics.

Roads

We stood in awe, gaping at the sheer expanse that someone had to ascend in order to reach the cave pocket in the sandstone cliff. Inside that pocket alcove high above us was a structure. Hand-and-toe holds ascended to the alcove aerie; but even with those aids, it was still a daunting climb a thousand years ago. Just the thought of doing it once was fear-inspiring. Yet, someone had man-handled wood beams, heavy containers of wet adobe mud and dressed stones — as well as himself — up that cliff face. And he had to have done it not once, but over and over again in order to have built that structure. No wonder the old Navajo travelers thought these ancient people had been able to fly! We find these hand-and-toe hold trails often in our backcountry excursions. But we never attempt to climb them; they have weathered through the centuries, and are no longer viable routes.

Hand-and-toe holds are just one kind of trail one finds in the American Southwest. Trails range from these hand-and-toe holds, to paths, to what some people refer to as highways. And seemingly everywhere you look there are traces of ancient trails crisscrossing the desert landscape.

Radiating out from Chaco Canyon in north-central New Mexico are good prehistoric roads. So good are these roads that they are sometimes referred to as highways. They point in all directions; the largest and best known is the great North Road which aims toward the San Juan River. The extent of these roads is still being mapped, but they are known at this time to extend for hundreds of miles.

These are well-constructed roads even by today's county road standards. They are wide, sometimes as much as forty-five feet wide, and are complete with raised berms — like curbs — at their sides. They are amazingly straight, cutting across landforms without wavering much off their original course. When natural obstacles blocked the way, staircases were cut up cliff faces and off canyon rims. Being as there were no livestock animals for transportation in prehistoric times, these roads are a wonder of ancient engineering and mysterious because one wonders why they built them.

To our modern, practical way of thinking we would assume their original purpose was to facilitate transportation. And in some instances, they may well have served that purpose. Along some of these practical-appearing roads have been found much broken pottery. But just as many of the roads do not fit that assumption. For example, some roads are well-developed in the smooth, straight segments where travel was easy, but then in the rough places where road work would have been most useful to a traveler, they are only poorly developed. Some roads run parallel to one another only a short distance apart. Others circle great pueblos in Utah, Colorado and New Mexico. Some roads connect pueblos with ancient, uninhabited pueblo ruins of their ancestors. Other roads lead to shrines.

These and other facts have led archaeologists to look for other possible meanings for the roads. It is known that in other cultures roads can be ceremonial, meant for ritual purposes and not necessarily practical. Some of these Chaco highways may well fall into that category, especially the roads that appear to run parallel to one another or circle a Great House.

Another North American culture, the Woodland culture in the eastern part of the United States, was also crisscrossed with trails and "roads." In the book, *Historic Highways of America: Indian Thoroughfares,* Volume 2, by Archer Butler Hulbert (published in 1902), he described the network of trails in the eastern part of the continent. Some of these trails were better than others. The most common thoroughfares were mere footpaths that had humble beginnings, perhaps even as buffalo trails. They wound around obstacles and crossed streams at their narrowest ford points, even if it was miles out of the way. These paths meandered.

The best roads were the War Paths, but everyone avoided them, even in peaceful times. These trails were deeper and straighter than the other paths. They were better thought-out and were lined with secret hiding places and places for camping. If you should happen to encounter someone while you were on a War Path, you could be immediately killed, so everyone took the less well-developed other paths instead. (Could this be the origin of the saying that someone is "on the War Path?") We wonder if some of the Chacoan roads might have been used in such a fashion.

We have tracked some of their trails in the landscape and we have also tracked the *idea* of roads, paths and trails through the Puebloan ethnographic literature. The Hopi say that the rising sun marks the road taken at the emergence of their ancestors from the underworld — their third world. When their ancestors emerged from their third world through the Great Sipapu, they forged an agreement with their god Maasau that gave them stewardship of this, their fourth world, as long as they followed the Hopi Road of Life. The Hopi people still travel this road through life today.

According to Pueblo beliefs, everyone and everything has a life-line, a road of life that he should follow. Even the sun itself has a road it must follow. The Zuni people say, "Life is a road." Every Puebloan child probably heard the admonishment over and over again while growing up: "Always follow the Hopi (or Taos, or etc.) Sun Trail," that is: Do the right thing, do what you are supposed to do.

The "road of life" is a theme that appears repeatedly in the ethnographic literature of the Puebloan People. This life-line or road of life theme appears on some ancient as well as modern pots, as we discussed in the chapter on pottery. But it is also a theme in this prayer:

> There, far off, my Sun Father arises, ascends the ladder, comes
>   forth from his place.
> May all complete the *road of life*, may all grow old.
> May the children inhale more of the sacred breath of life.
> May all my children have corn that they may complete the
>   *road of life*.
> Here, sit down; here remain; we give you our best thoughts . . .
>
> — Zuni prayer, Matilda Coxe Stevenson
> [Italics ours]

Archaeoastronomy: Waiting for Pleiades

For ancient farmers, knowing when to plant, cultivate, water and harvest their crops was a matter of life or death. Recall the average frost-free growing time on the Colorado Plateau is about 130 days. Corn requires at least 120 days to mature, more if the weather is cool or dry, which extends corn's maturation time. Planting just a few days off one way or another could spell disaster. So how did they manage to become such successful farmers when they were bracketed by such narrow margins? The sky told them.

In ancient times people spent their evenings engrossed in the night sky and its wonders. They learned to track the movements of the sun, the moon and the stars. They also tracked the seasons, all with their naked eyes. Today this seems impossibly sophisticated to us because only highly trained astronomers on huge telescopes do that now. But the reality is that we have lost our early knowledge gained from watching the sky. Fortunately, the naked-eye astronomy the ancients used is still available to us today. The study of how the ancients studied the skies is called *archaeoastronomy*.

As we discussed earlier, archaeologists have noticed that the ancient unit pueblos on the Colorado Plateau were often aligned to the four cardinal directions: north, south, east and west. The cliff dwellings in the Colorado Plateau frequently inhabit caves facing south, but not always. Woven throughout modern Puebloan culture is a desire for their universe to be in balance, for everything to be in harmony, and their search for the "center place." One wonders if these early celestial alignments were their ancestors' expression of this same desire. These cardinal direction orientations are fairly simple and straightforward. However, in some places, their astronomical observations became quite sophisticated.

In many ways it is as though the sky was an ancient cosmic timepiece to the people: The sun told of the season, the moon indicated the months and the stars were the minutes and hours.

The Sun

The Puebloan people worship the sun and call him their father. Their Father Sun is an old man and needs their help through prayers to make his daily trip from his eastern house (or kiva) in the morning to his western house (or kiva) in the evening.

Besides tracking the sun daily, they also track his progress through the seasons. Landmarks sometimes catch the sun's rays and light up ancient features at certain times of the year — of particular interest are the summer solstice, winter solstice and the equinoxes. Fajada Butte is a famous example at Chaco Canyon. On Fajada Butte are stone slab boulders that hide a spiral petroglyph pecked on the butte's face behind them. At the summer solstice — the longest day of the year — a dagger of sunlight pierces the darkness behind the boulder and bisects the center of the spiral. On the equinoxes, when the daylight hours and the hours of darkness are equal, two daggers of light frame the outside edges of this same spiral. Apparently some ancient person was carefully charting these days at this site. Sites like this pepper the backcountry in the Greater American Southwest.

The sun shrine at Ma-tsa-ki as pictured in the #23rd Bureau of American Ethnology, Stevenson. This shrine no longer exists.

Knowing these key times of the year would give ancient farmers a much-needed edge in a marginal environment for farming.

Another solar/landmark alignment that happens at certain times of the year was described by early ethnographer Frank Cushing: "At dawn, the Sun Priest . . . went to the ruined city of Ma-tsa-ki . . . He slowly approached a [shrine] and seated himself just inside . . . and before a pillar sculptured with the face of the sun . . . There he awaited with prayer and sacred song the rising of the sun . . . and [for] the shadows of the solar monolith, the monument of Thunder Mountain, and the pillar of the gardens of Zuni, [to] 'lie along the same trail.' Then the priest blesses, thanks and exhorts his father, and hastens back to call from the house-tops the glad tidings of the return of spring...." The shrine at Ma-tsa-ki, described by Frank Cushing and pictured by Matilda Coxe Stevenson, is no longer there, according to Ray Williamson, noted Southwestern archaeoastronomer.

Sometimes observers noticed that the ancients built structures that created an interplay between the sun's rays and certain room features. A beam of sunlight entered an opening and lit up certain features, such as a built-in niche, or a mural on the opposite wall just two days a year. Frank Cushing explained it: "Many are the houses in Zuni with scores on their walls or ancient plates imbedded therein, while opposite, a convenient window or small port-hole lets in the light of the rising sun, which shines but two mornings in the three hundred and sixty-five on the same place. Wonderfully reliable and ingenious are these rude systems of orientation, by which the religion, the labors, and even the pastimes of the Zunis are regulated." Sometimes the beam of light had to penetrate deeply into the structure through a series of labyrinths in

The Sun Chief at Zuni in the 1880s. Bureau of 23rd Bureau of American Ethnology, Stevenson.

order to light up the feature. This can be seen at Holly House at Hovenweep National Monument. Towers sometimes incorporated one or both of these features: The whole structure casting a shadow aligned to the heavens or a light ray penetrating the interior to light up a special mark.

The Moon

The moon also figures in the ancient cosmic timepiece. The crescent moon is more important in their ceremonies than is the full moon. This is probably because the crescent moons are easier to time than the full moon, which stays full for several days before it wanes. The crescent moons come quickly and then go just as quickly. When the crescent moon lies on its back with the horns up, it is not good. There will be no rain. When the crescent moon's horns are down it is good; there will be rain.

According to Florence Ellis in *A Thousand Years of the Pueblo Sun-Moon-Star Calendar,* the moons are given different names. For example, the March moon is called the Cactus Moon because by this time the stores from the previous summer's harvest are running short so they must begin to rely on cactus for food. The January moon is the Play Moon, it is a time for games. When there has been no moon for two days, followed by a new moon, that moonless time is called "moon none."

The Stars

The Morning Star, Orion and Pleiades are the most important stars to the Puebloans. The Morning Star is not actually a star but a planet — Venus. The Morning Star is used as a timing device; it signals the beginning of the new day.

It also signals the end of some night ceremonies, such as the end of The Old Year Ceremony as described by Frank H. Cushing: "As the morning star was rising, the music ceased, the congregation became silent, and the chief dancer was led to the center of the room, where he was elaborately costumed. Then the Priest of the Sun took him up the ladder to the roof, where, facing the east, he pronounced … a prayer to the waning Sun of the Old Year."

Pleiades also acted as a timing device for ceremonies. In one case, early ethnographer Alexander Stephen in the 1890s attended a kiva ceremony at Hopi. The ceremony was scheduled to end precisely when Pleiades appeared in the hatch opening of the kiva. But on that particular night it happened to be cloudy. When the Kiva Chief signaled the end of the ceremony, Stevens discreetly checked his watch. He was surprised to find the chief had called the end of the lengthy ceremony only ten minutes off in his timing!

When Pleiades appeared in the hatch of the kiva, it signaled the end of the ceremony.

The 10th Hayden Survey of 1878 pictures this round tower among its pages. Photographer William H. Jackson said of this tower: "It is one of the best preserved specimens of the ruined towers, and seems to have been built with much skill."

Towers

According to archaeologist Mark Varien, free-standing towers first appeared in and around Mesa Verde about A.D. 1150. These towers can be of several different shapes — there are square towers, round towers and even D-shaped towers.

What towers mean is not well understood. Some appear to be defensive. Once when we were in a very remote area we saw a type of tower that appeared to be the components of a unit pueblo, but the rooms were simply stacked on top of one another. This type of tower was divided into three floors: the bottom floor appeared to be for storage, the second floor was the

A square tower.

living room, and the open space on top was like a courtyard, open to the sky. The entry was a T-door on the second floor, and they apparently came and went by ladder. When trouble appeared or at night, they could pull up the ladder after them. There were no windows. These towers are thought to overlook farm fields; perhaps they were used just during the planting season and were field houses.

Others, however, do not appear to be defensive. A tower combined with a kiva sometimes occurs in the Chaco complexes; however, these were built before the cliff dwelling era. We do sometimes encounter tower/kiva structures in our backcountry travels.

Towers sometimes were incorporated into astronomy. At the largest pueblo city ruin in southwestern Colorado, there is an alignment among some of the towers, but not all of them, and rock art and certain towers are lit up by rays of the rising sun on the Summer Solstice.

Towers are one of the elements that did not make the move during the ancient people's Great Migration. Free-standing towers are generally considered a part of the Mesa Verde complex.

Shrines

There is a charming pueblo farmhouse deep in a remote area that we often like to visit. Ruined walls still stand six and seven feet high. They outline a fistful of rooms. Perhaps there was only a single extended family that lived here at one time. It is hard to say today. The roof is missing now and probably has been since ancient times. But now instead of people, the rooms are filled with rice grass that tosses in the wind. There is something timeless about this place and we like visiting it.

The pueblo farm-stead we found deep in a remote area.

Above left is the probable shrine we saw that day at the ancient farmhouse. On the right is a shrine photographed by A.V. Kidder in 1919. Although they are easily a hundred miles apart, they are so nearly alike they could have been built by the same hands. He wrote: "Low circular walls seem to be a favorite type of shrine enclosure." From: Bureau of American Ethnology, Bulletin #65, Kidder and Guernsey.

Standing alone perhaps 30 or 40 feet to the east of the farmstead is a low stone structure. It is round, perhaps two feet high and probably about five feet in diameter. The first several times we visited this place we thought it might have been a tumbled down tower, although there were no fallen stones that would indicate the structure had at one time been much taller.

Then on a visit to the Hopi village of Walpi more than a decade ago, we happened to show up on a ceremonial day. The usually quiet village was alive with preparations for the ceremony. Hopi people were coming and going and nodding at one another as they passed. The air buzzed with excitement, and there was smoke coming from the kiva stovepipe. And at the edge of the mesa overlooking the cliff was a stone structure about the size of a wishing well but without the cover. It reminded us of the lone structure at the remote farmhouse we liked to visit. However, inside the Walpi structure dozens of willow whips with feathers attached to them by cotton string danced in the wind.

These were shrines! And the eight hundred years separating these two places seemed to be bridged in an instant. The structure we had wondered about at the ancient remote farmhouse had more than likely been a shrine.

The willow whips with feathers attached to them that day at Walpi were pahos. Most of the feathers were probably turkey feathers, but we thought we recognized the distinctive blue of bluebird feathers and some that were the telltale rusty-orange of the American kestrel. Our guide asked us to be

Above is a shrine documented in the 23rd Bureau of American Ethnology, Stevenson. Inside are prayer stick offerings for rain.

careful not to step on any of the feathers that fluttered from their place on the ground. And sure enough, we passed several pahos fluttering from where they had been attached to the bedrock.

Pahos are made in different sizes and different shapes, and some are considered male and others are female. The cotton string is referred to as its life-line.

Santa Clara Puebloan Rina Swentzell in the book *Anasazi Architecture and American Design* relates that the pueblos have shrines marking the territory surrounding the pueblo. The markers begin in the plaza area — the center place of the pueblo. Then they radiate outward like ripples on a pond when a stone is tossed in. Some shrines mark areas that are traditionally for men only, and others mark places where women traditionally go, such as to plant-gathering sites.

A shrine could also be in a cave or a spring or a low structure devoted to a specific deity. Among modern Puebloan farmers, some have shrines in their fields. A shrine can also be an ancestral village that is connected to a modern pueblo by a trail and still visited by the residents of the modern pueblo. Often the trails to certain shrines are worn deep by the sandals of people who have walked to them for all these years.

There are other shrines that archaeologists are beginning to recognize, such as *herraduras.* Herradura is the Spanish word for horseshoe, and indeed, these shrines are shaped like a horseshoe. They are about the same height and width as other shrines, but they are not near a structure. These shrines are found along trails and seem to be marking the trail.

And so a thousand years of Puebloan people left their sandal tracks across the Greater American Southwest — in the form of shrines, roads and trails, structures such as towers, rock art and potsherds just to name a few. Each one of these artifacts has its own voice, its own song, if we just know how to listen for it. Now that you have read this book, it is our sincerest hope that you will be able to hear the songs from the ancient past as they echo down the canyons. That if you listen closely to wind on the mesa tops, you will hear the soft murmurings of the cliff dwellings as they speak.

Above, an ancestral Puebloan blanket and blurry old photograph of a cliff dwelling dated 1896. If these items had been separated through the nearly one hundred years of passing from owner to owner, this story could never have been told. Photographs, courtesy of the Telluride Historical Museum, Telluride, Colorado. Photographer: Jonas Grushkin.

14

ADVENTURES IN REVERSE ARCHAEOLOGY

Reverse Archaeology is a process by which artifacts in museums or private collections are reconnected to their original discovery sites, based on various clues from old letters, field records, photographs, rock inscriptions and so forth . . . Reverse Archaeology is extremely important to our understanding of our archaeological record . . . The [Telluride] blanket and the [old] photograph are the focus of one of our most persistent and interesting problems in Reverse Archaeology.

— *Archaeologist Winston Hurst,* Blue Mountain Shadows Journal.

If an enlightened explorer knows it is wrong to collect artifacts — even to place them on museum rocks — and also knows that it is illegal to dig for artifacts or to treasure hunt, then how can one participate meaningfully in the mysteries of the Southwest?

Today there is a new hunt afoot. Since it is illegal to dig for artifacts, people have turned to finding lost places instead. Fascinating artifacts sit in museums with their *provenances* — that is, their origins — blurred and incomplete. It is very important for museums to authenticate their artifacts and verify their authenticity — that is, their artifacts' provenances must be complete. Also, artifacts are much more interesting and informative when their discovery context is known.

The research related to key museum artifacts discovered a century or more ago is sometimes scattered: Maybe the excavation records are in one place and the field notes and artifacts are in another. Other important documents might well be at a third location, like the university that managed the excavation. Some of the early collections and their records were sent back East a century ago, and now no one knows exactly what the collections contained or where those collections are today.

In other instances, early records described places by names that were well-known at the time but have since been renamed, and the original names have been forgotten. For example, an early explorer might have described a site at the junction of Bear Creek and Trout Creek. Today those creeks might have different names and no one is sure where this site is located. There is a great need to track down this information and, through modern photographs and photocopies of the original documentation, reunite the information,

Above is the 1896 photograph of a cliff dwelling that accompanied the blanket. On the bottom was written: "Prehistoric ruin in S E Utah Taken by Ed Turner, Given to Wheeler." Wheeler was an early collector.

artifacts and field notes once again. This type of exploration requires lots of museum research time and our favorite part — interviewing old-timers — as well as patience and stick-to-it-iveness along with the exciting backcountry explorations.

Guide, former ranger and author Fred Blackburn and a team of his colleagues did this in the 1980s when they succeeded in retracing the steps of the Wetherill brothers' discovery of the Basketmaker site in "Cave 7" in the 1890s. No one alive today knew where Cave 7 was. Blackburn coined a new term for this type of archaeology, *Reverse Archaeology*. The purpose of Reverse Archaeology is to reunite artifacts with the information about their origins. The Wetherill collection still existed in a museum, but the whereabouts of Cave 7 had been lost to time. In this end Blackburn and his colleagues spent many weeks in the backcountry searching for this cave, and it also involved trips to New York City to research at the American Museum of Natural History. After much exploration and research they indeed found the mysterious Cave 7. The books *Cowboys and Cave Dwellers* and *Anasazi Basketmaker: Papers from the 1990 Wetherill-Grand Gulch Symposium* resulted from their efforts.

These publications documenting the endeavor also protect the information that the artifacts generated from future loss. This has been a major

Bill Sagstetter's 1968 photograph of the first "wild" cliff dwelling he had ever discovered. College friend Jim Hoskins is in the foreground.

accomplishment that will benefit those who are interested in the Southwest for generations to come. New research and new insights have already occurred from this work they accomplished.

This is the legacy for today's generation of explorers — not just the search for more artifacts, but the search and detective work of giving extant artifacts in the museums a new life by rediscovering their original location — and returning to them their provenance.

Another Case in Reverse Archaeology

Our adventures in Reverse Archaeology began in 2004 when we were in southeast Utah, as we frequently are. The beauty of the region keeps luring us back, even after 40 years. As usual, we stopped at the Edge of the Cedars Museum in Blanding, Utah, to see their latest exhibits and buy a number of books on the region. On the way out the door I picked up a copy of the *Blue Mountain Shadows Journal* and saw an article by Winston Hurst, well-known archaeologist, longtime friend of ours and member of the Grand Gulch Project team. Since we had just paid for a stack of books, I set it down and walked out. But something made me go back in and buy the magazine.

Driving to Bluff, Utah, Beth was reading aloud Hurst's article on "The Mysterious Telluride Blanket." Hurst and Blackburn were trying to locate the site where the ancient blanket on display at the Telluride Historical Museum had originally been found. Accompanying the article was a blurry black-and-white photograph of a "lost" cliff dwelling dated 1896. The shock that jolted me almost caused me to lose control of our vehicle. *Pictured there was the very first cliff dwelling I had ever found!*

I was immediately transported back to 1968. I remember looking for "wild" cliff dwellings using William H. Jackson's 1876 *Hayden Survey Report*. I was very discouraged because for several years I could not find a single cliff dwelling, even in an area rich in cultural remains.

Being young and inexperienced and in a very remote area, I got lost reading the USGS topographical maps incorrectly. Running low on gas and water, I was headed back to civilization. Then suddenly I thought I glimpsed a window out of the corner of my eye about a half a mile away. This had actually happened frequently, and when I would go to investigate, it never panned out. But still I hiked to it, losing it in the trees on the way and then spotting it again. Finally, there it was — my first cliff dwelling! As cliff dwellings go, this one is modest. But to me, since it was my first cliff dwelling, it was the most spectacular structure I had ever seen. I photographed it extensively and revisited it for several years.

It was then we noticed the date on the *Blue Mountain Shadows Journal* — it was ten years old (1994)! Disappointed, we did not call Hurst immediately because we thought that the BLM, a rancher or backcountry traveler surely would have found the site in that time. When we arrived home we went through all our old photographs and found our original photographs of the ruin from 1968.

After a few weeks I called Hurst and asked him who had found the cliff dwelling pictured in the *Blue Mountain Shadows Journal*. Hurst said the site had not been identified, so I immediately emailed the photos to him. One of the photographs was taken from near the same vantage point that the original photographer had used so many years before. Hurst emailed me back in just a day or two and confirmed that this was indeed the same cliff dwelling depicted in the 1896 photograph.

It turned out that in 1974 the Telluride Historical Museum had received, as part of an estate, a mysterious locked suitcase. When the suitcase was opened, inside was an old Native American blanket that was white with black, brown and red stripes and tassels at each corner. With the blanket was an old blurry black-and-white photograph of a cliff dwelling, a tattered

Winston Hurst stands at the mouth of the alcove above the cliff dwelling.

newspaper article and a large skein of white yarn. It was always assumed that the cliff dwelling in the photograph was where the blanket had been originally found. The newspaper article was dated August 14, 1896, and was from Telluride, Colorado's *Daily Journal*. It related this story:

In 1896 and Mel Turner and his nephew, Ed, were riding the range looking for stray cattle. High on a mesa something caught their eyes and they stopped to investigate, as they often did. Scrambling up several sandstone ledges, they kept ascending up and up, until finally a large alcove cave yawned before them. They realized upon entering the sandstone alcove that it had seen much use since ancient times: The ceiling was blackened from countless fires.

Ed Turner described the cave as being forty feet long and twenty feet wide with a roof of ten feet or more in height. In an old hearth they spotted "A white fleecy substance protruding from the fine ashes. It was pulled out and was found to resemble a mass of woolen [sic] strings. It had been used as a stopper to a large earthen vessel perfect in condition and of native workmanship. Scraping aside the ashes, the vessel was lifted out and its contents deposited on the floor of the cavern." The olla contained a

magnificent blanket such as they had never seen before: It was white with red and brown and black stripes and tassels at the four corners. It measured about 57 inches by 59 inches.

The blanket had been carefully folded before being put in the olla, and as the Turners unfolded it, they could see between the folds "a bone awl and a string of beads 16 feet long, containing about 7000 beads. The beads were … very small, black and red, brittle as glass and shiny as ebony."

In the cave they also found "corn husks, stalks, a few beans, pottery…. Sandals were found. A basket was also found."

A Puebloan man spinning thread in 1883. Cushing, The Century Magazine.

As they continued to explore the area, they discovered two other ruins, cliff dwellings built in what an archaeologist might describe as a somewhat Mesa Verde Pueblo III (A.D. 1150–1300) style, with dressed, blocky stones laid in irregular courses with adobe mud as the mortar.

It is important to note that in 1896 it was not illegal to dig in ruins. The first Antiquities Act did not pass until 1906. At that point it was not known how ancient the ruins were that peppered the American Southwest. For all people like Mel knew, the ruins might have been fairly recent, or as many at the time believed, relics of the Aztecs.

The blanket now known as the Telluride Blanket is thought to have been sold to a private collector about the time of the newspaper article. From that original collector it passed through several hands, all the time keeping the newspaper article, the photograph and the skein of yarn together with it. It is known that at one time it was nearly sold at a garage sale. If the three objects had been separated at any point in its journey, this story would have been lost forever.

The blanket Mel and his nephew Ed found that day in 1896 is probably an exceptionally fine example of a "wearing blanket." A wearing blanket was handy to have around: Of course you could wear it wrapped around yourself when it was cold, and at night you slept in it. If you had a heavy load, the load could be packed in the blanket and it could be used to haul the load. It could be spread out on the ground for sitting. A baby could be wrapped in it and the ends of the blanket brought around you and tied, leaving your hands free to do another job. And when a person died, sometimes he would be buried in it. It was certainly true that a wearing blanket was a handy thing to have around.

When the Spanish arrived in the northern Southwest perhaps 300 years later in A.D. 1540, the Pueblo people still wore wearing blankets, but the style had changed. The Hopi people at that time preferred blankets that were white with blue and black stripes.

In his book *Sun Chief,* Don Talayesva related when he was a child he loved hanging out in his grandfather's kiva. The men would be busy with their traditional duties of weaving and spinning. As their

A Puebloan weaver, 1883. Cushing, *The Century Magazine.*

fingers worked they told their ancient stories and young Don was enthralled. As a matter of fact, archaeologists often find loom anchors in the floors of ancient kivas. Perhaps the Telluride blanket was created in such a way, by ancient Puebloan men in their kivas with their ancient stories on their lips.

The blanket now known as the Telluride Blanket was woven of cotton (not wool as suggested in the old newspaper account) on a loom with what is called a twill weave, according to textile expert Kate Peck Kent. Twill is the weave used to create blue jeans today. Twill is a sophisticated and difficult weave to master, so it is assumed the blanket was woven by an expert weaver, a person who really knew what he was doing. Kate Peck Kent in her evaluation of the blanket for the museum noted: "No other complete specimen exists. There are only two other patterned prehistoric blankets that match this when it comes to its undamaged state."

The blanket is thought by textile expert Laurie Webster to be a superb example of Pueblo III workmanship and design, and that it would date from A.D. 1200 to 1300.

Winston Hurst states the area where the blanket was found is too high and northerly for successful cotton production, which requires warmer growing conditions than this area can provide. This means that the blanket, or at least the cotton from which it was woven, must have come from the lower elevation areas of the lower San Juan River, Glen Canyon or someplace farther south.

With the acquisition of the ancient blanket, the small-town, volunteer-run Telluride Historical Museum suddenly found itself with a world-class art object on its hands, one worthy of any of the large world-famous museums. Carl Patterson, Chief Conservator of the Denver Art Museum, called the blanket "a national treasure."

But the tiny museum did not have the resources to conserve the blanket nor to store it securely. It required a special cabinet that would preserve the delicate ancient weaving. It needed state-of-the-art security so as not to become a target of art thieves. They had no choice but to be creative since they had no funding. In the early days of the blanket's acquisition, in order to protect it from being stolen, they stored the prehistoric ancestral Puebloan blanket in the same case with the historic Navajo blankets. They knew only an expert would be able to tell them apart.

The plan worked, but there were consequences. After more than a decade and having changed curators several times, even the museum was a little vague as to which Native American blanket was the rare prehistoric one.

Fred Blackburn was born in Telluride, Colorado, in the same hospital building that today serves as the museum building. Blackburn and his wife, Victoria Atkins, archaeologist for the Anasazi Heritage Center in Dolores, Colorado, were visiting family in Telluride and stopped by the museum. They immediately recognized the one blanket that was of cotton; the other, historic blankets were of wool. Since sheep came with the Spaniards, the ancient blanket could only have been made of cotton. Atkins arranged for the blanket to be kept in the proper storage facilities at the Anasazi Heritage Center.

Blackburn contacted Winston Hurst and together they began to place articles in local newspapers that included the old, blurry picture of the cliff dwelling that had survived with the blanket, asking local people if they recognized this cliff dwelling. A few people responded, but when they checked out the dwellings, they were not a match. Then in 1994 Winston wrote a story about the blanket and the missing dwelling in the *Blue Mountain Shadows Journal*. There were a few responses, but none of them panned out until ten years later and my phone call to Winston.

The Story of Discovery Continues

That fall we went back to the cliff dwelling again, this time with an archaeological team led by Hurst and Blackburn. Besides ourselves, Susan

The insription painted in red on the cave wall: M R Turner, above, and E D Turner, below it. The date 1896 is on the far right, out of the picture.

and Terry Tice and Sue and John Mansfield also were present, as well as BLM archaeologist Jim Carter. As we all explored the ruin, Hurst immediately saw that this could not have been the resting place of the blanket for all those years. First of all, the ruin is sitting on bedrock — there is not enough dirt and sand on the floor of the cave to bury an olla in, nor was there any sign of an old hearth. Also, the cave is wet; moisture permeates everything. No textile could have survived in that environment for eight hundred years. The actual resting place had to be somewhere else — somewhere nearby and *dry*.

The Tices and Mansfields carefully read the old newspaper account from 1896 of the discovery, and found an excerpt explaining that above the cliff dwelling about 300 feet there was an alcove, and this is where the pot containing the blanket and other artifacts had actually been found.

They scaled the steep escarpment and about 300 feet above found a wide, grassy ledge that they followed. It let them straight to a cave — a *dry* cave — that fit the description. And if that were not enough, when they searched around the cave, they found two inscriptions painted in red on the wall above an old hearth: *M R Turner* and *Ed Turner 1896*. This was it! We had found the resting place of the blanket-filled pot from so long ago. The blanket, its story and the location had been reconnected once again after more than a hundred years. The provenance of the ancient blanket was now complete.

In 1968 if you had asked me about this cliff dwelling, all I could have answered was, "It's really neat." Today when we revisit this old ruin, we see it in a whole different light. After 40 years of exploring cliff dwellings and writing this book, we see it with new eyes. We can see this fistful of rooms was originally intended as a two-story structure because part of the second-story wall remains. But because so much of the second-story walls are missing, it's impossible to say how large it had been intended to be. The walls were constructed with sandstone blocks that were not as carefully dressed as are those at Mesa Verde National Park. The gaps between the sandstone blocks were heavily mortared with adobe, more adobe mud than was typically used at Mesa Verde National Park ruins.

Also, the cliff dwelling faces the "wrong" direction. It is not south or southwest facing as cliff dwellings typically are in this area. There is no kiva attached to the complex. Not much that could be considered a courtyard exists in front of it, either, and there could not have been a courtyard in front of the ruin since it is situated under a pour-over. Nor is there much in the way of household debris surrounding the ruin. Only a half dozen or so sherds of pottery were spotted on the surface below the dwelling. One was "diagnostic," as archaeologists would say — that is, part of the rim is present on the black-and-white sherd. It indicates this sherd might have been part of a serving bowl. Arranged along the rim fragment are telltale dots. From having read this book, you will recognize this as a sherd of probable classic Mesa Verde black-on-white pottery.

What I thought were windows in 1968 are more than likely storage room or granary doorways. The lintels are set back to accommodate a sandstone slab door, and also to be sealed shut. However, there is a lack of corncobs scattered about as one would typically see at a granary.

Remains of one room could have been a possible living room: It is the largest room in the complex, but there is no sooting on the walls, and no trace of a hearth. What remains of the doorway does have a low threshold. It's impossible to tell today if it was intended to be a T-door.

There is light sooting on the *cave* walls, which could imply the cave was used in ancient times. But the man-made stone walls have no sooting on them.

What this cliff dwelling represents more than likely is an unassuming version of a Mesa Verde-type ruin — certainly it is not an example of the highest form of the Mesa Verde building arts. Perhaps it was intended as storage. Or perhaps the unit was never completed and never occupied.

But still, this unpretentious little ruin has a special place in our hearts. The discovery of it back in 1968 has inspired 40 years of exploration of cliff ruins. It has solved the mystery of the origins of the Telluride Blanket by pointing the way to the cave where the blanket was actually found in 1896. And the story of discovery it inspired has resulted in this book you hold in your hands. Not a bad track record for what would otherwise have been an unremarkable little ruin.

In the end, the adventure is truly not what you find — such as this unexceptional dwelling — but what you find out.

Since the acquisition of the blanket, the Telluride Historical Museum has reinvented itself as a place worthy of curating a world-class art object. Under the leadership of executive director Lauren Bloemsma the museum now has state-of-the-art security and conservation facilities. Because its provenance is known, the blanket that had been in storage for many years, can now be displayed in the Telluride Historical Museum. Tests are being conducted on the blanket to verify its age and where the cotton originated. In the near future, tests will be done to study the ancient dyes that were used in the piece. Next to nothing is known about the ancient dying practices of this prehistoric era. New insights into not only this particular blanket, but also new knowledge of textile practices of the ancient Southwestern people are being discovered. If you are interested in becoming involved in this fascinating project, contact:

Stewards of the Telluride Blanket
The Telluride Historical Museum
P. O. Box 1579
Telluride, CO 81435
(970) 723-3344
www.telluridemuseum.org

A stylized image of a bird takes wing. Surrounding him are seven stylized stars, according to early archaeologist J. W. Fewkes in the 33rd Annual *Bureau of American Ethnology.* The bird's body is made up of an eagle tail feather with its telltale stairstep design. Above the stairstep design are blanket-type designs. We do not know the significance of the three legs. This design was on a bowl from the ancient pueblo of Sikyatki on the Hopi Mesas in Arizona.

EPILOGUE

We struggled up the steep slope most of the morning. The rising sun was at our backs, hot and suffocating without a breeze. Each step we took kicked up a cloud of red dirt that choked us. Trails of sweat trickled down our backs and dampened our clothing. Still we kept pushing upward, one foot in front of the other, zigzagging our way up the backside of the ridge.

When we finally topped the spine of the ridge, we were greeted with a strong, blasting wind. Although it was a hot wind, it was still refreshing and we stripped off our backpacks and threw ourselves down side-by-side in the dry grass. The hot wind flapped our wet clothing and dried it almost immediately.

Suddenly a shadow blotted out the sun in the cloudless sky. And then just over our heads appeared two red-tailed hawks, wing tip to wing tip. They had slid over the ridge, just barely clearing the landmass — playing with the wind. We must have looked strange from their perspective. They paused and hovered over us checking out the two humans spread-eagled beneath them. They cocked their heads and casually looked us over, curious but unafraid. They were so close, if we had been standing we could have reached out and touched them. We could see the wind rippling their feathers. We could almost smell the mustiness of their feathers. They made long, lingering eye contact with us, and then let the wind catch them and propel them down slope. That was when we realized we both had been holding our breaths.

We know we'll never be able to soar with the red-tailed hawks, nor to see the world from their unique perspective. Our feet must always remain earthbound. But our encounter with them has changed us nonetheless; we see things from a new angle. Our view is wider and longer and deeper now. Since we are more observant, we "see" things we never saw before — and the things we saw before, we now see in a new light. It's been a transforming experience, and we will never be the same again.

This highly stylized image of a bird from the ancient pueblo of Sikyatki was painted in a bowl. It speaks to us from across the ages. The bird image seems to incorporate a spiral and its grace and spirit fascinate us still today.

From: 33rd Bureau of American Ethnology. Fewkes.

APPENDIXES

Appendix A

Below are sites to visit that are related to the ancient people of the Greater American Southwest. Not all are cliff dwellings, however, some are pueblo ruins in the open. Some you can enter the ruin and look around, some you can only stand outside. Others are museums. But all will have fascinating information on the culture and will help you learn more about the ancient people of the Southwest. This is not intended to be a complete list; it is meant to merely whet your curiosity and to let you know many of the options available for people interested in the ancient Southest.

Acoma Pueblo (Sky City)
P.O. Box 309
Acoma, NM 87034
(800) 747-0181 or (505) 552-6017

The Amerind Foundation
2100 North Amerind Road
Dragoon, AZ 85609
(520) 586-3666
www.amerind@amerind.org

Anasazi Heritage Center/Canyon of the Ancients
27501 Highway 184
Dolores, CO 81323
(970) 882-5600
www.blm.gov/co

Aztec National Monument
#84 County Road
Aztec, NM 87410
(505) 334-6174
www.nps.gov/azru

Bandelier National Monument
15 Entrance Rd.
Los Alamos, NM 87544
(505) 672-3861
www.nps.gov/band

Canyon de Chelly National Monument
P.O. Box 588
Chinle, AZ 86503
(928) 674-5500
www.nps.gov/cach

Canyonlands National Park
2282 SW Resource Blvd.
Moab, UT 84532
(435)719-2313
www.nps.gov/cany

Canyonlands Natural History Association
3015 South Highway 191
Moab, UT 84532
(800)840-8978
www.cnha.org

Casa Grande National Monument
(singular, as opposed to Casas Grandes, Mexico, plural)
1100 W. Ruins Dr.
Coolidge, AZ 85228
(520) 723-3172
www.nps.gov/cagr

Chaco Culture National Historical Park
P.O. Box 220
Nageezi, NM 87037
(505) 786-7014
www.nps.gov/chcu

Chimney Rock Archaeological Area
P.O. Box 1662
Pagosa Springs, CO 81147
www.chimneyrockco.org

Cochiti Pueblo
P.O. Box 70
Cochiti Pueblo, NM 87072
(505) 465-2244

Coronado State Monument
(at Bernalillo, NM)
P.O. Box 2087
Santa Fe, NM 87504
(505) 476-1150
www.nmmonuments.org

Deming Luna Mimbres Museum
301 South Silver
Deming, NM 88030
(505) 546-2382
www. deminglunamimbresmuseum.com

Edge of the Cedars State Park Museum
600 W. 400 N.
Blanding, UT 84511-4000
(435) 678-2238
www.stateparks.utah.gov/parks/edge-of-the-cedars

El Morro National Monument
HC 61 Box 43
Ramah, NM 87321
www.nps.gov/elmo

Gila Cliff Dwelling National Historic Park
HC 68 Box 100
Silver City, NM 88061
(505) 536-9461
www.nps.gov/GICL

Grand Canyon National Park
P.O. Box 129
Grand Canyon, AZ 86023
(928) 638-7888
www.nps.gov/grca

Grand Gulch/Cedar Mesa Plateau
BLM Field Office
365 No. Main St.
Monticello, UT
(435) 587-1510
www.blm.gov/ut (then do a BLM site search for
Grand Gulch and Cedar Mesa)

Homolovi Ruins State Park
HCR 63 Box 5
Winslow, AZ 86047
(928) 289-4106
azstateparks.com/parks/hour

Hopi Land
Hopi Cultural Center
P.O. Box 67
Second Mesa, AZ 86039
(928) 734-2401
www.hopiculturalcenter.com

Hovenweep National Monument
McElmo Route
Cortez, CO 81321
www.nps.gov/hove

Isleta Pueblo
P.O. Box 1270
Isleta Pueblo, NM 87022
(505) 869-3111

Jemez Pueblo
P.O. Box 100
Jemez Pueblo, NM 87024
(505) 834-7235
www.jemezpueblo.org

Laguna Pueblo
P.O. Box 194
Laguna Pueblo, NM 87026
(505) 552-6654

Mesa Verde National Park
P.O. Box 8
Mesa Verde, CO 81330
(970) 529-4465
www.nps.gov/meve

Montezuma Castle National Monument
P.O. Box 219
Camp Verde, AZ 86322
(928) 567-3322
www.nps.gov/moca

Monument Valley/Navajo Tribal Park
P.O. Box 2520
Window Rock, AZ 86515
(928) 871-6647
www.navajonationparks.org

Museum of Northern Arizona
3101 N. Ft. Valley Rd.
Flagstaff, AZ 86001
(928) 774-5213
www.musnaz.org

Museum of Indian Arts and Culture
Laboratory of Anthropology
710 Camino Lejo
Santa Fe, NM 87505-7511
(505) 827-6344

Nambe Pueblo
Governor's Office, Rt. 1, Box 117-BB
Santa Fe, NM 87501-9702
(505) 455-2036

Natural Bridges National Monument
HC-60 Box1
Lake Powell, UT 84533
(435) 692-1234
www.nps.gov/nabr

Navajo National Monument
Kiet Siel and Betatakin
HC 71 Box 3
Tonalea, AZ 86044
(928) 672-2700
www.nps.gov/nava

Paquimé
Museo de las Culturas Paquimé
Nuevas Casas Grandes, Chihuahua,
Mexico.

Pecos National Historic Park
P.O. Box 418
Pecos, NM 89552

(505) 757-7200
www.nps.gov/peco

Picuris Pueblo
P.O. Box 127
Penasco, NM 87553
(505) 587-2519

Pojoaque Pueblo
Poeh Cultural Center
78 Cities of Gold Road
Santa Fe, NM 87506
(505) 455-3334
www.poehcenter.com

Salmon Ruins
6131 U.S. 64
Bloomfield, NM 874139554
(505) 632-2013
www.salmonruins.com

Sandia Pueblo
P.O. Box 6008
Bernalillo, NM 87004
(505) 867-3317
www.sandiapueblo.nsn.us

San Felipe Pueblo
P.O. Box 4339
San Felipe Pueblo, NM 87001
(505) 867-3381

San Ildefonso Pueblo
Rt. 5, Box 315-A
Santa Fe, NM 87501
(505) 455-2273

San Juan Pueblo
P.O. Box 1099
San Juan Pueblo, NM 87566
(505) 852-4400

Santa Ana Pueblo
2 Dove Rd.

Bernalillo, NM 87004
(505) 867-3301
www.santaana.org

Santa Clara Pueblo
P.O. Box 580
Espanola, NM 87532
(505) 753-7330

Santo Domingo Pueblo
P.O. Box 99
Santo Domingo Pueblo, NM 87052
(505) 465-2214

Taos Pueblo
P.O. Box 1846
Taos, NM 87571
(505) 758-1028
www.taospueblo.com

Telluride Historical Museum
P.O. Box 1579
201 W. Gregory
Telluride, CO 81435
(970) 723-3344
www.telluridemuseum.org

Tesuque Pueblo
Rt. 5, Box 360-T
Santa Fe, NM 87501
(505) 983-2667

Tonto National Monument
26260 N. AZ Hwy 188 #2
Roosevelt, AZ 85545
(928) 467-2241
www.nps.gov/tont

Tuzigoot National Monument
P.O. Box 219
Camps Verde, AZ 86322
(928) 634-5564
www.nps.gov/tuzi

Ute Mountain Tribal Park
P.O. Box 109
Towaoc, CO 81334
(800) 847-5485
www.utemountainute.com

Walnut Canyon National Monument
6400 N. Hwy. 89
Flagstaff, AZ 86004
(928) 526-3367
www.nps.gov/waca

White Mountain Apache Tribe
(Kinishba Ruin)
P.O. Box 710
Fort Apache, AZ 85926
(928) 338-1230
www.wmatoutdoors.org

Wupatki National Monument
6400 N. Hwy 89
Flagstaff, AZ 86004
(928) 679-2365
www.nps.gov/wupa

Zia Pueblo
135 Capitol Square Dr.
Zia Pueblo, NM 87053-6013
(505) 867-3304

Zuni Pueblo
P.O. Box 1009
Zuni, NM 87327
(505) 782-4403

SITE STEWARDSHIP PROGRAMS

Appendix B

Arizona Site Steward Program
Arizona State Parks
1300 W. Washington St.
Phoenix, AZ 85007
(602) 542-4174
www.azstateparks.com

NW New Mexico Site Stewards Program
Salmon Ruins
6131 U.S. 64
Bloomfield, NM 87413-9554
Email: clay-nwnmssp@msn.com
www.nmstewards.org

San Juan Mountains Association
Ruth Lambert, Ph.D.
Cultural Program Director
P.O. Box 2261
Durango, CO 81302
(970) 385-1267
www.sjma.org

Utah Site Stewards
Edge of the Cedars Museum
600 W. 400 N.
Blanding, UT 84511-4000
(435) 678-2238

GLOSSARY

Anasazi: The ancient people of the Colorado Plateau. The word is thought to be Navajo in origin; the translation of the word is open to debate. It was thought to mean "ancient others" when the term was officially adopted into archaeological terminology at the First Pecos Conference in 1927. Modern Pueblo people resent being named by their enemies and prefer the term "ancestral Puebloans" instead.

Archaeoastronomy: The study of the ancient astronomical practices — how they determined the solstices and the equinoxes and which stars they watched, and so on.

Athapaskans: Speakers of the Athapaskan language that are thought to have migrated from Canada to the American Southwest in the 1400s. Today these people are known as the Apache and the Navajo people.

Atlatl: An Aztec word for a spear-thrower. The atlatl basically lengthened the arm of the hunter, thereby increasing the speed and the distance he could throw a spear.

Bahana: The Hopi word for white-man. It is sometimes spelled *pahana*.

Basketmakers: The beginning era of the ancient Pueblo people. The name derives from Richard Wetherill who noticed differences in skull shapes with the later people, and he also noticed they did not have pottery. He thought they might be a different race of people.

BLM: Bureau of Land Management, a government agency charged with caring for certain government land.

Breath line: Also called a heart line or a spirit line. A person's essence. It is sometimes been referred to as the soul.

Chapalote: An early race of corn that was grown in the early days of farming.

Check dam: Terracing that was intended to slow the flow of run-off water, or to redirect it to their crops. A form of water control.

Cloud-blower: A pipe for smoking tobacco. It is typically made from clay.

Colorado Plateau: An enormous geological uplift extending from mid-Arizona and New Mexico north through most of the Four Corners states: Arizona, Colorado, New Mexico, and Utah. Sagebrush is the "indicator" plant of the Colorado Plateau.

Core: A large piece of stone that a flake is chipped from in order to create a stone tool.

Dado: The lower half of an interior wall that is treated differently than the top half. In the case of the ancient ones, the lower half of the wall was usually plastered a darker brown and a lighter shade on the top half.

Dendrochronology: Dating a site by the tree rings in wooden beams in the building. It is one of the most accurate ways to date a ruin.

Desert varnish: A dark patina on sandstone that is composed of hydrous iron and manganese oxides. It is easy to remove with a sharp instrument, thereby exposing the lighter stone beneath it, making a perfect "canvas" for rock art.

Dropped Lintel: A peeled stick that rests an inch or two below the top of the doorway. It is thought it was for the stone slab door to rest against.

Duck Pot: A ceramic pot that is in the shape of a bird. A type of effigy pot.

Ethnography: The in-depth study of a single culture. Today an ethnographer might learn the language of a people and then live with them awhile.

Ethnology: The study of man. Usually this means traits that are common to all cultures, worldwide.

Flintknapper: A person who makes stone tools.

He'we: The Zuni word for the wafer thin bread that the Pueblo people are known for. Usually it is colorful because it is made from the different colored corn.

Herraduras: Spanish for horseshoe. A shrine that is typically found along ancient trails and roadways in the American Southwest. They are thought to mark turns in the road and are usually round with one end open, hence the name.

Hohokam: One of the great cultures of the American Southwest, centered in Arizona near where the town of Phoenix is today. They are best known for the 600 miles of irrigation canals they constructed with stone tools and hand labor. Some of these canals are still in use today.

Hoodoo: A pinnacle of sandstone, usually wind-sculpted into odd shapes and sizes.

Hunter/gatherers: Ancient nomadic way of life before the ancient people settled down to a farming way of life. Usually the men did the hunting of wild game and the women gathered wild foodstuff.

Jacal: (huh-CALL) Sticks woven together into a wall, then covered heavily with mud.

Knife Wing: A bird image on pottery or rock art. Knife Wing faces the viewer with wings outstretched and often ending in sharp points. The bird's talons are prominent and so is his sharp beak.

Lithic scatter: The small stone chips that are the debris from making a stone tool.

Maiz de Ocho: Corncobs that have eight rows of kernels around their perimeter.

Mano: A hand-held grinding stone.

Metate: (Meh TAH tay) The heavy base stone of the grinding stones.

Mimbres: A subgroup of the Mogollon people who lived along the Mimbres River in southwestern New Mexico. The Mimbres people are best remembered for their magnificent pottery.

Misfire: Dark clouds on a pot caused from problems that arose while firing the pot. Much experience was required to effectively fire a pot.

Mogollon: One of the great cultures of the American Southwest who lived in the highlands between central Arizona and New Mexico. The Mogollon created brownware pottery.

Mogollon Rim: The southern tip of the Colorado Plateau in mid-Arizona. It forms a major boundary between habitats. Farming techniques are very different above and below the Mogollon Rim. And the cultures were different above and below the rim.

Moqui: An early name for the Hopi people of Arizona.

Museum rock: Visitors place artifacts they have found at a site on a convenient table-sized stone or a window ledge to display them for future visitors to the site. They attempt to re-create a museum-like atmosphere in the wild. Apparently they think this does not constitute removing the artifact from a site. Archaeologists and preservationists discourage this practice.

Olla: (Oy-ah) The Spanish word for a water jug.

Pahos: Prayer feathers. There are many different kinds: Some prayer feathers are attached to long willow whips, others are on small, wide wooden boards. Some are large and elaborate, others are small and simple.

Paquimé: The ancient name of the city that is now called Casas Grandes (great houses). The ruins of this once great city are located near the modern town of Nuevo Casas Grandes in the state of Chihuahua, Mexico. There is a museum adjacent to the site. Note that Casas Grandes is plural, there is another site in Arizona called Casa Grande (singular).

Pecos Classification: During the first Pecos Conference in 1927 archaeologists created a list of traits to characterize the different phases of the Anasazi culture at different times. It began with the Basketmakers and proceeded through Pueblo I, II, III, and IV (and today is abbreviated PI, PII, PIII and PIV). It has been revised and updated repeatedly since then. Cliff dwellings are in the PIII range of the Pecos Classification.

Petroglyph: Rock art that has been pecked onto the face of the rock. Petroglyphs are the most common of all rock art.

Pictograph: Rock art that has been painted on the face of the rock.

Piki: (Pee kee) The Hopi word for the wafer thin bread that the Pueblo people are known for. Usually it is colorful because it is made from the different colored corn.

Prehistory: The time before written records. Since the ancient people of the American Southwest did not have their own written language, history and documents arrived with the Spaniards.

Provenance (or provenience): A complete accounting of an artifact's history of ownership. Every person or place that has ever owned a particular art object is listed, thereby lessening the chance for the artifact to be a fake.

Pueblo: The Spanish word for "town."

Quetzalcoatl: The feathered or plumed snake, an important deity among the Mayans.

Quicksand: When ordinary sand has a subterranean water source it becomes unstable and seems to "suck" under anything that comes in contact with it.

Ramada: A post-and-beam structure that is not enclosed with building materials; instead the open spaces are filled-in with branches and leaves. This provides shade and allows a breeze to flow through it, and is a comfortable place in the desert heat. Native Americans of today still construct ramadas and use them.

Refuge site: Our definition is: a wall on an inaccessible ledge that was probably used as protection when danger appeared. There is only one choke point entrance. There is no sign that anyone ever lived at such a site — no black smoking on the walls, no sign of a hearth, no vents. But there will be loopholes.

Sipapu: (See PAH poo) A small hole near the center of a kiva floor that represents the place of emergence from the previous underworld.

Slickrock: The sandy bottoms of ancient seas, visible today in the form of sandstone. It can stretch for miles.

Slip: Since the potter preferred a crisp white background for her pottery designs, and pottery was either grayware or brownware, the potter wiped or painted the surface of the pot with a thin emulsion of white clay before painting on her designs. This is called slip.

T-Door: A doorway shape that is unique to the Greater American Southwest — one that is larger on the top half of the door than the narrower bottom half of the door. T-shaped doorways usually lead into habitation rooms, public areas or ceremonial rooms.

Teosinte: The wild Mexican grass that is probably the parent plant of maize or corn.

Tlaloc: The Mayan/Aztec god of water, among other things. Tlaloc is one of the images that diffused north to the American Southwest. His most recognizable feature is his huge goggle eyes that can take up half his body. Among the Mayans the goggle eyes were actually two coiled snakes.

Tradeware: Pottery that does not belong where it is found. It was created in one place, as determined by its designs and clay type, but is found far away from that location. Archaeologists assume it was traded for, and that is how it made its way to this location.

Trinchera: The Spanish word for a check dam. It is terracing that was intended to slow the flow of run-off water, or to redirect it to their crops.

Unit pueblo: A semi-subterranean pithouse or early kiva with an arc of surface rooms behind it. It is an early form of a pueblo and they are scattered all over the Colorado Plateau. They are older than cliff dwellings and most were farmsteads operated by an extended family.

Vernacular architecture: "Folk" architecture, that is, buildings that were designed and built by their owners for their own use. Buildings that were not designed by professional architects. Pueblos and cliff dewllings are an outstanding example of vernacular architecture.

BIBLIOGRAPHY

10ᵗʰ Annual Report of the United States Geological and Geographical Survey of the Territories Embracing Colorado and Parts of Adjacent Territories by F. V. Hayden. "Report of the Ancient Ruins Examined in 1875 and 1877." Washington D.C.: Government Printing Office, 1878.

Adams, E. Charles. "The Architectural Analogue to Hopi Social Organization and Room Use, and Implications for Prehistoric Northern Southwestern Culture." *American Antiquity.* 48 no. 1 (1983) 44-61.

Adler, Michael A., ed. *The Prehistoric Pueblo World A.D. 1150–1350.* Tucson: University of Arizona Press, 1996.

Allen, Hubert A. Jr. *The Petroglyph Calendar: An Archaeoastronomy Adventure.* Albuquerque: Hubert Allen and Associates, 1998.

Allen, Marti Lu, and Baker, Shane A. eds. *Of Earth, Stone, and Corn: The Anasazi and Their Puebloan Descendants.* Museum of Peoples and Cultures: Popular Series 2. Provo, Utah: Brigham Young University, 2000.

Amsden, Charles Avery. *Prehistoric Southwesterners from Basketmaker to Pueblo.* Los Angeles: Southwest Museum, 1949.

Arhhenius, Olof W. *Stones Speak and Waters Sing: The Life and Works of Gustaf Nordenskiold.* Mesa Verde National Park, Colorado: Mesa Verde Museum Association, Inc., n.d.

Athearn, Frederic J. *A Forgotten Kingdom: The Spanish Frontier in Colorado and New Mexico 1540 – 1821.* Cultural Resource Series no. 29. Denver: Bureau of Land Management, 1992.

Atkins, Victoria M., ed. *Anasazi Basketmaker: Papers from the 1990 Wetherill-Grand Gulch Symposium.* Cultural Resource Series no. 24. Salt Lake City: Bureau of Land Management, 1993.

Aveni, Anthony F. ed. *Native American Astronomy.* Austin: University of Texas Press, 1977.

Bagwell, Elizabeth A. "Architectural Patterns along the Rio Taraises Northern Sierra Madre Occidental, Sonora." *Kiva: The Journal of Southwestern Archaeology and History.* 70 no. 1, (Fall, 2004): 7-30.

Bahn, Paul, ed. *Written in Bones: How Human Remains Unlock the Secrets of the Dead.* Toronto, Canada: Firefly Books, Ltd., 2002.

Baldwin, Anne R., and Bremer, J. Michael. *Walnut Canyon National Monument: An Archeological*

Survey. Publications in Anthropology no. 39. Tucson, Arizona: Western Archeological and Conservation Center, 1986.

Barnett, Franklin. *Dictionary of Prehistoric Indian Artifacts of the American Southwest.* Flagstaff: Northland Press, 1973.

Benedict, Jeff. *No Bone Unturned: The Adventures of a Top Smithsonian Forensic Scientist and the Legal Battle for America's Oldest Skeletons.* New York: HarperCollins Publishers, 2003.

Berger, Joanne H., and Berger, Edward F. *Insights into the Ancient Ones.* 2nd ed. Cortez, Colorado: Interdisciplinary Supplemental Educational Programs, Inc., 1984.

Bernardini, Wesley. "Conflict, Migration, and the Social Environment: Interpreting Architectural Change in Early and Late Pueblo IV Aggregations." In *Migration and Reorganization: The Pueblo IV Period in the American Southwest* by K. Spielmann, ed. Anthropological Research Papers no. 51. Tempe: Arizona State University, 1998.

Bernardini, Wesley. *Hopi Oral Tradition and the Archaeology of Identity.* Tucson: University of Arizona Press, 2005.

Blackburn, Fred M. *The Wetherills: Friends of Mesa Verde.* Durango, Colorado: Durango Herald Small Press, 2006.

Blackburn, Fred M., and Williamson, Ray A. *Cowboys and Cave Dwellers: Basketmaker Archaeology in Utah's Grand Gulch.* Santa Fe: School of American Research Press, 1997.

Bloomer, William W. "Moon House: A Pueblo III Period Cliff Dwelling Complex in Southeastern Utah." Dissertation, Washington State University, May, 1989.

Boissiere, Robert. *Meditations with the Hopi.* Santa Fe: Bear & Company, 1986.

Bolton, Herbert E. *Pageant in the Wilderness: The Story of the Escalante Expedition to the Interior Basin, 1776.* Salt Lake City: Utah State Historical Society, 1972.

Bostwick, Todd W. *Byron Cummings: Dean of Southwest Archaeology.* Tucson: University of Arizona Press, 2006.

Bradley, Bruce A. "Architectural Petroglyphs at Sand Canyon Pueblo Southwestern Colorado." *Kiva.* 54 no. 2 (1989) 153-161.

Breternitz, David A., (princ. inv.) *Dolores Archaeological Program: Anasazi Communties at Dolores: Early Small Settlements in the Dolores River Canyon and Western Sagehen Flats Area.* Denver: U.S. Department of the Interior, May 1986.

—. (princ. inv.) *Dolores Archaeological Program: Research Designs and Initial Survey Results.* Denver: U.S. Department of the Interior, June 1986.

—. (princ. inv.). *Dolores Archaeological Program: Synthetic Report 1978-1981.* Denver: U.S. Department of the Interior, June 1984.

—. (princ. inv) *Dolores Archaeological Program: Field Investigations and Analysis – 1987.* Denver, Colorado: U.S. Department of the Interior, November 1983.

Brody, J. J. *Anasazi & Pueblo Painting.* School of American Research Book. Albuquerque: University of New Mexico Press, 1991.

—. *Mimbres Painted Pottery.* School of American Research Book. Albuquerque: University of New Mexico Press, 1977.

Brody, J. J.; Catherine J. Scott; Steven A. LeBlanc. *Mimbres Pottery: Ancient Art of the American Southwest.* New York: Hudson Hill Press, 1983.

Bunting, Bainbridge. *Early Architecture in New Mexico.* Albuquerque: University of New Mexico Press, 1976.

Bunzel, Ruth L. *The Pueblo Potter: A Study of Creative Imagination in Primitive Art.* Reprint, 1929. New York: Dover Publications, 1972.

Calvin, William H. *How the Shaman Stole the Moon: In Search of Ancient Prophet-Scientists from Stonehenge to the Grand Canyon.* Authors Guild Backinprint.com Edition, originally published by Bantam Books. Lincoln: iUniverse.com, Inc., 1991.

Cameron, Catherine M. *Chaco and After in the Northern San Juan: Excavations at the Bluff Great House.* Tucson: University of Arizona Press, 2008.

—. *Hopi Dwellings: Architecture at Orayvi.* Tucson: University of Arizona Press, 1999.

—. Ed. *Invisible Citizens: Captives and Their Consequences.* Salt Lake City: University of Utah Press, 2008.

Chapin, Frederick H. *The Land of the Cliff Dwellers.* Appalachian Mountain Club. Boston: W.B. Clarke and Company, 1892.

Childs, Craig. *House of Rain: Tracking a Vanished Civilization across the American Southwest.* New York: Little, Brown and Company, 2006.

Ciolek-Torrello, Richard S. and Lange, Richard C. "The Gila Pueblo Survey of the Southeastern Sierra Ancha." *Kiva: The Journal of Southwestern Archaeology and History.* 55 no. 2 (1990): 127-154.

Clark, Jeffery J. *Tracking Prehistoric Migrations: Pueblo Settlers among the Tonto Basin Hohokam.* Anthropological Papers no. 65. Tucson: University of Arizona Press, 2001.

Cole, Sally J. *Legacy on Stone: Rock Art of the Colorado Plateau and Four Corners Region.* Revised edition. Boulder: Johnson Books, 2009.

Colton, Harold S. *Hopi Kachina Dolls*. Albuquerque: University of New Mexico Press, 1949.

—. *Potsherds: An Introduction to the Study of Prehistoric Southwestern Ceramics and the use in Historic Reconstruction*. Bulletin 25, Museum of Northern Arizona. Flagstaff: Northern Arizona Society of Science and Art, 1953.

Cordell, Linda S. *Ancient Pueblo Peoples*. Exploring the Ancient World Series. Washington, DC: Smithsonian Institution, 1994.

—. *Archaeology of the Southwest*. 2nd ed. San Diego: Academic Press, 1997.

Cornet, James W. *How Indians Used Desert Plants*. Palm Springs: Nature Trails Press, 2002.

Courlander, Harold. *The Fourth World of the Hopi: The Epic Story of the Hopi Indians as Preserved in Their Legends and Traditions*. Albuquerque: University of New Mexico Press, 1971.

Crotty, Helen K. *Honoring the Dead: Anasazi Ceramics from the Rainbow Bridge-Monument Valley Expedition*. Museum of Cultural History Monograph no. 22. Los Angeles: University of California, 1983.

Cummings, Byron. "The Ancient Inhabitants of the San Juan Valley." *Bulletin of the University of Utah*. III no. 3 (November 1910) 1-45.

Cunkle, James R. *Talking Pots: Deciphering the Symbols of a Prehistoric People*. Phoenix: Golden West Publishers, 1993.

—. *Treasures of Time: A Guide to Prehistoric Ceramics of the Southwest*. Phoenix: Golden West Publishers, 1994.

Cushing, Frank Hamilton. "My Adventures in Zuni I." *The Century Magazine*. (1st ed.) 25, no. 2 (December, 1882): 191-207.

—. "My Adventures in Zuni II." *The Century Magazine*. (1st ed.) 25, no. 3. (January, 1883): 500-511.

—. "My Adventures in Zuni III." *The Century Magazine*. (1st ed.) 26, no. 1 (May, 1883): 28-47.

—. *My Adventures in Zuni*. Reprint. Palo Alto, California: American West Publishing Company, 1970.

—. *A Study of Pueblo Pottery as Illustrative of Zuni Culture-Growth*. 4th Annual Report of the Bureau of American Ethnology. Smithsonian Institution: Washington, D.C., 1882-1883.

Dean, Jeffrey S. *Chronological Analysis of Tsegi Phase Sites in Northeastern Arizona*. Papers of the Laboratory of Tree-Ring Research no. 3. Tucson: University of Arizona Press, 1969.

—. ed. *Salado.* Amerind Foundation Publication, Dragoon, Arizona. Albuquerque: University of New Mexico Press, 2000.

Di Peso, Charles C. *Casas Grandes: A Fallen Trading Center of the Gran Chichimeca.* Vols. I, II, III. Amerind Foundation no. 9. Flagstaff: Northland Press, 1974.

Dittert, Alfred E. Jr. "The Acoma Culture Province during the Period A.D. 1275 – 1500: Cultural Disruption and Reorganization." In *Migration and Reorganization: The Pueblo IV Period in the American Southwest* by K. Spielmann, ed. Anthropological Research Papers no. 51. Tempe: Arizona State University, 1998.

Doyel, David E. and Dean, Jeffrey S., eds. *Environmental Change and Human Adaptation in the Ancient American Southwest.* Salt Lake City: University of Utah Press, 2006.

Dozier, Edward P. *The Pueblo Indians of North America. Case Studies in Cultural Anthropology.* New York: Holt, Rinehart and Winston, Inc., 1970.

Duff, Andrew I. "The Process of Migration in the Late Prehistoric Southwest." In *Migration and Reorganization: The Pueblo IV Period in the American Southwest* by K. Spielmann, ed. Anthropological Research Papers no. 51. Tempe: Arizona State University, 1998.

Dunmire, William W. and Tierney, Gail A. *Wild Plants and Native Peoples of the Four Corners.* Santa Fe: Museum of New Mexico Press, 1997.

Ehrilich, Paul R.; Dobkin, David S.; Wheye, Darryl. *The Birder's Handbook: A Field Guide to the Natural History of North American Birds.* New York: Simon & Schuster, Inc. 1988.

Elliott, Melinda. *Great Excavations: Tales of Early Southwestern Archaeology 1888-1939.* Santa Fe: School of American Research Press, 1995.

Ellis, Florence Hawley. "A Thousand Years of the Pueblo Sun-Moon-Star Calendar." A paper presented at the American Association for the Advancement of Science meeting, June 20, 1973, Mexico City.

Ellis, Rueben. *Stories and Stone: Writing the Anasazi Homeland.* Boulder: Pruett Publishing Co., 1997.

Fagan, Brian. *The Great Warming: Climate Change and the Rise and Fall of Civilizations.* New York: Bloomsbury Press, 2008.

—. *The Little Ice Age: How Climate Made History 1300 – 1850.* New York: Basic Books, 2000.

Fedoroff, Nina V. "Prehistoric GM Corn." *Science.* 302 (November 14, 2003): 1158 – 1159.

Ferg, Alan and Mead, Jim I. *Red Cave: A Prehistoric Cave Shrine in Southeastern Arizona.* no. 26. Phoenix: Arizona Archaeological Society, 1993.

Ferguson, T. J. *Historic Zuni Architecture and Society: An Archaeological Application of Space Syntax.* Anthropological Papers of the University of Arizona, no. 60. Tucson: University of Arizona Press, 1996.

Ferguson, William M. and Rohn, Arthur H. *Anasazi Ruins of the Southwest in Color.* Albuquerque: University of New Mexico Press, 1987.

Ferguson, William M. *The Anasazi of Mesa Verde and the Four Corners.* Niwot, Colorado: University Press of Colorado, 1996.

Fewkes, J. Walter. "The Winter Solstice Ceremony at Walpi." *The American Anthropologist.* XI, no. 3. (March, 1898): 65–105.

—. *Antiquities of the Mesa Verde National Park: Spruce-Tree House.* Bureau of American Ethnology, Bulletin no. 41. Washington DC: Smithsonian Institution, 1909.

—. *Antiquities of the Mesa Verde National Park: Cliff Palace.* Bureau of American Ethnology, Bulletin no. 51.Washington, DC: Smithsonian Institution, 1911.

—. *Designs on Prehistoric Hopi Pottery.* 23rd Annual Report of the Bureau of American Ethnology. Washington, DC: Smithsonian Institution, 1919.

—. *Preliminary Report on a Visit to the Navaho National Monument Arizona.* Bureau of American Ethnology. Bulletin no. 50. Washington DC: Smithsonian Institution, 1911.

Fiero, Kathleen. *Balcony House: A History of a Cliff Dwelling.* Archaeological Research Series no. 8A. Mesa Verde National Park, Colorado: National Park Service, 1999.

Fletcher, Maurine S., ed. *The Wetherills of the Mesa Verde: Autobiography of Benjamin Alfred Wetherill.* London: Associated University Presses, 1977.

Flint, Richard and Flint, Shirley Cushing, eds, trans. *Documents of the Coronado Expedition, 1539–1542: "They Were Not Familiar with His Majesty, nor Did They Wish to Be His Subjects."* Dallas: Southern Methodist University Press, 2005.

Flint, Richard. *Great Cruelties Have Been Reported: The 1544 Investigation of the Coronado Expedition.* Dallas: Southern Methodist University Press, 2002.

Fowler, Don D. *A Laboratory for Anthropology: Science and Romanticism in the American Southwest, 1846-1930.* Albuquerque: University of New Mexico Press, 2000.

Frazier, Kendrick. *People of Chaco: A Canyon and Its Culture.* 3rd ed. New York: W. W. Norton & Co., 2005.

Fuller, Glen E. *Anasazi: Builders of Wonders.* N.p.: 1991.

Gabriel, Kathryn. *Roads to Center Place: A Cultural Atlas of Chaco Canyon and the Anasazi.* Boulder: Johnson Books, 1991.

Gibson, Daniel. *Pueblos of the Rio Grande: A Visitor's Guide.* Tucson: Rio Nuevo Publishers, 2001.

Gillmor, Frances and Wetherill, Louisa Wade. *Traders to the Navajos: The Story of the Wetherills of Kayenta.* Albuquerque: University of New Mexico, 1953.

Gilman, Patricia A. "Architecture as Artifact: Pit Structures and Pueblos in the American Southwest." *American Antiquity.* 52 no. 3 (1987) 538-564.

Glassie, Henry. *Vernacular Architecture.* Bloomington: Indiana University Press, 2000.

Grant, Campbell. *Canyon de Chelly: Its People and Rock Art.* Tucson: University of Arizona Press, 1978.

—. *Rock Art of the American Indian.* Golden, Colorado: Outbooks, 1981.

Graves, Michael W. "Anomalous Tree-Ring Dates and the Sequence of Room Construction at Canyon Creek Ruin, East Central Arizona." *Kiva: The Journal of Southwestern Archaeology and History.* 47 no. 3 (1982): 107-131.

—. "Growth and Aggregation at Canyon Creek Ruin: Implications for Evolutionary Change in East-Central Arizona." *American Antiquity.* 48 (1983) 290-315.

Green, Jesse, ed. *Zuni: Selected Writings of Frank Hamilton Cushing.* Lincoln: University of Nebraska Press, 1979.

Greenlee, Bob. *Life Among the Ancient Ones: Two Accounts of an Anasazi Archaeological Research Project.* Boulder, Colorado: Hardscrabble Press, 1995.

Gulliford, Andrew, ed. *Preserving Western History.* Albuquerque: University of New Mexico Press, 2005.

—. *Sacred Objects and Sacred Places: Preserving Tribal Traditions.* Boulder: University Press of Colorado, 2000.

Gumerman, George J. *A View from Black Mesa: The Changing Face of Archaeology.* Tucson: University of Arizona Press, 1984.

—, ed. *Themes in Southwest Prehistory.* Advanced Seminar Series. Santa Fe: School of American Research, 1994.

Haas, Jonathan and Creamer, Winifred. *Stress and Warfare Among the Kayenta Anasazi of the Thirteenth Century A.D.* Fieldiana, Anthropology no. 21. Chicago: Field Museum of Natural History, 1993.

Hadingham, Evan. *Early Man and the Cosmos.* New York: Walker and Company, 1984.

Hafen, Leroy R. and Hafen, Ann W. *Far West and the Rockies Historical Series 1820 —1875.* Vol. X, "Diaries of William Henry Jackson, Frontier Photographer." Glendale, California: Arthur H. Clark Co., 1959.

Hamm, Jim. *Bows & Arrows of the Native Americans: A Complete Step-by-Step Guide to Wooden Bows, Sinewbacked Bows, Composite Bows, Strings, Arrows & Quivers.* n.p.: Lyons Press, 1989.

Harper's Weekly Magazine, (May 22, 1875): 420.

Haury, Emil. W. *The Canyon Creek Ruin and the Cliff Dwellings of the Sierra Ancha.* Medallion Papers no. XIV. Globe, Arizona: n.p., January, 1934.

Hayes, Alden C. and Windes, Thomas C. "An Anasazi Shrine in Chaco Canyon." In *Collected Papers in Honor of Florence Ellis* by Theodore R. Frisbie, ed. Papers of the Archaeological Society of New Mexico 2: Santa Fe.

Hayes, Alden C. *The Archeological Survey of Wetherill Mesa.* Archeological Research Series no. 7A. Mesa Verde National Park, Colorado: National Park Service, 1964.

—. *Two Raven House: Wetherill Mesa Excavations.* Archaeological Research Series no. 7E. Mesa Verde National Park, Colorado: National Park Service, 1998.

Hayes, Alden C.; Brugge, David M.; Judge, W. James. *Archeological Surveys of Chaco Canyon New Mexico.* Publications in Archeology no. 18A, Chaco Canyon Studies. Washington DC: National Park Service, 1981.

Hayes, Allan and Blom, John. *Southwestern Pottery: Anasazi to Zuni.* Flagstaff: Northland Publishing, 1996.

Heacock, Laura A. "Archaeological Investigations of Three Mesa Verde Anasazi Pit Kilns." *Kiva: The Journal of Southwestern Archaeology and History.* 60 no. 3 (1995): 391-410.

Hobler, Philip M. and Hobler, Audrey E. "An Archeological Survey of the Upper White Canyon Area, Southeastern Utah." Antiquities Section Selected Papers, Department of Development Services. 5, no. 13. (1978) Salt Lake City: Utah State Historical Society.

Holmes, William H. *Pottery of the Ancient Pueblos.* 4th Annual Report of the Bureau of Ethnology. Washington, DC: Smithsonian Institution, 1882-1883.

Hopi Dictionary Project. *Hopi Dictionary: A Hopi-English Dictionary of the Third Mesa Dialect.* Tucson: University of Arizona Press, 1998.

Huckel, J.F. ed. *American Indians: First Families of the Southwest.* 2nd ed. Kansas City, Missouri: Fred Harvey, 1920.

Hulbert, Archer Butler. *Indian Thoroughfares. Historic Highways of America,* Vol.#2. Cleveland: Arthur H. Clark Company, 1902.

Hurst, Winston and Till, Johathan. "Mesa Verdean Sacred Landscapes." In *The Mesa Verde World* by David Grant Noble, ed. Santa Fe: School of American Research Press, 2006.

Hurst, Winston. "The Mysterious Telluride Blanket." *Blue Mountain Shadows* 13 (Summer, 1994): 68–69.

Hutchinson, Art and Smith, Jack E., eds. *Proceedings of the Anasazi Symposium 1991.* Mesa Verde National Park: Mesa Verde Museum Association, Inc., 1991.

Iowa, Jerome. *Ageless Adobe: History and Preservation in Southwestern Architecture.* Santa Fe: Sunstone Press, 1985.

Jackson, John Brinckerhoff. *A Sense of Place, A Sense of Time.* New Haven: Yale University, 1994.

Jackson, William H. *8ᵗʰ Annual Report of the United States Geological and Geographical Survey of the Territories Embracing Colorado and Parts of Adjacent Territories by F. V. Hayden.* "Ancient Ruins in Southwestern Colorado."Washington DC: Government Printing Office, 1876.

Jackson, William Henry. *Time Exposure: Autobiography of William Henry Jackson.* New York: Van Rees Press, 1940.

Jaenicke-Despres, Viviane; Buckler, Ed S.; Smith, Bruce D.; Gilbert, M. Thomas P.; Cooper, Alan; Doebley, John; Paabo, Svante. "Early Allelic Selection in Maize as Revealed by Ancient DNA." *Science.* 302 (November 14, 2003): 1206–1208.

James, Harry C. *Pages from Hopi History.* Tucson: University of Arizona Press, 1974.

Jennings, Jesse, ed. *Anthropological Papers: Miscellaneous Collected Papers 11-14.* No. 83. Salt Lake City: University of Utah Press, 1966.

Jett, Stephen. *House of Three Turkeys: Anasazi Redoubt.* A Noel Young Book. Santa Barbara: Capra Press, 1977.

Judd, Neil M. *Men Met Along the Trail: Adventures in Archaeology.* Norman: University of Oklahoma Press, 1968.

Kamp, Kathryn A., ed. *Children in the Prehistoric Puebloan Southwest.* Salt Lake City: University of Utah Press, 2002.

—. *Life in the Pueblo: Understanding the Past through Archaeology.* Prospect Heights, Illinois: Waveland Press, Inc., 1998.

Kankainen, Kathy, ed. *Treading in the Past: Sandals of the Anasazi.* Salt Lake City: Utah Museum of Natural History, 1995.

Kantner, John. *Ancient Puebloan Southwest.* Cambridge, United Kingdom: University of Cambridge, 2004.

Kavena, Juanita Tiger. *Hopi Cookery.* Tucson: University of Arizona Press, 1980.

Kent, Kate Peck. *Prehistoric Textiles of the Southwest.* School of American Research Book. Albuquerque:

University of New Mexico Press, 1983.

Kidder, A.V. "Notes on the Archaeology of the Babicora District, Chihuahua." In *So Live the Works of Man: Seventieth Anniversary Volume Honoring Edgar Lee Hewett.* Albuquerque: University of New Mexico Press, 1939.

—. "Reminiscences in Southwest Archaeology: I." *Kiva: Journal of the Arizona Archaeological and Historical Society.* 25 no. 4 (April 1960): 1-32.

—. "Explorations in Southeastern Utah in 1908." *Papers of the School of American Archaeology.* 15 (1910) 337-359.

Kidder, Alfred Vincent and Guernsey, Samuel J. *Archeological Explorations in Northeastern Arizona.* Bureau of American Ethnology, Bulletin no. 65. Washington DC: Smithsonian Institution, 1919.

Kluckhohn, Clyde M. *To the Foot of the Rainbow.* Reprint. 1927. Glorieta, New Mexico: The Rio Grande Press, 1980.

Knipmeyer, James H. *Butch Cassidy was Here: Historic Inscriptions of the Colorado Plateau.* Salt Lake City: University of Utah Press, 2002.

—. *In Search of a Lost Race: The Illustrated American Exploring Expedition of 1892.* Reprint. N.p.: n.n., 2006.

Kooyman, Brian P. *Understanding Stone Tools and Archaeological Sites.* Albuquerque: University of New Mexico Press, 2000.

Krupp, E.C., ed. *In Search of Ancient Astronomies: Stonehenge to von Daniken.* New York: McGraw-Hill Book Company: 1979.

Lambert, Ruth E. "Investigations of Small Structures in the Citadel District of Wupatki National Monument." Dissertation, University of New Mexico, 2006.

Lange, Charles H. and Riley, Carroll L. eds. *The Southwestern Journals of Adolph F. Bandelier 1880-1892.* Vols. 1-4. Albuquerque and Santa Fe: University of New Mexico Press and School of American Research, 1966-1984.

Lange, Richard C. ed. *Echoes in the Canyons: The Archaeology of the Southeastern Sierra Ancha, Central Arizona.* Arizona State Museum Archaeological Series no.198. Tucson: University of Arizona and Arizona State Museum, 2006.

LeBlanc, Steven A. "Settlement Consequences of Warfare during the Late Pueblo III and Pueblo IV Periods." In *Migration and Reorganization: The Pueblo IV Period in the American Southwest* by K. Spielmann, ed. Anthropological Research Papers no. 51. Tempe: Arizona State University, 1998.

—. *Constant Battles: Why We Fight.* New York: St. Martin's Press, 2003.

—. *Prehistoric Warfare in the American Southwest.* Salt Lake City: University of Utah Press, 1999.

—. *The Mimbres People: Ancient Pueblo Painters of the American Southwest.* New York: Thames and Hudson, 1983.

LeBlanc, Steven A. and Rice, Glen E., eds. *Deadly Landscapes: Case Studies in Prehistoric Southwestern Warfare.* Salt Lake City: University of Utah Press, 2001.

Lekson, Stephen H. *A History of the Ancient Southwest.* Santa Fe: School for Advanced Research, 2008.

—. *Salado Archaeology of the Upper Gila, New Mexico.* Anthropological Papers no. 67. Tucson: University of Arizona Press, 2002.

—. *The Chaco Meridian: Centers of Political Power in the Ancient Southwest.* Walnut Creek, California: AltaMira Press, 1999.

—. ed. *The Architecture of Chaco Canyon, New Mexico.* Salt Lake City: University of Utah Press, 2007.

Lightfoot, Ricky R. *The Duckfoot Site.* Archaeology of the House and Household, Vol 2. Cortez, Colorado: Crow Canyon Archaeology Center, 1994.

Lipe, W.D. and Hegmon, Michelle, eds. *The Architecture of Social Integration in Prehistoric Pueblos.* Cortez, Colorado: Crow Canyon Archaeological Center, 1989.

Lipe, William D. "Final Report for the Surface Cleanup of Cultural Sites in Grand Gulch." Flagstaff: Museum of Northern Arizona, 1974.

—. "Value and Meaning in Cultural Resources." Approaches to the Archaeological Heritage, Henry Cleere, ed. Cambridge, United Kingdom: Cambridge University Press, 1984.

Lipe, William D.; Matson, R. G. and Haase William R. IV. "Adaptational Continuities and Occupational Discontinuities: The Cedar Mesa Anasazi." *Journal of Field Archaeology.* 15 (1988) 245-264.

Lister, Florence C. and Lister, Robert H. *Earl Morris and Southwestern Archaeology.* Albuquerque: University of New Mexico Press, 1968.

Lister, Florence C. *Behind Painted Walls: Incidents in Southwestern Archaeology.* Albuquerque: University of New Mexico Press, 2000.

—. *Pot Luck: Adventures in Archaeology.* Albuquerque: University of New Mexico Press, 1997.

—. *Prehistory in Peril: The Worst and Best of Durango Archaeology.* Niwot, Colorado: University Press of Colorado, 1997.

—. *Troweling through Time: The First Century of Mesa Verdean Archaeology.* Albuquerque: University of New Mexico Press: 2004.

Lister, Robert and Lister, Florence C. *Those Who Came Before: Southwestern Archeology in the National Park System.* Tucson: University of Arizona Press, 1983.

Lister, Robert H. "Survey of Archaeological Remains in Northwestern Chihuahua." *Southwestern Journal of Anthropology.* 2 no. 4 (1946) 433-451.

—. *Archaeological Excavations in the Northern Sierra Madre Occidental, Chihuahua and Sonora, Mexico.* University of Colorado Studies, Series in Anthropology no. 7. Boulder: University of Colorado Press, 1958.

Lister, Robert H. and Lister, Florence C. *Aztec Ruins on the Animas: Excavated, Preserved, and Interpreted.* Tucson: Southwest Parks and Monuments Association, 1987.

Lister, Robert H. and Lister, Florence C. *Chaco Canyon: Archaeology and Archaeologists.* Albuquerque: University of New Mexico Press, 1981.

Lister, Robert H. and Lister, Florence C. *The Earl H. Morris Memorial Pottery Collection: An Example of Ten Centuries of Prehistoric Ceramic Art in the Four Corners Country of Southwestern United States.* Boulder: University of Colorado Press, 1969.

Longacre, William A., ed. *Reconstructing Prehistoric Pueblo Societies.* School of American Research Book. Albuquerque: University of New Mexico Press, 1970.

Loomis, Charles F. "The Indian Who is not Poor." *Scribner's Magazine.* XII (1892) 361-373.

Love, Marian F. "A Survey of the Distribution of T-Shaped Doorways in the Greater Southwest." In *Collected Papers in Honor of Florence Ellis* by Theodore R. Frisbie, ed., pp 296–311. Papers of the Archaeological Society of New Mexico 2: Santa Fe.

Lucius, William A. and David Breternitz. *Northern Anasazi Ceramic Styles: A Field Guide for Identification.* Phoenix: Center for Indigenous Studies in the Americas, 1992.

Lumholtz, Carl. *Unknown Mexico: A Record of Five Years' Exploration Among the Tribes of the Western Sierra Madre; In the Tierra Caliente of Tepic and Jalisco; and Among the Tarascos of Michoacan.* First edition. Vols. I and II. New York: Charles Scribner's Sons, 1902.

Lyons, Patrick D. *Ancestral Hopi Migrations.* Anthropological Papers no. 68. Tucson: University of Arizona Press, 2003.

Mails, Thomas E. and Evehema, Dan. *Hotevilla: Hopi Shrine of the Covenant, Microcosm of the World.* New York: Marlow & Company, 1995.

Malotki, Ekkehart, ed. *Hopi Ruin Legends: Kiqötutuwutsi.* Flagstaff: Northern Arizona University, 1993.

—. *Kokopelli: The Making of an Icon.* Lincoln: University of Nebraska Press, 2000.

Malville, J. McKim and Claudia Putnam. *Prehistoric Astronomy in the Southwest*. Revised ed. Boulder: Johnson Books, 1993.

Manchester, William. *A World Lit Only by Fire: The Medieval Mind and the Renaissance*. Boston: Little, Brown and Company, 1992.

Markovich, Nicholas C.; Preiser, Wolfgang F. E.; Sturm, Fred G., eds. *Pueblo Style and Regional Architecture*. New York: Van Nostrand Reinhold, 1990.

Matheny, Ray T., ed. *New Dimensions in Rock Art Studies*. Museum of People and Cultures, no. 9. Provo, Utah: Brigham Young University, 2004.

McGregor, John C. *Southwestern Archaeology*. 2nd ed. Urbana: University of Illinois, 1977.

McGuire, Randall H. "The Mesoamerican Connection in the Southwest." *Kiva*. 46, no. 1–2 (1980): 3–38.

McIntosh, Jane. *The Practical Archaeologist: How We Know What We Know about the Past*. New York: Checkmark Books, 1999.

McKern, W. C. *Western Colorado Petroglyphs*. Cultural Resources Series no. 8. Denver: Bureau of Land Management, 1983.

McMillon, Bill. *The Archaeology Handbook: A Field Manual and Resource Guide*. New York: John Wiley & Sons, Inc., 1991.

McNitt, Frank. *Richard Wetherill: Anasazi*. Albuquerque: University of New Mexico Press, 1966.

McPherson, Robert S. *Comb Ridge and its People: The Ethnohistory of a Rock*. Logan: Utah State University, 2009.

—. *Sacred Land Sacred View: Navajo Perceptions of the Four Corners Region*. Charles Redd Monographs in Western History no. 19. Provo: Brigham Young University, 1992.

Mills, Barbara J. and Crown, Patricia A., eds. *Ceramic Production in the American Southwest*. Tucson: University of Arizona Press, 1995.

Mills, Barbara J. "Migration and Pueblo IV Community Reorganization in the Silver Creek Area, East–Central Arizona." In *Migration and Reorganization: The Pueblo IV Period in the American Southwest* by K. Spielmann, ed. Anthropological Research Papers no. 51. Tempe: Arizona State University, 1998.

— ed. *Identity, Feasting, and the Archaeology of the Greater Southwest: Proceedings of the 2002 Southwest Symposium*. Boulder: University Press of Colorado, 2004.

Mindeleff, Cosmos. *The Cliff Ruins of Canyon de Chelly, Arizona*. 16th Annual Report of the Bureau of American Ethnology. Washington, DC: Smithsonian Institution, 1897.

Mindeleff, Victor. *A Study of Pueblo Architecture: Tusayan and Cibola*. 8th Annual Report of the Bureau of Ethnology. Washington, DC: Smithsonian Institution, 1891.

Moore, Charles G. "An Example of Rock Art Exhibiting the Transition Between the Representational and Nonrepresentational." *Kiva*. 54 no. 4 (1989) 415-417.

Moore, Michael. *Medicinal Plants of the Desert and Canyon West*. Santa Fe: Museum of New Mexico Press, 1989.

Morris, Earl H. *Preliminary Account of the Antiquities of the Region Between the Mancos and La Plata Rivers in Southwestern Colorado*. 23rd Annual Report of the Bureau of American Ethnology. Washington, DC: Smithsonian Institution, 1919.

Morrow, Baker H. and Price, V. B., eds. *Anasazi Architecture and American Design*. Albuquerque, New Mexico: University of New Mexico Press, 1997.

Motsinger, Thomas N. "An Inside View of Hohokam Architecture." *Kiva*: 59 no. 4 (1994) 395-418.

Nabokov, Peter and Easton, Robert. *Native American Architecture*. New York: Oxford University Press, 1989.

Nabokov, Peter. *Architecture of Acoma Pueblo: The 1934 Historic American Buildings Survey Project*. Santa Fe: Ancient City Press, 1986.

Nequatewa, Edmund. "The Morning Echo Days, The Old Hopi Way of Life." *Plateau Journal*. 12:18 (July 1939): 15-16.

Neuzil, Anna A. "Corrugated Ceramics and Migration in the Pueblo III to Pueblo IV Transition, Silver Creek, Arizona." *Kiva: The Journal of Southwestern Archaeology and History*. 71 no1 (Fall 2005): 101-124.

—. *In the Aftermath of Migration: Renegotiating Ancient Identity in Southeastern Arizona*. Anthropological papers of the University of Arizona, no. 73. Tucson: University of Arizona Press, 2008.

Nichols, Deborah L. and Crown, Patricia L., eds. *Social Violence in Prehispanic American Southwest*. Tucson: University of Arizona Press, 2008.

Nickens, Paul R.; Larralde, Signa L.; Tucker, Gordon C. Jr. *A Survey of Vandalism to Archaeological Resources in Southwestern Colorado*. Cultural Resource Series no. 1. Denver: Bureau of Land Management, 1981.

Axel E. Nielsen and Walker, William H., eds. *Warfare in Cultural Context: Practice, Agency, and the Archaeology of Violence*. Tucson: University of Arizona, 2009.

Noble, David Grant, ed. *In Search of Chaco: New Approaches to an Archaeological Enigma*. Santa Fe: School of American Research Press, 2004.

— ed. *New Light on Chaco Canyon*. Santa Fe: School of American Research Press, 1984.

— ed. *The Mesa Verde World: Explorations in Ancestral Pueblo Archaeology*. Santa Fe: School of American Research Press, 2006.

Nordby, Larry V. "Control Point/Defensive Architecture at Mesa Verde During the 13th Century." Paper presented at the 67th Annual Meeting of the Society for American Archaeology, Denver, Colorado, March, 2002.

—. *Prelude to Tapestries in Stone: Understanding Cliff Palace Architecture*. Archeological Research Series, Architectural Studies no. 4. Mesa Verde National Park: Mesa Verde National Park Division of Research and Resource Management, 2001.

Nordenskiold, Gustaf. *The Cliff Dwellers of the Mesa Verde*. 1893. Reprint. Glorieta, New Mexico: Rio Grande Press, 1979.

Nusbaum, Jesse L. *The 1926 Re-Excavation of Step House Cave, Mesa Verde National Park*. Mesa Verde Research Series no. 1. Mesa Verde National Park: Mesa Verde Museum Association, Inc., 1981.

Nusbaum, Rosemary. *Tierra Dulce: Reminiscences from the Jesse Nusbaum Papers*. Santa Fe: The Sunstone Press, 1980.

Oppelt, Norman T. *Earth, Water and Fire: The Prehistoric Pottery of Mesa Verde*. Greeley, Colorado: Oppelt Publications, 1998.

Ortiz, Alfonso, ed. *New Perspectives on the Pueblos*. School of American Research Book. Albuquerque: University of New Mexico Press, 1972.

Parsons, Elsie Clews, ed. *Hopi Journal of Alexander M. Stephen*. Contributions to Anthropology, no. 23. Vols. I and II. Reprint. 1936. Mansfield Centre, Connecticut: Martino Fine Books, n.d.

—. *Pueblo Indian Religion*. Reprint. 1939. University of Chicago. Vols. I and II. Bison Books Edition. Lincoln: University of Nebraska Press, 1966.

Patterson-Rudolph, Carol. *On the Trail of Spiderwoman: Petroglyphs, Pictographs, and Myths of the Southwest*. Santa Fe: Ancient City Press, 1997.

—. *Petroglyphs and Pueblo Myths of the Rio Grande*. 2nd edition. Albuquerque: Avanyu Publishing Inc., 1993.

Patterson, Alex. *Hopi Pottery Symbols*. Boulder: Johnson Books, 1994.

Peckham, Stewart. *From this Earth: The Ancient Art of Pueblo Pottery*. Santa Fe: Museum of New Mexico Press, 1990.

Peet, Stephen D. " A Study of the High Cliff-Dwellings and Cave-Towns." *The American Antiquarian*. 18 no. 5 (n.d.): 285-302.

—. "Agriculture Among the Pueblos and Cliff-Dwellers." *The American Antiquarian.* 21 no. 4 (July and August 1899) 209-232.

—. "Great Houses and Fortresses." *The American Antiquarian.* 20 no. 6 (November and December 1889): 315-338.

—. "The Military Architecture of the Emblematic Mound Builders." *The American Antiquarian.* 3 no. 2 (January, 1881) 81-94.

Pepper, George H. *Pueblo Bonito.* Reprint. Anthropological Papers of the American Museum of Natural History, vol. 27. 1920. Albuquerque: University of New Mexico Press, 1996.

Peterson, Roger Tory. *A Field Guide to Western Birds.* The Peterson Field Guide Series. 3ʳᵈ ed. Boston: Houghton Mifflin Company, 1990.

Pike, Donald. *Anasazi: Ancient People of the Rock.* Palo Alto, California: American West Publishing Co., 1974.

Plog, Stephen. *Ancient Peoples of the American Southwest.* London: Thames and Hudson, Ltd., 1997.

Poore, Henry R. "A Harvest with the Taos Indians." *The Continent: An Illustrated Weekly Magazine.* (1st ed.) 3, no. 61. (April 11, 1883): 449-458.

Powell, John Wesley. *The Exploration of the Colorado River and Its Canyons.* 1875. Reprint. New York: Simon & Schuster, 1996.

Powell, Shirley and Smiley, Francis E., eds. *Prehistoric Culture Change on the Colorado Plateau: Ten Thousand Years on Black Mesa.* Tucson: University of Arizona Press, 2002.

Powers, Margaret A. *The Salvage of Archaeological Data from Turkey Pen Ruin, Grand Gulch Primitive Area, San Juan County, Utah.* Contributions to Anthropology Series, no. 808. Farmington, New Mexico: San Juan County Museum Association, 1984.

Prudden, T. Mitchell. "A Summer Among Cliff Dwellings." *Harper's New Monthly Magazine.* 93 no. 556 (1896) 545-561.

Prudden, T. Mitchell. "The Circular Kivas of Small Ruins in the San Juan Watershed." *American Anthropologist.* 16 (1914) 33-58.

—. "The Prehistoric Ruins of the San Juan Watershed in Utah, Arizona, Colorado, and New Mexico." *American Anthropologist.* 5 (1903) 224-288.

—. *On the Great American Plateau: Wanderings among Canyons and Buttes in the Land of the Cliff-Dweller, and the Indian of To-Day.* New York: The Knickerbacker Press, 1906.

Qoyawayma, Polingaysi. *No Turning Back: A Hopi Indian's Struggle to Live in Two Worlds.*

Albuquerque: University of New Mexico Press, 1964.

Reed, Paul F. ed. *Foundations of Anasazi Culture: The Basketmaker–Pueblo Transition.* Salt Lake City: University of Utah Press, 2000.

— ed. *Chaco's Northern Prodigies: Salmon, Aztec, and the Ascendancy of the Middle San Juan Region After A.D. 1100.* Salt Lake City: University of Utah Press, 2008.

Reid, J. Jefferson and Doyel, David E., eds. *Emil W. Haury's Prehistory of the American Southwest.* Tucson: University of Arizona Press, 1986.

Reid, Jefferson and Whittlesey, Stephanie. *Grasshopper Pueblo: A Story of Archaeology and Ancient Life.* Tucson: University of Arizona Press, 1999.

Reid, Jefferson and Whittlesey, Stephanie. *The Archaeology of Ancient Arizona.* Tucson: University of Arizona Press, 1997.

Rhine, Stanley. *Bone Voyage: A Journey in Forensic Anthropology.* Albuquerque: University of New Mexico Press, 1998.

Riggs, Charles R. *The Architecture of Grasshopper Pueblo.* Salt Lake City: University of Utah Press, 2001.

Robbins, Chandler S.; Bertel Bruun; Herbert S. Zim. *Birds of North America: A Guide to Field Identification.* New York: Golden Press, 1983.

Roberts, David. *In Search of the Old Ones: Exploring the Anasazi of the Southwest.* New York: Simon & Schuster, 1996.

—. *Sandstone Spine: Seeking the Anasazi on the First Traverse of the Comb Ridge.* Seattle: Mountaineers Books, 2006.

—. *The Pueblo Revolt: The Secret Rebellion that Drove the Spaniards out of the Southwest.* New York: Simon & Schuster, 2004.

Roberts, Frank H. H., Jr. "The Development of a Unite-Type Dwelling." *So Live the Works of Men: Seventieth Anniversary Volume Honoring Edgar Lee Hewitt.* Albuquerque: University of New Mexico Press, 1939.

—. *The Village of the Great Kivas on the Zuni Reservation New Mexico.* Bureau of American Ethnology, Bulletin no. 111. Washington DC: Smithsonian Institution, 1932.

Rohn, Arthur H. *Mug House.* Archaeological Research Series no. 7D. Mesa Verde National Park: National Park Service, 1971.

Sagstetter, Beth and Bill. *Unraveling the Mysteries of the Telluride Blanket.* Telluride, Colorado: Telluride Historical Museum, 2008.

Sanders, Ronald D. *Rock Art Savvy: The Responsible Visitor's Guide to Public Sites of the Southwest.* Missoula, Montana: Mountain Press Publishing Company, 2005.

Sando, Joe S. *The Pueblo Indians.* N.p.: The Indian Historian Press, 1976.

Saunders, Charles Francis. *Indians of the Terraced Houses: An Account of the Pueblo Indians of New Mexico and Arizona. 1912.* Reprint. Glorieta, New Mexico, Rio Grande Press, 1973.

Sayles, E. B. *An Archaeological Survey of Chihuahua, Mexico.* Medallion Papers no. XXII. Globe, Arizona: Gila Pueblo, May, 1936.

Schaafsma, Polly. *Indian Rock Art of the Southwest.* School of American Research Book. Albuquerque: University of New Mexico Press, 1980.

—. *Indian Rock Art of the Southwest.* School of American Research Book. Albuquerque: University of New Mexico Press, 1980.

—. *The Rock Art of Utah: A Study from the Donald Scott Collection.* Salt Lake City: University of Utah Press, 1971.

—. *Warrior, Shield and Star: Imagery and Ideology of Pueblo Warfare.* Santa Fe: Western Edge Press, 2000.

Schwartz, Jeffrey H. *What the Bones Tell Us.* Tucson: University of Arizona Press, 1993.

Seaman, P. David, ed. *Born a Chief: The Nineteenth Century Hopi Boyhood of Edmund Nequatewa.* Tucson: University of Arizona Press, 1993.

Sibley, David Allen. *The Sibley Guide to Birds.* The National Audubon Society. New York: Alfred A. Knopf, 2000.

Simmons, Leo, ed. *Sun Chief: The Autobiography of a Hopi Indian.* New Haven: Yale University Press, 1942.

Slifer, Dennis. *Kokopelli: The Magic, Mirth, and Mischief of an Ancient Symbol.* Salt Lake City: Gibbs Smith, Publisher, 2007.

Smith, Jack E. *Mesas, Cliffs, and Canyons: The University of Colorado Survey of Mesa Verde National Park, 1971-1977.* Mesa Verde Research Series, Paper 3. Mesa Verde National Park: Mesa Verde Museum Association, Inc., n.d.

— ed. *Proceedings of the Anasazi Symposium, 1981.* Mesa Verde National Park, Colorado: Mesa Verde Museum Association, Inc., 1981.

Smith, Watson. gen. ed. *Prehistoric Ceramics of the Mesa Verde Region.* Museum of Northern Arizona Ceramic Series no. 5. Flagstaff: Northern Arizona society of Science and Art, Inc., 1974.

—. *Kiva Mural Decorations at Awatovi and Kawaika-a.* Papers of the Peabody Museum of Archaeology and Ethnology, vol. 37. Reprint. 1952. Cambridge: Harvard University, 2005.

—. *Painted Ceramics of the Western Mound at Awatovi.* Papers of the Peabody Museum of Archaeology and Ethnolgy, Harvard University, vol. 38. Cambridge, Massachusetts: Peabody Museum, 1971.

—. *When is a Kiva? And other Questions about Southwestern Archaeology.* Tucson: University of Arizona Press, 1990.

Stevenson, Matilda Coxe. "Dress and Adornment of the Pueblo Indians." *The Kiva.* 52, no. 4 (1987).

—. *The Zuni Indians: Their Mythology, Esoteric Fraternities, and Ceremonies.* 23rd Annual Report of the Bureau of American Ethnology. Washington DC: Smithsonian Institution, 1904.

Stokes, William M. and Stokes, William Lee. *Messages on Stone: Selections of Native Western Rock Art.* Salt Lake City: Starstone Publishing Co., 2000.

Stuart, David E. *Anasazi America: Sixteen Centuries on the Road from Center Place.* Albuquerque: University of New Mexico Press, 2000.

—. *Glimpses of the Ancient Southwest.* Santa Fe: Ancient City Press, 1984.

Stuart, David E. and Gauthier, Rory P. *Prehistoric New Mexico: Background for Survey.* Albuquerque: University of New Mexico Press: 1984.

Sturtevant, William C. gen. ed., Alfonso Ortiz, vol. ed. *Handbook of North American Indians: Southwest.* vol. 9. Washington DC: Smithsonian Institution, 1970.

Swink, Clint. *Messages from the High Desert: The Art, Archaeology and Renaissance of Mesa Verde Pottery.* Bayfield, Colorado: Redtail Press, 2004.

Telluride Daily Journal. "Relics of a Past Age." Telluride, Colorado. August 14, 1896. Unsigned typed text on file at the Telluride Historical Museum.

Thayer, William M. *Marvels of the New West: A Vivid Portrayal of the Unparalleled Marvels in the Vast Wonderland West of the Missouri River.* Norwich, Connecticut: The Henry Bill Publishing Company, 1892.

Thiel, J. Homer. *Rock Art in Arizona.* Technical Report no. 94-6. Phoenix: Arizona State Parks, 1995.

Thomas, David Hurst. *Exploring Ancient Native America: An Archaeological Guide.* New York: Routledge, 1999.

Thompson, Ian. *The Towers of Hovenweep.* Moab, Utah: Canyonlands Natural History Association, 2004.

Titterton, Robert J. *Julian Scott: Artist of the Civil War and Native America.* Jefferson, North Carolina: McFarland & Company, Inc. 1997.

Tuchman, Barbara W. *A Distant Mirror: The Calamitous 14th Century.* New York: Ballantine Books, 1978.

Turner, Christy G. II and Turner, Jacqueline A. *Man Corn: Cannibalism and Violence in the Prehistoric American Southwest.* Salt Lake City: University of Utah Press, 1999.

Udall, Louise, ed. *Me and Mine: The Life Story of Helen Sekaquaptewa.* Tucson: University of Arizona Press, 1969.

Underhill, Ruth. *First Penthouse Dwellers of America.* New York: J. J. Augustin Publisher, n.d.

—. *Life in the Pueblos.* Santa Fe: Ancient City Press, 1991.

—. *People of the Crimson Evening.* N.p.: U.S. Indian Service, n.d.

Upton, Dell and Vlach, John Michael, eds. *Common Places: Readings in American Vernacular Architecture.* Athens: University of Georgia Press, 1986.

Varien, Mark D. and Wilshousen, Richard H. eds. *Seeking the Center Place: Archaeology and Ancient Communities in the Mesa Verde Region.* Salt Lake City: University of Utah Press, 2002.

Vitelli, Karen D. *Archaeological Ethics.* Walnut Creek, California: AltaMira Press, 1996.

Warner, Ted J., ed. *The Dominguez–Escalante Journal: Their Expedition through Colorado, Utah, Arizona, and New Mexico in 1776.* Salt Lake City: University of Utah Press, 1995.

Washburn, Dorothy K. *Living in Balance: The Universe of the Hopi, Zuni, Navajo and Apache.* Philadelphia: University of Pennsylvania Museum, 1995.

Webb, William and Weinstein, Robert A. *Dwellers at the Source: Southwestern Indian Photographs of A. C. Vroman, 1895-1904.* Albuquerque: University of New Mexico Press, 1973.

Welsh, Liz and Peter Welsh. *Rock-Art of the Southwest: A Visitor's Companion.* Berkeley: Wilderness Press, 2000.

Wenger, Gilbert R. *The Story of Mesa Verde National Park.* revised ed. Mesa Verde: Mesa Verde Museum Association, Inc., 1991.

Whalen, Michael E. and Minnis, Paul E. *The Neighbors of Casas Grandes: Medio Period Communities of Northwestern Chihuahua.* Tucson: University of Arizona, 2009.

Wheat, Joe Ben. *Mogollon Culture Prior to A.D. 1000.* Memoirs of the Society for American

Archaeology, no. 10. N.p.: American Anthropological Association, 1955.

White, Leslie A. *The Acoma Indians: People of the Sky City.* 1929. Reprint. 47th Annual Report of the Bureau of American Ethnology. Glorieta, New Mexico: The Rio Grand Press, Inc., 1973.

Whittaker, John C. *Flintknapping: Making & Understanding Stone Tools.* Austin: University of Texas, 1994.

Whittlesey, Stephanie M. ed. *Sixty Years of Mogollon Archaeology: Papers from the Ninth Mogollon Conference*, Silver City, New Mexico, 1996. Tucson: SRI Press, 1999.

Widdison, Jerold G. ed. *The Anasazi: Why Did They Leave? Where Did They Go?* A panel discussion at the Anasazi Heritage Center, Dolores, Colorado, Bureau of Land Management. Albuquerque: Southwest Natural and Cultural Heritage Association, 1991.

Williamson, Ray A. *Living the Sky: The Cosmos of the American Indian.* Boston: Houghton Mifflin Company, 1984.

Wills, W.H. *Early Prehistoric Agriculture in the American Southwest.* Santa Fe: School of American Research Press, 1988.

Winship, George Parker. *The Coronado Expedition, 1540 – 1542.* Reprint. 1896. Annual Report of the Bureau of American Ethnology. Chicago: The Rio Grande Press, 1964.

Woodbury, Richard B. *Sixty Years of Southwestern Archaeology: A History of the Pecos Conference.* Albuquerque: University of New Mexico Press, 1993.

Wright, Barton, ed. *The Mythic World of the Zuni: As Written by Frank Hamilton Cushing.* Albuquerque: University of New Mexico Press, 1988.

Wright, Kenneth R. *Water for the Anasazi: How the Ancients of Mesa Verde Engineered Public Works.* #22. Boise, Idaho: Essays in Public Works History, 2003.

Yeager, C. G. *Arrowheads & Stone Artifacts: A Practical Guide for the Amateur Archaeologist.* Boulder: Pruett Publishing Company, 2000.

Zaslow, Bert. *Pattern Dissemination in the Prehistoric Southwest and Mesoamerica: A Comparison of Hohokam Decorative Patterns with Patterns from the Upper Gila and from the Valley of Oaxaca.* Anthropological Research Papers no. 25. Phoenix: Arizona State University, 1981.

ABOUT THE AUTHORS . . .

Elizabeth M. Sagstetter and William E. Sagstetter are a writer/photographer/research team living in Denver, Colorado. This book is a culmination of over forty years of exploring cliff dwellings.

The Sagstetter byline has appeared on hundreds of magazine articles to date. They have been on the staff of a national magazine and were a correspondent/photographer team for the *Denver Post.* This is their fourth book. Their book on the historical archaeology of the ghost towns, *The Mining Camps Speak,* continues to be a best seller even after more than a decade.

They produced several documentaries about the American Southwest and Mexico that aired on primetime television. Their film, *The Mystery of Huajatolla* (wah-ha-TOY-ah), went on to win a Special Award at the Aspen Arts Film Festival in 1978. They also produced the film, *The Tarahumara: The People Who Run,* on the remote, little-known tribe in Mexico.

Bill was an honorarium instructor in filmmaking at the University of Colorado/Denver for several years. Besides filmmaking, he has also taught Colorado history and filmmaking at the college level as an honorarium instructor. His students at Community College at Auraria in Denver voted him the best teacher of the year. Today, his slide/Powerpoint lectures are very popular and he still gives dozens of these lectures every year.

Bill's name appears on over forty patents to date. Approximately 25 of these are U.S. patents, the rest are foreign.

ABOUT THE BOOK . . .

A book requires many experts to create — as does a house — in order for it to come into existence. We feel privileged to have worked with a talented group of publishing professionals in bringing this book to fruition. Thanks to each of them for doing such an outstanding job!

Graphic Designer:	Patte Smith, Graphic Design
Cover Art:	Rob Bartee, Bartee Photography
Editing:	Mary Anne Maier
Marketing Consultant:	Cassandra Leoncini, Leoncini Consulting
Printed by:	Sheridan Book Co.

This book is for people who have visited ghost town sites and were disappointed because there was "nothing left." It takes up where other ghost town guide books end. Readers are guided around a site Sherlock Holmes fashion. They unravel the secrets of the ghost towns, even is all that's left is rubble. It is essentially the historical archaeology of gold rush sites. The techniques it offers are valid anywhere there has been gold or silver mining history, not only in the American West, but also in Alaska.

Cover:	Paperback
Size:	8½ x 11"
# of pages:	304
Illustrations:	Nearly 400 b/w photographs and antique engravings
Biblio:	Yes
Index:	Yes
ISBN:	978-0-9645824-1-5
Retail price:	$22.95

"For anyone who is drawn by the lure of the mountains, *The Mining Camps Speak* is an intense, visually descriptive and absorbing look at the way it was. Highly entertaining and intriguing, it goes far beyond mere storytelling."
Clive Cussler, *Raise the Titanic!*

Contact:
BenchMark Publishing of Colorado LLC
2217 Grove Street
Denver, CO 80211-4613
(303) 455-0789
benchmarkcolo@worldnet.att.net